HOW I BECAME MY FATHER... A DRUNK

An Inspirational True Story by

WILLIAM G. BORCHERT

STORY MERCHANT BOOKS
LOS ANGELES
2015

THE STORY MERCHANT

www.williamborchert.com

ISBN: 978-0-9963689-2-6.

Story Merchant Books
400 S. Burnside Avenue #11B
Los Angeles, CA 90036

http://www.storymerchant.com/books.html

Cover art design & interior format by IndieDesignz.com

AUTHOR'S NOTE

Being an author and screenwriter, I was invited to speak at a very large social convention in West Palm Beach, Florida. There were quite a few senior citizens in the audience that day which is probably what prompted me to share some personal reflections about my dad who had passed on some years before at the young age of seventy one.

I mentioned what a great relationship we had developed in the later years of his life after traveling a rocky road together as father and son during those earlier times. I talked about the intimate conversations we would have, the fishing trips and interesting places we would go, the many enjoyable things we did together, and also the joy I got from watching the close, loving bond he and my mom developed after too many years of marital strife.

Later that evening, the gentleman who chaired the convention invited me for a cup of coffee and some polite conversation. He said he enjoyed my talk and then asked if I had ever considered writing a book about my father and how we managed to mend fences after years of anger and resentment.

"I think it would make a wonderful story since I've always believed that a bad beginning and a great ending is much better than a good beginning and a terrible ending," he explained. "And that's apparently the story of your father's life and yours which I gathered from your remarks."

"I don't think I would be particularly interested in re-visiting a past filled with considerable pain and shame," I replied, "and re-examining a man I had made peace with before he passed away. Why stir up something already covered with a lot of dust?"

After apologizing for probing into an obviously still sensitive area, the gentleman made one more observation.

"There's something else I believe," he said with a caring smile. "I believe that hope and love spring eternal and what more people need today is hope. Perhaps telling his story and your relationship with him could give many still in difficult relationships hope that things can change for the better...like yours did. Just think about it."

It took awhile, but I finally did get around to thinking about his suggestion. However, it wasn't until I stopped thinking about my own possible discomfort and began thinking about the hope and love the gentleman spoke of that I finally put pen to paper. That's when I discovered that the man I never wanted to be like, I had become. I became my father, a drunk.

The result has been a somewhat difficult and painful journey but, in the daylight of sobriety, it has proven to be a journey more pleasing and satisfying than I ever expected. I invite you to take this journey with me.

ACKNOWLEDGMENTS

Trying to recall things that happened many years ago, especially painful, life-changing incidents, is a significant challenge to say the least. But maybe the so-called memory experts are correct when they say the older you get the easier it is to remember the long-ago than it is to remember what happened yesterday.

Since I fit into that "older" category, perhaps I shouldn't have been all that surprised that I could recall so many incidents from my childhood. I guess some of those tapes never get erased and can be replayed rather clearly when dusted off.

Still, I needed a lot of help with the digging and the dusting. I am deeply grateful that four people in particular were willing to grab onto their own shovels and uncover some of the long-ago with me, despite the discomfort it may have resurrected for them too.

First there was my sister, Mrs. Marilyn Dean, who I don't believe ever said a bad word about my father in her life and never would, even though, as she admits, her childhood wasn't always "peaches and cream." Her memories were quite helpful in confirming many of my own.

I also want to thank my younger sister, Patricia Gass, for sharing so much of her troubled life with me and helping me at times when I really needed help.

My younger brother, Robert Borchert, was my dad's pride and joy because he was born on "VJ Day," August 14, 1945 when America was finally victorious over Japan to end World War II. But Bobby didn't completely escape the wrath of my father's drinking either.

My dear wife, Bernadette, also helped shed a great deal of light on the later stages of my dad's alcoholism while she herself was caught in the downward spiral of my own drinking problem. She loved my father for who he was deep down inside and because he was her saving grace many times.

I also wish to express my gratitude to my dear friend, John Donnelly, who despite being seriously ill took time to read every chapter as I wrote it and offer me invaluable advice, suggestions and encouragement. John died five weeks after I finished the book.

Finally, I want to acknowledge and thank my Higher Power Who, every time I became uncertain about writing this book, kept urging me on in His usual quiet but reassuring way. He kept filling my head with thoughts of the past and helped me find notes and letters and diaries written by my father that convinced me this was a project I had to complete.

With His help and the support of Marilyn, Patricia, Robert and Bernadette and my dear friend John, I did. Thank you all.

Note: Some names in this book have been changed in order to protect the anonymity of those involved.

THIS BOOK IS DEDICATED TO:

MY LOVING WIFE, BERNADETTE...
FOR NEVER GIVING UP.

TABLE OF CONTENTS

Prologue.. 1

Chapter One: The Unexpected 1

Chapter Two: The Fruit and Vegetable Wagon 6

Chapter Three: Twenty-Eight Flavors of Ice Cream.............24

Chapter Four: Overnight the Whole World Changed.........42

Chapter Five: Joy in The Midst of Gloom.....................59

Chapter Six: Escaping the Chaos 77

Chapter Seven: What Will I Tell My Mother? 96

Chapter Eight: What Should She Tell the Neighbors?....... 116

Chapter Nine: Great Opportunities Come and Go 143

Chapter Ten: Becoming My Father....................................... 161

Chapter Eleven: How Far Is Down?....................................... 184

Chapter Twelve: A Man Named Benny 212

Chapter Thirteen: Hope and Love Spring Eternal 240

Chapter Fourteen: Carrying the Message 265

Dear Reader.. 313

About the Author.. 315

PROLOGUE

What can you do when the pressure gets so great you really need a few drinks just to relax? You have to do what comes naturally. But why did it almost always lead to trouble? And every time I would ask God for some help, why would He always turn me down while taking good care of everyone else? What can you do when the whole world seems to be stacked against you?

Perhaps that's why I was on my way to Moochie's Bar & Grill that morning intending to see my father. This way I could thank him for being such a great role model when I was growing up. I would kiss him on the cheek and express my gratitude for showing me how to wreck a loving family and a promising career. Maybe I would pat him on the back for always being there when I needed to talk over a problem or get some direction.

As I drove down to my favorite watering hole, I found myself blaming everyone but myself for the situation I was in. I had a wife whom I felt didn't love me anymore, a City Editor who refused to understand my problems, a father who was an uncaring drunk and a God Who wanted no part of me. My self-pity was growing exponentially, my blame-game was in high gear and my resentments were popping out my eyeballs. Yes, it was everybody else's fault, especially my father's.

Sure enough when I pulled to the curb on South Street and walked into the smoky saloon, he was standing there bellied up to the bar as usual. He was on his break after the first edition had gone to press, the edition that should have carried my story about Tommy Manville and his stupid, meaningless, almost laughable thirteenth marriage.

The moment my dad saw me, he knew there was something terribly wrong. My clothes were wrinkled, my eyes were bloodshot and I needed a shave. Even before he said hello, he looked at me with a frown and asked:

"What's wrong? You look like hell."

I nodded to Frank Moochie, the owner who was tending bar. He knew my drinking habits as well as he knew my father's. He poured me a double shot of rye and a beer chaser. As I picked up the shot glass, my father grabbed my arm and said:

"I asked you what's wrong."

"I screwed up," I responded rather sharply. "I missed an assignment and Mahar wanted to fire me. He demoted me instead." Then I downed the shot and beer.

"Maybe he's just trying to teach you a lesson. From what I hear, things aren't going well on the home front either. If I were you I'd get back in my car and head for home. Drinking's not going to solve anything. Believe me, I know."

Maybe I took his remarks the wrong way because it was like someone just threw a bucket of hot water in my face. I saw red. That's when I remember suddenly losing control.

"Who the hell are you to be giving me advice!" I said loud enough to attract attention. "I should go home? What about you? You think you're some kind of great role model?"

"That's enough!" was my father's angry reply.

"Why? Aren't you proud of the way I've followed in your footsteps? I'm a drunk just like you and doing what drunks do—fuck up!"

"I said that's enough!" he insisted.

"Enough?" I responded. "Who says it's enough? Come on, let's have another drink. It's never enough, is it?"

CHAPTER ONE

The Unexpected

Perhaps there's been a time in your life when some kind of tragedy struck someone close to you, and you were there to help. Remember how deeply grateful you were for being there.

That's how it was for me on February 14, 1982 when my father passed away at the young age of seventy-one and my mother needed me...and I was able to be there for her. Even though it was a very sad occasion, my being able to help became one of those positive memories you want to hang on to, hoping it might somehow replace some of the bad ones you've been trying to forget. And I had a truckload of those.

So, as the now dependable older son, I made all the funeral arrangements, only taking Mom with me to pick out Dad's casket. She wanted something special. She also wanted him waked for two days. That began on a Thursday afternoon. I took her to the funeral home early to check on things. Since I had other related errands to run, my two sisters and younger brother came along just in case she had another emotional breakdown.

Despite her pain, Mom wanted to make sure that before anyone else arrived, all the flowers were properly arranged, the Mass card stand was in place and the funeral cards were exactly what she had ordered...my father's full name, William Henry Borchert, in bold print on the back of the card just above his favorite prayer, "The Serenity Prayer":

"God grant me the serenity to accept the things I cannot change, courage to change the things I can, and wisdom to know the difference."

After we inspected the undertaker's fine work and shed a few more tears, I left and drove over to St. Mary Gate of Heaven Catholic Church to check with the priest who was speaking at the wake, finalize the Mass arrangements, the services at the cemetery and a luncheon to follow for all the mourners. By now I was running late.

I hit some heavy traffic on the way back. As I started to turn into the parking lot of the James Funeral Home in Ozone Park, Queens, which was one of those typical working class neighborhoods that surround New York City, I couldn't believe my eyes. Passersby probably thought some celebrity or very prominent personage was being waked that freezing cold February afternoon. There was an unbelievably long line of people waiting outside the funeral home.

While it was quite an impressive sight to see so many folks shivering out there on that cold and windy street, I was soon to be stunned by something even more imposing inside...something that moved my entire family almost to a state of incomprehension.

I entered and weaved my way through the throng of men and women already inside who had come to pay their last respects, stopping every few feet to accept heartfelt condolences from relatives and friends. As I finally eased my way into the seat my mother had saved for me next to her and directly in front of my father's handsome bronze casket, I leaned over to kiss her on the cheek. I was a bit taken aback by the flood of warm tears I felt pouring down her still attractive and almost unwrinkled face. You wouldn't guess she was now in her 70's.

Yes, I knew how deeply she missed my dad and the anguish she felt from his passing, even though it had been expected. He had been diagnosed with inoperable liver cancer and died a short time later. They had been married over fifty years. It was the last fifteen when they fell in love all over again and became totally devoted to each other. So it was only natural that her deep emotions would continue to flow from her eyes.

But then as I began to notice all the people approaching her, I suddenly realized the tears now gushing down her cheeks came more from the comments they were making as they knelt in front of her and held her hand. I saw something special, maybe even spiritual, on their faces as they spoke. Then I saw the look on the faces of my sisters and brother as they listened. They too were overwhelmed by what we were hearing. It was all so unexpected.

"Bill was the finest man I ever knew," whispered a thin balding gentleman named Phil who was struggling to control his own emotions. "I wouldn't be here if it wasn't for him. I'll still be looking for him at our meetings every Monday and Thursday nights because I know he'll be there in spirit."

Then there was Eleanor, a lovely white-haired lady with a black fur hat who could hardly speak from crying. "Your husband was always there for my Frank, even during his many slips. He could have been with you but you let him be with my Frank instead. And then he finally got sober and your husband brought love and peace back into our home again. Thank you, Ruthie. Thank you."

But it wasn't until a handsome young man in his early 30's, his red hair messed from the wind and his eyes filled with tears, knelt down in front of my mother. His very attractive wife who was obviously pregnant stood behind him also weeping. That's when mom really broke down.

"Your husband saved my life." he said for all to hear. "Bill saved my life. I had to tell you that. I had given up. So had my wife. I would have died. I wanted to, but he wouldn't let me go. He said God needed me here...to help others. Now I know what he meant. God bless you and your whole wonderful family."

I put my arm around my mother to steady her. My older sister Marilyn handed her some more tissues. After a moment she nodded that she was okay. She lifted her head and smiled at the next person who approached.

As I listened again, I began to ask myself why was I so surprised by all this? Why was it so unexpected? After all, dad had developed a very close relationship with God during his later years. He had found the path to spirituality and was walking it. And since God works through people, weren't we hearing now how God worked through him?

That's when I turned and stared at my father lying quietly in front of us, his eyes closed, his handsome features still there, his curly brown hair now thin and almost completely gray He was dressed in his favorite dark blue suit and light blue tie with a white shroud pinned neatly around him like he was floating on a cloud.

This man was my father, not some doctor or lawyer or clairvoyant. And I certainly wasn't observing a priest or clergyman or some kind of saint. In other words, my father didn't fit the profile of people who do save lives from time to time. He had been a simple pressman for a large New York City newspaper most of his life, not well educated or worldly. Yes, he did have a kind and caring side but, early on, it was rarely seen due to the fact that for many years he had been a man with a serious drinking problem.

No, that's soft-peddling it. My father was a drunk. He was a terrible, hard-drinking alcoholic who hurt his wife and children and brought much shame and devastation into his home. He was a man I sometimes loved but often hated. There were times I wished I wasn't named after him. There was one thing for sure, at least in my opinion. He had been a lousy father for a long, long time.

My mother tried her best to change him. When she would get tired of screaming and hollering, she would sometimes talk him into taking a pledge for thirty or sixty days, hoping it might help him stop. Or she'd encourage him to give up drinking for Lent. I don't believe he ever made it through those forty days and forty nights. And every time he failed, he would use the same old excuse: "You can't teach old dogs new tricks." And the dysfunction would start all over again. My mother would go back into her rage and take her anger at him out on us kids.

As I continued to stare at my father while listening at the same time to all the glowing tributes, I was strangely taken back to those days when he was described by many in far less flattering terms. For some reason I became aware of one particular shameful event that happened when I was six years old. I don't know why it suddenly popped into my mind. It was something I thought I had buried so deep that it would never surface again. But here it was, as vivid an image in my brain at this moment as was my father there in the casket in front of me.

It transported me back to a time that I never wanted to return to or think about, only here it was and there was nothing I could do about it. I certainly didn't want to lose the feelings I now had about my father, good feelings that were a long time in coming and were being reinforced by all these people sharing their own thoughts about him with my mother.

But here I was six years old once more and back in a world I was all too familiar with, a world far different from the one I had become accustomed to.

CHAPTER TWO

The Fruit and Vegetable Wagon

It was a hot August day and we were moving again, this time from a nice three-bedroom house in Ozone Park which we rented to a small apartment over a grocery store just three blocks away. I was only six-years-old at the time. It was one of my first vivid childhood memories of a day I'll never forget...even though I tried many times.

It was 1939 and the country was nearing the end of The Great Depression. The banks had failed and all that most people had left was the money they hid under their mattresses. They were like my father, living from paycheck to paycheck and praying they wouldn't lose their jobs.

President Franklin Delano Roosevelt was everybody's hero for trying to make things better. My parents had his picture plastered all over the house. But despite the President's optimistic oratory, few could see good things coming. There was still a lot of gloom and doom in the air...and a lot of drinking that only created false hope.

Prohibition hadn't worked. In fact, it actually helped make booze more available through moonshiners who filled the underground pipeline and illegal importers like Joseph "Joe" Kennedy from Massachusetts who became a multi-millionaire from selling illicit Scotch whiskey brought in by mobsters.

But for every moonshiner and every Joe Kennedy there were many like my father who made booze in his own bathtub and strained it through an old felt hat like his father had taught him. At the same time, he struggled mightily just to hold on and support his family. Little did my dad and others like him realize that drinking was often the curse that tore families apart.

My father was a strong, handsome man with brown curly hair and dark brown eyes who yearned to be five feet ten inches tall so he could become a New York City policeman. But despite a brief stint at strenuous stretching exercises, he never made it beyond five feet eight which he deeply resented.

"That big fat Irish police commissioner ain't no taller than I am," he would argue, "yet he walks around like he's ten feet tall because his damn brother-in-law is the mayor "

It wasn't that my dad hated his job as a pressman for the New York Journal-American, the largest evening newspaper in the world at that time. In fact, he liked it and most of the men he worked with. He just hated scrubbing the black ink from the presses off his body every single day.

I don't believe my father was really an angry man. He just seemed to be extremely disappointed by what life had handed him. He simply wanted more, to better himself, to share it with my mother. And when it didn't happen, I guess he found solace in the bottle. Maybe that's why the only times I would see him smiling or laughing was when he was drinking.

He wasn't a man to show his affection in public, or even in private for that matter. I'm sure he loved me in his own way but never said so. He would rustle my hair sometimes but I never remember him hugging me. He considered that "sissy stuff." Instead he would tell me things like "real men don't cry. They learn how to take their punishment without complaining." Sometimes he would add: "Real men understand that most things they want in life don't work out no matter how hard you work for them. You simply accept whatever happens and go on from there."

Perhaps that's why he didn't seem so upset about moving again. It was simply another one of life's inconveniences. Of course I didn't learn until some years later that most of these "inconveniences" had to do with the lack of money. In this case, the landlord also needed money which is why he had to sell our house.

He was hoping my dad would buy it. Little did he know that because of my father's drinking problem, he could barely pay the rent which was thirty three dollars a month. That may sound like a real bargain now, but it's about what things were going for back in the 1930's when the average salary was under $2,000 a year.

The landlord wanted $3,000 for the attached six-room brick house with a large basement, a garage and a big fenced-in yard. He was asking for a down payment of three hundred dollars and a monthly mortgage payment that would be roughly the same amount as the current rent. Not a bad deal.

The problem was, my father couldn't beg, borrow or steal three hundred dollars at the time. He had absolutely no credit or other resources. What he had was a great deal of false pride. He told people for years after that he didn't buy the house because it was falling apart and the landlord "was trying to pawn it off on me."

On the other hand, my mother loved that house and I'm sure she did everything she could to keep it which included begging the landlord for more time to raise the money. But her side of the family had no money either. Not only that, there was a lot of alcoholism in her family too, including her father, my granddad, Robert Archibald McLintock.

I always figured with a Scotch name like Archibald McLintock you had to be a big drinker. But he was also a caring, loveable man who, when sober or not too drunk, would tell funny stories about people he knew, his working on the New York City docks and also about his life back in Glasgow, Scotland before coming to America as a very young man. I remember how much I enjoyed being with him.

He and my grandmother, "Lizzy," McLintock lived in a small apartment in a place called City Line which was a neighborhood right on the border between Brooklyn and Queens. My grandmother's maiden name was Elizabeth Grant but everybody called her Lizzy.

She was kind of a stern woman compared to my grandfather, but with a lovely square face surrounded by dark gray hair. Her family had come to this country from Dublin, Ireland many years before. In fact, after knocking down a few good shots of Irish whisky, she would often claim she was the fourth cousin of the great Civil War General Ulysses S. Grant. I remember checking on that once but found they apparently sawed his limb off our family tree.

Their apartment was about a twenty-five minute trek on foot from where we lived. I'll never forget the long walks I'd take with my grandfather which would usually wind up at the ice cream parlor. I have a hunch he spiked his Coca Cola. Then it seemed like one day he got sick and suddenly died. I heard people say it was his liver. I really missed him. So did my mother. She loved her father dearly. She had tears in her eyes for days which wasn't really like her.

When I think about it, perhaps that's when she began to change. Perhaps it was that one more pain, that one more heartache she didn't have room for. It made all the anger she held inside begin to burst out.

The change in her confused me because the mother I knew from my earliest childhood was a beautiful, loving woman with jet black hair, high cheekbones and sparkling hazel eyes. She had the prettiest smile and a laugh that was infectious. As the Irish used to say, her laughter "could warm the cockles of your heart" which Webster's Collegiate Dictionary translates as "reaching the core of one's being." And that it did, for my mother's smile and laughter would touch you deep inside.

But then as the years past and the hurt, anger and disappointment affected her more and more, her insides began to show on the outside. It was sad to see the smile fade, her eyes darken and the laughter all but disappear. So by the time I was seven or eight, I had come to realize I now had two mothers—the one who would kiss and hug me when I was frightened or hurt and the one who would yell and slap me at times for no reason other than she was angry at my father and I was in the way.

"I'm sorry," she would say later. "I didn't mean to hit you like that." I could sense her guilt as she'd hand me some ginger snaps from the cookie jar, unable to embrace me at the moment like I wanted her to. It was always so confusing and most of all fearful because I knew it would be happening again.

As I said, her change from a warm, loving mother into a near-tyrant at times didn't happen overnight. It happened gradually as my sisters and I grew older and her problems with my father seemed to overcome her ability to accept them without striking out at him or at us.

I remember late one night when I got up to go to the bathroom, I heard my mother in her bedroom nearby sobbing as my father who was terribly drunk was rolling back and forth on the floor trying to get his clothes off. I heard her sob:

"I never should have had these children. Then I wouldn't have to stay here and put up with this."

I went back to bed with tears in my eyes.

I think before her own father's death and my father's drinking worsened, the only thing that really bothered my mother believe it or not was her first name. She had been christened "Euphemia" which she always hated because she said it sounded like a disease. She would plead with her mother to change it especially since everyone at school would laugh whenever her name was mentioned. It was particularly embarrassing when her teacher would call out "Euphemia" in class and she would have to stand up to answer a question.

Finally when she was twelve years old and received the Sacrament of Confirmation in the Catholic Church, she had the opportunity to choose a "Confirmation name." She picked the name "Ruth" and from that point on demanded that everyone call her Ruth. It took a while especially with her schoolmates, but finally she was able to "bury Euphemia" and live the rest of her life as "Ruth." The only one who would dig up the grave once in a while was my father when he'd get drunk and tease her. There was usually hell to pay.

When I was first told we were moving again for the third time in my young life, I remember feeling frightened. I had a sense of suddenly being lost and alone. My bedroom was where I felt safe. I could pretend there and dream away my unhappy feelings. When my parents would get into one of their loud, screaming arguments late at night, I would lock my bedroom door, scrunch deep down under the covers and try to block it all out.

But what was going to happen now when we moved? Would I have my own room again or would I have to face all those things I didn't want to face...all those things that made me scared, angry and confused? But I was afraid to ask. My parents didn't like talking about "problems."

And then I got more bad news. In preparation for the move, we would have to downsize some of our possessions, some of those things that wouldn't fit into the smaller apartment a few blocks away, some of those things that are important to a child.

My sister, Marilyn, who was two years older than I, couldn't take her big old cardboard dollhouse. There was no room for it, my mother said. But then she compromised and told my sister she could take all the dollhouse furniture to play with.

Marilyn had my mother's beautiful face except her eyes were blue, her hair was brown and she had a real stubborn streak that sometimes gave my parents fits. If she wanted something or didn't want to do something, she'd stand her ground. It seemed like she didn't mind getting hit or punished in some other way which is why my parents—my mother in particular—would usually compromise with her.

There was much that didn't seem to bother my sister like it did me. Our moving again was a good example, although I think she was glad to be getting away from "Pops."

He was the old man who lived with his wife in the house attached to ours. He was in his seventies, had a homely wrinkled face and body odor. But he seemed nice enough. My father used to invite him in to drink beer and kibitz once in awhile. But Marilyn always called him "that dirty old man next door." I learned later on why.

One day my sister was bringing her girlfriend, Nancy Wheeler, over to play with the new loom she had gotten for her birthday. "Pops" was sitting on his front steps when they arrived. He suddenly got up, grabbed little Nancy around the waist and said with a big friendly smile, "Give Pops a big hug."

Being a very outgoing eight-year-old, Nancy thought nothing of it...that is, until she felt the old man's hand slipping up under her dress

11

and into her panties. She started to yell and began slapping "Pops" across the face. He quickly put her down, opened his door and disappeared inside. When I heard that story, I asked Marilyn why she didn't tell our parents what happened. She said something strange in reply. At least I didn't understand it at the time.

"If I told Daddy, he would have killed 'Pops', especially if Daddy was drinking," she tried to explain. "That's why I told Nancy to keep quiet too. And if I had told Mom, she would have said it was my fault and, that I was probably leading him on. Then she would have hit me with that rubber hose she was always waiting to use on us.

"With Mom, I was the first one to blame for anything. She seemed to be mad at me all the time."

Then she added:

"I think her screaming bothered me a lot more than daddy's drinking."

When my sister said that, I realized her relationship with our mother was as bad as my relationship with our father. That's what can happen when drinking creates so much confusion in a family. Once I understood that, it drew Marilyn and me much closer together, and we still are today. We also had a baby sister, Patricia, who was only two. She would cry a lot whenever there was loud arguing going on in the house. I didn't realize what a sensitive nature Patty had until a few years later.

As for downsizing our possessions before moving, the first things I insisted on keeping were the souvenirs I had from The 1939 New York World's Fair. I was one of the few kids on our block who had been to the Fair and those souvenirs gave me bragging rights.

The Fair had opened on April 30, 1939 which coincided with the hundred and fiftieth anniversary of George Washington being inaugurated as President in the City of New York. That was before there was any Washington, D.C. I had the good fortune to be spending a few days with my Aunt Maggie in Williamsburg, Brooklyn around the same time the Fair was opening.

Aunt Maggie was my Grandmother McLintock's first cousin. She was also a lonely widow in her late sixties who loved company. She would take Marilyn and me off my mother's hands separately at times, bring us to her cold water flat and treat us like we were something special. I used to look forward to spending time with her because she loved to tell stories, laugh a lot and make sure we were having a great time. She was slightly over five feet tall and on the plump side. She'd love to take out her false teeth to scare you but she would laugh so hard doing it there was no way you could be frightened.

I apologize for continuing to get sidetracked like this but I have to tell you just a little bit about my Aunt Maggie because she was a very special person to me, especially when I learned what a difficult life she had. While I didn't realize it at the time, she taught me that a person can be happy even when they have pain and sorrow in their life.

Her full name was Mary Margaret Frye and I learned from family gossip her husband had died of a sudden heart attack when their only child, Willie, was five. Some said his heavy drinking caused the attack which shouldn't have been a surprise in a family like ours so riddled by alcoholism. While he left her some insurance, Aunt Maggie decided to save it to educate her son and give him a good start in life. So she made her living sewing for two tailors and cleaning clothes and apartments for her neighbors.

Instead of going off to college like his mother had planned, "Uncle Willie"—which is what we called him—became a New York City cop. That made my aunt very proud, especially when she was able to brag about how quickly her son was promoted to sergeant. However, she never talked about why he was suddenly fired from the police force. She managed to blame all of her son's troubles on "that Jewish hussy from Bensonhurst, Brooklyn he married against my wishes."

Sometimes my aunt would hug me and say, "I always hoped your Uncle Willie would give me some wonderful grandchildren like you and your sister so I wouldn't be lonely in my old age. But that Jewish wife of his never wanted to have any children. She didn't want to ruin her figure. That's why your uncle divorced her."

Family gossip told a different story. Supposedly he got drunk one night, pulled out his police revolver and threatened to kill her for cheating on him. She was gone before he woke up the next morning and never came back.

I would only see Uncle Willie when he'd drop by to briefly visit his mother while I was staying there. I remember he'd sit glumly with her at the kitchen table drinking shots of whisky while his mother would watch him with a sad look on her face. Then he'd follow her into the parlor where they'd chat for a few minutes. I'd notice her slipping money into his jacket pocket. Then he'd kiss her goodbye, force a smile at me and leave.

Aunt Maggie only talked about what a great policeman her son had been and that it was his whole life. She never ever mentioned the night Uncle Willie was found dead in his small apartment with empty bottles of booze scattered around the room. He was slouched in a chair after doing what too many cops still do. He put his gun in his mouth and pulled the trigger.

All this happened a year or so before the New York World's Fair rolled into town. As I said, I was staying with my aunt when she asked if I'd like to go with her to the Fair. I had no idea what she was talking about except that it sounded exciting. So we took a trolley car from Williamsburg, Brooklyn to Forest Hills, Queens and then another trolley to the Fair which was located on 1,216 acres of Flushing Meadow Park, just across the East River from Manhattan.

Back then, there were hundreds of trolley car lines running throughout the city. Trolley cars looked a bit like buses except they ran on steel tracks imbedded in the street and were powered by an overhead electric cable. They were similar to the ones still operating in San Francisco except these are pulled by an underground cable.

The first thing I remember seeing as we approached the Fair was its emblem, The Trylon and the Perisphere. The Trylon was a tall, pointed tower that stood next to this huge round silver ball called The Perisphere.

Big industrial and commercial Fairs like this were held on occasion all over the world as well as throughout the United States, primarily to introduce breakthroughs in science, business and technology and to build imports and exports between nations. The major goal of The 1939 New York World's Fair, however, was primarily to help jump-start the economy of the city and the state and end the lingering Depression.

I remember how my eyes popped open as we walked through the various exhibits and came across a brown wooden box with knobs that looked like a large radio. But there was a round glass picture on the front that showed people singing and dancing, like in the movies. Little did I know that this was the first commercially-feasible television set being introduced to America and the world by The Radio Corporation of America, RCA. Before long those boxes with pictures controlled by an antenna on top called "rabbit ears" were showing up in homes across the United States, at least in those that could afford it.

There were a myriad of such exciting exhibits ranging from futuristic cars and trains to the introduction of fluorescent lamps and air conditioning. There was also a large amusement area that featured a roller coaster, a high-speed train ride and an exciting one hundred and ninety foot high parachute jump. The parachute jump was so unique it was later moved to the Coney Island resort area in Brooklyn where it still remains today.

I wanted to see all the exhibits and go on all the rides, but my Aunt Maggie's legs and feet would only take her so far. After a few hours of enjoying what we could and eating too many waffles covered with whipped cream and drinking too many malted milk shakes, we headed for the trolley car to take us back to Williamsburg.

I remember my Aunt Maggie taking off her shoes on the trolley, rubbing her feet and saying to me:

"I could have walked a lot further if I didn't have these darn corns on my feet. Don't you ever grow old and get corns." Then she kissed me on the cheek and smiled: "I'm glad you had such a good time."

I did have a great time but I suffered for it for two days with a bellyache from stuffing myself with so many sweets.

There was one other aunt my parents used to park Marilyn and me with on occasion whom I'll never forget because of the bizarre way our relationship ended. Her name was Aunt May, another one of my grandmother Lizzy McLintock's cousins. She was married to a World War I army veteran named Frank Reardon. The sad thing was they could never have children. She was still quite attractive for a woman in her late fifties who dyed her hair bright red and wore a lot of makeup. She and Uncle Frank were also heavy drinkers.

Family gossip said Uncle Frank suffered from "battle fatigue" which I believe is what they now call PTSD or "post-traumatic stress disorder." I heard stories that he would get drunk, put on his old army uniform and helmet and march around his apartment with his rifle on his shoulder. Aunt May always denied it.

However, late one night when my sister and I were asleep in their spare bedroom, we were suddenly awakened by Aunt May's booming voice screaming profanities at her husband. I still remember her shouting things like:

"Put that rifle down you stupid bastard before I shove it right up your ass!"

Marilyn and I crawled to the bedroom door and opened it a crack. We could see they were both obviously drunk. Uncle Frank was dressed in his World War I army uniform and was pointing his rifle at Aunt May as he shouted back:

"Don't you ever call me a good for nothing old drunk again, you hear me! I shot a lot of Krauts in those trenches in France so I won't have any trouble shooting you!"

We were both quite scared so we closed the bedroom door and leaned against it praying Uncle Frank wouldn't shoot his wife and us too. The argument probably only lasted a few minutes but it seemed like hours to us. It was very difficult to go back to sleep. But in the morning we all had breakfast together as though nothing had happened.

I was reluctant to say anything to my parents but Marilyn wasn't. She even made the incident sound worse than it was. We didn't see Aunt May or Uncle Frank for a long time after that. The good news was he never shot his wife.

As I've said, from my earliest memories it seemed like no matter where I went or who I was with I was surrounded by the diabolical effects of drinking. So why would I ever want to pick up a drink myself when I got older? That's the most baffling part of this terrible disease of alcoholism.

Now, getting back to our moving… the good news was my parents let me keep all of my World's Fair souvenirs. The bad news was, I had to get rid of my closest and dearest friend, my pet duck Petey who I raised from right out of his shell.

We were all at dinner one night just a few weeks before moving when I was told there would be no room for Petey in our new small apartment.

"We won't have a yard or any open space for him to roam around," my father tried to explain. "And that's what ducks need—plenty of space."

"We certainly couldn't keep him in the house," my mother added. "You can't walk him like you do a dog, so he'd be going to the bathroom all over the house."

Naturally I couldn't believe what I was hearing. I remember I started pounding the table and shouting out something like: "It's not fair! He's my pet! You can't take him away from me!"

"Calm down!" my father said raising his voice. "Things are tough enough right now without you acting like a little baby!" Then he took a deep breath and said more sympathetically:

"Look, son, we know how much you love Petey but I don't think Petey would be very happy cooped up with nowhere to run around. So I talked to a friend of mine who owns a small farm way out on Long Island. He has a big pond with lots of other ducks in it that Petey could play with. Don't you think he'd be better off in a place like that?"

As much as I didn't want to admit it, what my dad said made sense. And even though he lied to me a lot—mainly promising to take me places we never went to or getting me things I never got—this time I wanted to believe him. If Petey went to live on a farm on Long Island, at least I could go visit him. So I calmed down and went quietly off to my room so I could sulk all by myself.

A few nights before we moved, however, we had Petey for dinner. I know it sounds horrible. Even at age six, I felt it was monstrous. My father had told me the biggest lie ever and my mother kept insisting it was a large chicken. But she was a worse liar than my father. She could never look you in the eye.

As my sister and I recall that painful incident, I stood there with tears rolling down my cheeks pointing at the large bird in the roasting pan and shouting:

"That's Petey! That's Petey!"

"That's not Petey," my mother kept insisting. "I told you it's a large chicken I bought today for our supper. So just sit down and stop crying!"

"No!" I continued to shout. "That's Petey! That's Petey!"

My father glared at me and said very angrily, "You sit down like you mother said or you'll get the worse spanking of your life!"

My mother turned to my sister. "Tell him that's not Petey!" she demanded.

Tears welled up in Marilyn's eyes too. She looked back at my mother and simply said, "No I won't." My mother reached out and slapped her right across the face. My sister jumped up and ran upstairs to her room. I ran after her, still sobbing.

I was sitting at the edge of my bed when my father walked in a few minutes later. I tensed up waiting for his large hand to start swatting my bare behind. I had been through that before and it was no fun. Instead he sat down next to me on the bed and started speaking very softly. I can't recall his exact words but I do remember the sense of what he said and the sadness in his voice.

"You know I'm getting pretty sick and tired of you being such a cry baby. You're going on seven and I keep telling you that real men take the good with the bad. It's better you learn now so you won't still be crying when you're forty years old.

"Besides, you're old enough now to understand that things can't always be your way. Times are tough and like they say, money doesn't grow on trees. Your mom and I do the best we can to feed you and put clothes on your back and that's not always easy to do. Do you hear what I'm saying?" I nodded.

Then he got up, rustled my hair and added:

"Someday you'll understand why things are the way they are and there's not much we can do to change them." He walked slowly out the door leaving me sad and confused but very grateful I didn't get that spanking. I went to sleep very hungry that night, still shedding tears for Petey.

Finally moving day arrived. It was Saturday and it started off as a very hot and humid morning. When I came downstairs for breakfast, I could see that all my clothes, shoes, toys and other stuff I helped my mother pack into two large suitcases were now parked near the front door. My older sister was still arguing with my frustrated mother over some stuff she still wanted to take with her. My baby sister was in her highchair playing with a bowl of oatmeal. My father was nowhere in sight.

As I poured myself a bowl of Wheaties I remember glancing into the dining room and parlor and seeing stacks of furniture that had been brought down from the upstairs rooms. All of a sudden I realized...we really are moving. I just wanted to sit there and pretend it wasn't happening. I kept staring into my cereal bowl until my mother came over and nudged me. She had to clean up the kitchen, pack the rest of the dishes, pots and silverware and be sure we all had everything out of our rooms. I remember she kept saying:

"I only have two hands so I need your help. I know you don't like it but it's what we have to do."

So I finished quickly and went back upstairs. As I glanced around my empty room, that feeling of being lost and alone came back worse than ever. I tried to stop the tears running down my cheeks but couldn't until I heard my mother shout, "What's taking you so long up there? Get down here and take care of your little sister."

When I reached the bottom of the stairs, my dad came charging in the front door clapping his hands and shouting,

"The moving van's here! Let's get the show on the road!"

I could always tell when my father was drinking. He was happy and filled with energy. Here it was not quite ten in the morning and he was already walking hand in hand with his friend John Barleycorn. Behind him were three of his drinking buddies from Monahan's Bar and Grill which, by the way, was right down the street from the apartment we were moving into. They all came to help us move.

I recognized one of the men because he was often at our house on weekends drinking beer with my father, smoking cigarettes and eating that terribly stinky old Limberger cheese with raw onions on crackers. My father was a heavy smoker all his life. My mother used to open up all the windows so the smell of the smoke and limburger cheese wouldn't get into the furniture and rugs. That's how bad it was.

The man I knew was named Charley, but everybody called him Charley the Vegetable Man because he sold fruits and vegetables around the neighborhood from his horse-drawn wagon. He and my dad were very good friends and drinking buddies.

There was this one Sunday afternoon I brought my friend Ricky into the house to play a game I had gotten for my birthday. Charley and my father were in the kitchen half loaded and smearing Limberger cheese with raw onions on some Pumpernickel bread. Ricky grabbed his nose and bolted out the door. He later told some other friends of mine he thought someone had gone to the bathroom on our kitchen floor. That's what Limberger cheese smelled like, a huge bowel movement. Boy was I teased about that.

My father and his drinking buddies started carrying our furniture out of the house. I remember looking through the doorway to see how big the moving van was. There was no moving van. The only thing parked at the curb was Charley's empty fruit and vegetable wagon.

As I watched Charley help my father and the others pile our furniture into the dilapidated vegetable wagon, I stood there with my mouth open. I had this feeling that I was in some strange place watching something very strange happening right before my eyes. And for some reason, I also began to feel a sense of shame deep down in my stomach.

It took them four trips to move all our furniture and belongings to the smaller apartment three blocks away, not counting a few side trips to Monahan's Bar and Grill. That's something I learned later that night when my parents had a furious argument because my father was so drunk he could hardly put the bed up in their room so they could go to sleep. .

But the worse thing I remember was that last trip over those three long blocks to our new home. My father insisted that we all ride in the vegetable wagon together.

"Come on. Get in. It'll be fun," he kept saying with a big silly grin on his face. "When did any of us ever have a chance to ride in a horse and wagon? I won't go fast, I promise."

My mother would have none of it. She put my sister Patty in her baby carriage and walked the three blocks. My father gave in and let Marilyn go with them. But he wasn't letting me out of all the "fun." He put me right up in the front of the wagon between him and Charley and told me to hang on tight as if the old nag could clomp down the street at a hundred miles an hour.

Charley let my dad drive the final leg. When he grabbed the reins and shouted "Giddyap," perhaps all the whisky he drank made him think we were some Wild West pioneers moving across the fruited plains in a Conestoga wagon. Instead, we were simply some poor, lost souls going to a place we really didn't want to go in a broken down cart still smelling from the rotting fruits and vegetables that had been in it the day before.

But the worst was yet to come. It was late afternoon now and the kids in the neighborhood were still playing stickball in the middle of the street. I saw them up ahead. Some were slightly older guys I looked up to and wanted to be accepted by as a friend.

Suddenly I was so embarrassed riding atop this old wagon with our belongings piled high in the back that I wanted to disappear. I tried to crawl down into the wagon but my father grabbed me and pulled me back up.

"No, I want to get off," I kept saying. "Let me go. I want to get off."

But my father wouldn't let go of me. He was apparently so proud to be driving a horse and wagon or so drunk that he was in another world that he began waving at all the kids as they stepped aside to let us pass.

I closed my eyes to blot out the scene. But I could still hear the derisive laughter and whistles and the insulting remarks made by some of them like "Hey look! The stagecoach just came to town" and "Hey, anybody need some used furniture" and "I hope that nag don't crap all over our street." Then one of the meaner kids pointed to me and shouted, "Hey Billy boy. You plan to enter the rodeo?"

A feeling of absolute humiliation filled every part of me. Once again I hated the man sitting next to me, the man who was supposed to be my father, who was supposed to love and protect me and not let people make fun of me. I remember thinking that I would never be like him when I grew up. It may have been the first time I ever made that promise to myself so clearly, so emphatically, but I was to take that oath many more times in the future.

That whole episode may have bounced right off someone more mature or with a harder shell, but for a six-year-old already suffering from low self esteem, it was devastating. And there was nowhere to hide. I felt like I was on display, an object for people to deride.

I've often wondered why I felt that way as a young boy. In fact, those feelings continued as I grew older...like I didn't quite measure up...that I wasn't as good as...that I was different...that I didn't fit in. I know it sounds crazy but I used to blame it on my mother because as a child she let my hair grow into long blond curls.

You see, for some reason my mother wouldn't let me get a haircut until I was more than four years old. She loved the long blond hair that hung down in ringlets around my neck. In fact, every time she'd wash my hair and dry it, she'd twist it around her finger to make the blond curls longer. In some old family pictures I looked like Shirley Temple.

It takes a lot for me to admit that even today because I hated having those curls. And the older I got, the more anger I built inside because people would tease me incessantly about those damn blond curls. Finally my dad came to the rescue. He knew how much it bothered me. I think it bothered him too having a son who looked like a girl.

Without telling my mother, he brought me to Barney's Barber Shop one day and had Barney cut off all my curls and give me a regular boy's haircut. I remember how great I felt looking into the mirror and seeing a real boy looking back at me. That was one of those times when I think I loved my dad for being someone who showed he really cared about me. Maybe that feeling would have lasted longer if he hadn't started drinking more and doing things that hurt all of us.

There was hell to pay when we got home from the barber shop that day. I do remember my mother yelling and crying when she saw me. I don't remember what my father did when she started throwing things at him. He probably went out for a few more beers.

When my father finally pulled the horse and wagon to the curb in front of our new apartment building, I remember jumping down and running up the stairs. I ran past my mother who was arranging furniture in the parlor, rushed through the dining room which was being turned into my mom and dad's bedroom and into the kitchen looking for my own room. I spotted two bedrooms in the back. There was a larger one where I saw my baby sister's crib and Marilyn already unpacking and a very small one where my bags were piled at the entrance.

The bedroom was barely big enough to fit my dresser, a chair and my bed although it did have a small closet to hang my clothes. I closed the door and stood there trying to catch my breath. After a moment I walked to a back window and stared out at a bunch of tall trees behind the building. The window opened onto a small back porch. I wondered if there was a yard down below to play in. That made me think about Petey which only made me feel worse.

I sat down on the bed and glanced around at the bare walls. While I was relieved to be away from those kids on the street and their painful taunts, that feeling of being lost and alone came back again. As I sat in the gathering darkness, it wouldn't go away.

So I did what I always did when I got anxious and sad. I began to pretend. I pretended I was somewhere else. Only this time I also pretended to be someone else...a boy who owned a big toy store and everyone who came in wanted to be my friend hoping I would give them a toy or a game or something.

I pretended until it was dinner time and my mother called us into the small kitchen for something to eat. My father wasn't there. I was really glad.

CHAPTER THREE

Twenty-Eight Flavors of Ice Cream

One of the great things about the human psyche is that emotional pain can subside over time and even go away after awhile. That's especially true at the young age of seven which is what I turned on September 9th, just a month after we moved into our new apartment.

While I still felt the whole world would never forget seeing me sitting atop that horse-drawn vegetable wagon looking and feeling stupid, most of the kids I knew in the neighborhood did so rather quickly. When you're a kid, you usually don't live in the past. It's what's happening right now that counts. So I began venturing back out and joining into the various street games we played like Johnny-On-The-Pony, Kick the Can, Marbles and Caught-Caught-Ring-O-Leevio. I discovered little had changed. My real friends still liked me and invited me on their teams and those that didn't I tried not to bother with.

More importantly, my dad had cut way back on his drinking and was on his best behavior, coming home every night for dinner. I could tell, however, that my mother was still walking on eggs, waiting, as they say, for the other shoe to drop. I still kept my distance from him for awhile even when he'd invite me into the parlor to listen to "The Shadow" or "Gangbusters" on the radio, two of my favorite radio shows. I'll never forget how "The Shadow" began. A sinister voice would come on and utter:

"Who knows what evil lurks in the hearts of men; the Shadow knows."

Whenever my father would feel guilty about his actions and their impact on all of us, he'd try to think up something special to make amends. I always wanted to believe that deep inside was a kind and loving man as I've said before. I don't think he ever did anything intentionally to hurt us. The problem was I wanted that good side of him to be there all the time and because of his drinking it wasn't. That was something that confused me and would take years for me to understand. Right now I couldn't. None of us could.

Anyway, at supper one Friday night he announced that we'd be celebrating my birthday the following Sunday by driving out to Freeport, Long Island in his big old Hudson car for a very special treat. He said it was a surprise.

The time was just before the outbreak of World War II and Freeport was still basically a small boating and fishing community on an inlet near the Atlantic Ocean. It was about an hour drive from where we lived. There was only one main road then to and from Freeport. It was called Sunrise Highway and that's where a new concession chain called Howard Johnson's had recently set up shop to sell hot dogs, hamburgers and soft drinks to the summer tourist crowd. But its popularity suddenly exploded when the food chain introduced a brand new and exciting product line— twenty-eight flavors of delicious ice cream.

According to company propaganda, Howard Johnson, who started the fast-growing enterprise in Boston, Massachusetts, loved his mother's home-made ice cream, especially the wide variety of flavors she was able to create. Being a great salesman and promoter, Howard waited until his mother had the number up to twenty-eight different and distinct flavors. He then made a big splash about it in the ice cream world which essentially was getting by on vanilla, chocolate and strawberry.

Almost overnight, ice cream lovers began flooding into Freeport just to get a taste of one or more of Howard Johnson's twenty-eight flavors. For families like ours, it became a special place to go on a weekend, spending the day together swilling down hot dogs, hamburgers and particularly ice cream cones filled with one or more of the twenty eight flavors made by good old Howard Johnson's mother. Today Howard has hotels and motels and a broad variety of frozen foods distributed all across the country.

So that's where we went that warm and sunny Sunday afternoon to celebrate my birthday. The whole family enjoyed being together that day. All of us, including my mother, got so stuffed that we slept all the way home. I think our snoring helped keep my father awake at the wheel. I wish I could remember how many flavors of ice cream I had but I'm sure it was more than plain old vanilla, chocolate or strawberry.

I hadn't seen my parents so happy together in a long time. At least it seemed that way. There was a smile of confidence on my mother's face, hoping perhaps that the worst was over and that my father might be changing his ways. But looking back, it was simply one more time when her hopes rose only to be dashed again sooner than she expected.

The fall season was now upon us and the leaves were beginning to turn those beautiful autumn colors. Aunt Catherine called one day to invite us to her home in St. Albans, Queens for a cookout. She was married to Uncle Freddie, one of my dad's four brothers and another heavy drinker. In fact, three of my father's four brothers were alcoholics although, like my dad, none of them knew it or would admit it. In fact, the term "alcoholic" was reserved back then for the Bowery derelict and rarely applied to "family men," even if they were staggering, falling down drunks.

I always enjoyed visiting Uncle Freddie and Aunt Catherine because they had three boys, Georgie who was my age, Bobby who was my sister Marilyn's age and an older son Frederick named after my uncle. They also had a real big yard to play in. Aunt Catherine was one of my favorite aunts, maybe because she baked such great cookies and was very generous in handing them out. I always managed to take home a bagful.

I can't recall ever seeing her when she wasn't wearing an apron. She was a jolly, plain-looking woman on the stoutish side and stood at least three inches taller than her husband who was only five foot six. Uncle Freddie, who was balding and wore glasses, always seemed to be smiling but never spoke very much...that is, until after he had a few beers.

The small town of St. Albans was another working class community once famous for its St. Albans Golf Course which attracted rich and famous golfers as well as sports celebrities like Babe Ruth. The Depression, however, forced the golf course owners to sell to a private land development company but the deal fell through and the land sat idle.

With World War II breaking out, the federal government seized the property in 1942 and built the St. Albans Naval Hospital for wounded servicemen being shipped back to the United States. It had seventy-six wards and more than three thousand beds. Today it's part of the Veterans Administration, operating as a Primary and Extended Care Facility.

There was a small, wealthier section of St. Albans on the border of Hollis, Queens where many famous jazz musicians once lived, like the great trumpet player Louis Armstrong, also known as "Satchmo." Soul musician James Brown who sold millions of records also lived in the town. And then there was that other musician in St. Albans who thought he was famous too every time he got drunk and played his violin...and that was my Uncle Freddie.

We kids spent that Saturday playing tag and kickball and enjoying delicious steak and chicken fresh off the grill. Freddie, Jr. did most of the cooking while our fathers sat at the picnic table drinking lots of beer. That evening came the usual drunken concert. Against my Aunt Catherine's wishes, Uncle Freddie took out his violin and began playing every sour note he had ever learned. He made the famous fiddle-playing comedian, Jack Benny, sound like a virtuoso. And on top of that, my dad started singing along with him.

Actually, my father had a very nice voice when sober. Many people in our family—and certainly many of his drinking buddies—thought he sang better than Bing Crosby. From some stories I heard, it went to his head at one point and he tried to break into "show business." Some friends introduced him to some bands in the area that played at weddings and needed a vocalist. He was given several opportunities but since booze flows like water at weddings, it never worked out.

As Uncle Freddie would scratch the strings of his old fiddle with his worn-out bow, I remember my Aunt Catherine shouting at him:

"Don't you realize what a fool you're making of yourself? You've never taken a violin lesson in your life yet you think you belong in Carnegie Hall." Then she'd look at my father and say:

"You've got such a nice voice. How can you sing along with all that noise he's making on that damn thing?"

My father would usually come to his brother's defense.

"Leave him alone, Kate. He gets better and better every time he plays it. Sometimes I think you women are jealous just because we like good music."

That would always draw a laugh until the duet would keep drinking and drinking. The longer they performed at Uncle Freddie's that night, the more upset both Aunt Catherine and my mother became. The hopeful smile my mom had on her face only a week before was now completely gone. My father was getting very intoxicated. So was Uncle Freddie.

My mother kept demanding that we leave. She wanted to call a taxi since we lived only a half hour away. She felt my dad was too drunk to drive. My Aunt Catherine suggested we stay there overnight since she had plenty of room to put us up. But my father would have none of it. He said he was perfectly okay to drive. I think my mother was too embarrassed to start an argument in front of her in-laws.

It was kind of late by the time we all got into the car and headed for home. My parents were arguing every step of the way. I sat in the front seat on my mother's lap. Marilyn was in the back next to Patty's car crib. Children's car seats hadn't been invented yet. Also back in those days, street lights weren't as bright as they are today, so my father appeared to be having a problem seeing the road in front of him.

Every once in a while I'd see him stick his head out of his rolled-down window. I learned later through my own experience that this is the way drunken drivers try to keep their eyes open. Every time he stuck his head out my mother would yell:

"Pull over and park the car! I'm taking the children home in a taxi before you kill us all. Pull over I said!"

But that would only make my father angrier. He would shout back:

"I don't need any back seat driver telling me what to do! I can drive this car better with one eye than some damn taxi driver can do with two. So just stop yelling!"

I don't recall exactly where it happened. We were driving under one of those elevated train lines New York City was noted for in those days. All I remember was hearing a loud crashing noise as we came to a sudden, shocking stop. The passenger door flew open and I was hurled from my mother's arms out into the street. I smashed my head on the curb and opened a gash above my left eye. My mother was slammed up against the dashboard. I heard her screaming. I think it was more out of concern for me than for any injury to her.

The next thing I recall there were people gathered all around me. My mother was pressing her handkerchief against my forehead and asking if I was alright. I really didn't know at the time. I think I was crying more from fright than from pain. Soon the police showed up. I don't remember if they took my mother and me to the hospital or if they called an ambulance. It was all pretty much of a blur then as it is now.

I was told the doctor put ten stitches into the nasty cut above my left eye. I still have the scar. I do remember my mother saying that God saved our lives. I think she was afraid to say anything about my father's drinking with the doctor and nurses all around us. I know she was very grateful there were no other serious injuries. That was probably because my dad's big old Hudson was built like a tank.

My father showed up later at the hospital with Marilyn and Patty in tow. None of them had been injured either. I think my dad had been shocked into sobriety which may be why the police didn't arrest him for drunken driving. Of course there were no "breathalizer tests" back then and much less enforcement of the drinking and driving laws. After the doctor examined all of us, we took a taxi home.

Over the next several days I learned that my father had smashed into one of the steel pillars that held up the elevated train line. His car, despite being built like a tank, was damaged beyond repair.

As I've said, I didn't understand until many years later that alcoholism is a disease, a very progressive disease, and my dad had it from stem to stern. From my childhood through my teen years and into young manhood I watched his disease progress, and with it my anger and resentment and yes, my hatred toward him—again, mainly because I didn't understand. He went through periods when he struggled hard to control his drinking. That's when things weren't too bad at home. But then he would go through periods when he lost all control and things got horrendous.

Late one evening after the accident I was asleep in my room when some voices woke me up. My door was slightly ajar and I overheard my parents talking in the kitchen. It was right near my room so I used to hear a lot when I was awakened at night. Actually my mother was doing the talking and my father was doing the listening. He used to describe times like that as "being in the doghouse." But she took things much more seriously. She was crying and saying something like:

"The police told me at the hospital we could have all been killed in the accident. They were surprised there weren't more serious injuries. Why couldn't you have just pulled over and taken us home in a taxi like I begged you to do?"

I heard my father reply, "I'm sorry. I'm really sorry. It won't happen again. I'll make it all up to you."

Then my mother started to cry harder. "I used to love you so much. I don't know how I feel anymore. I know I can't trust your promises. All I know is that if something like this were to ever happen again, I think I'd take the children and leave you for good."

Then she got up and went into their bedroom leaving my father alone in the kitchen. I think I heard him crying too but maybe that was just my imagination. After all, he always said real men don't cry.

I'll never forget how her words that night affected me. There were times when my dad would be so drunk and they'd get into such terrible fights that my mother would drag us all out of bed and take us to my grandparents for a day or two. But the idea of her leaving my father for good...of not having a mother and a father to take care of us sent shivers of fear right through my entire body. In a way, I'm glad she never carried through on her threats.

Even though I'd get angry at them once in awhile, particularly when I thought they were treating me unfairly, I knew in my heart I needed both of them. What would I do? How would I grow up without them? My mother's words that night in the kitchen bothered me so much I didn't want to think about them anymore. So I scrunched down under the covers and tried to dream them away.

Somehow I knew my father loved my mother very much. He would always tell people how beautiful she was. And she was, with those attractive grayish eyes and jet black hair. Well actually, from what I learned some years later, my mother dyed her hair black because before she was thirty, her hair had turned completely gray. When they'd fight she would often shout that it was all the worry and anxiety my father brought into her life that made her hair turn prematurely gray.

The last thing I remember my father saying to her that night was that he'd work twice as hard to make things up to her...that he'd get them out of debt...that he'd move us to a nicer place so we could have a better life. What I know now is that drunks will promise the world in order to calm things down and get off the hook.

But my father really tried. I know he did. Looking back, I remember he started coming home late at night, not because he was drinking, but because he began working double shifts at the newspaper. He also worked at other newspapers on holidays because he could make double time. As a member of The Pressmens Union, he was allowed to work at different shops when extra help was needed.

Working overtime, he made enough money to buy another car, a used 1938 silver Ford coupe with a V8 engine and a radio. It certainly wasn't as large or as well built as his old Hudson, but my father bragged it was much better on gas. That's when gas cost eighteen cents a gallon. Even though it was a smaller car, we were all able to fit into it comfortably. Most importantly, my mother liked it.

Maybe she liked it because it seemed easier to drive and, since the accident, she had been thinking about taking driving lessons in order to get her license. She was afraid the same thing could happen again if my dad didn't stop drinking.

But there was one thing for sure. She wasn't going to let him teach her how to drive. She was quite emphatic about that. Instead, she began saving up her pennies to take driving lesions. It took almost two years before she had enough. In the meantime, life went on...but not without its painful incidents

I'm sure we've all had our embarrassing moments in life, situations we're reluctant to talk about and hope not too many people remember or find out about. Well, I've decided to share one of my own most embarrassing incidents only because it drew me in a strange way much closer to my father at the time, something I always wished had happened more often.

It was about three weeks before Christmas and the students in the first and second grades at St. Sylvester's grammar school which I attended were practicing for the annual Christmas pageant. A very strict nun named Sister Julia of The Sisters of Charity was directing the play. While it was essentially about the birth of Jesus, she had created different kinds of characters to sing and dance and generally intermingle with the shepherds, angels and Three Wise Men. This was so parents would have a child in the play they could enjoy watching.

I was practicing to be a Brownie. From what I understood, a Brownie was something like an elf or forest creature that ran with the sheep near Bethlehem. My father thought I should have played a manly character like a shepherd or one of the Wise Men but Sister Julia thought I'd make a perfect Brownie. My dad didn't particularly care for this particular Nun after meeting her once at some school activities which he rarely attended.

It was after class one afternoon and we were all on stage in the second floor auditorium practicing our various roles. I must have had something to eat at my grandmother's house that didn't agree with me. She was a widow now and Marilyn and me would go there everyday for lunch since there was no cafeteria at school. Also, it was closer than taking the three-mile round trip to our house. I began to feel a rumbling in my stomach that told me I had to go to the bathroom—and soon. So I raised my hand to be excused. All I got from Sister Julia was a dirty look. So I started waving my hand frantically. She simply yelled:

"William! Put your hand down. Whatever it is, it can wait!"

No it couldn't. I felt it coming. I ran off the stage and down two flights of stairs to the Boy's Room. Fortunately our school uniform called for a white shirt, dark blue tie and dark blue knickers. The knickers saved the day. The diarrhea stopped right at the bottom of my dark blue knickers. I remember standing just inside the Boy's Room wondering what to do. Panic set in. Do I try to clean myself off? How? With what? Then the answer hit me. I've got to get to my grandmother's house in a hurry.

But how do you hurry when your knickers are filled with you know what. So I slowly squished my way five long blocks with people staring at me, then up a long flight of stairs. When I knocked on my grandmother's door, she knew right away there was something wrong, especially as I squished my way past her with tears in my eyes and sat down on one of her dining room chairs.

"What happened?" she asked in a very worried tone. "Tell Nana what happened."

Immediately I began to sob. I think I said something like:

"Sister Julia wouldn't let me go to the bathroom so I went in my pants."

My grandmother's worried tone suddenly disappeared as she shouted:

"Get off that dining room chair!"

I jumped up and started crying harder. The shame I felt was beyond description. I think my grandmother sensed that. She came over, patted me on top of the head, and took me by the hand.

"Come on. Let me get you into the bath tub."

For some reason, I was always ashamed to take my clothes off in front of anyone, even my parents. Now here was my grandmother stripping me naked and I didn't care a wit. I just wanted all of this to be over. But it wasn't. For as she was washing me down, there was a knock on the door and a man I knew named Bob Scuddy stuck his head into the bathroom. He owned the two family house where my grandmother lived. He and his wife resided downstairs. He was a very nice man who would drop by occasionally to see if my grandmother needed anything from the store, or just to make sure she was okay.

"Hey Billy," he smiled when he saw me in the tub. "What happened to you?"

My grandmother replied innocently enough, "He was practicing to be a Brownie in a school play."

I never heard anyone laugh as loud as Bob Scuddy did that afternoon. Then he replied:

"I can see he got the part." Then he roared again with laughter. I wanted to disappear. I was glad when he finally did.

That story spread like wildfire throughout the family circle. Everyone thought it was really funny except my dad. When I told him what had happened and why it happened, he started breathing fire. Before my mother could dissuade him, he drove over to the Nun's convent near the school that weekend and gave Sister Julia a piece of his mind. I wish I could have been a fly on the convent wall that day. She claimed she had no idea what went on since she was so busy with the other children. But she did admit she wasn't really paying attention to why I was waving my hand and apologized to my father and me for the embarrassing incident.

That was one of those terrific things about my dad. He always stood up for people when he saw they were hurt or the underdog. Drunk or sober, he didn't believe anyone had the right to take advantage of people, whether they were a strict Nun or judgmental priest, a mean boss or a ruthless bully. He believed in fairness and caring for the other person's feelings—at least when he was sober.

I came to realize that was probably why he took me to Howard Johnson's in Freeport for my birthday. Perhaps when he sobered up, he understood how embarrassed I was riding on that fruit and vegetable wagon in front of all the kids in the neighborhood.

Even though my mother was still upset over his telling off Sister Julia, I looked at him in a whole new light. For now, the hurt he caused was gone. He was my hero. I could now walk back into her class with my chest out and my head held high. And I wasn't afraid of what she might say when I quit my role as a dumb Brownie in her Christmas pageant. Actually she said nothing and began treating me with a bit more kindness and respect.

While our family wasn't what you might call "staunch Catholics," my mother did make sure we all received The Sacraments of the Church and went to Mass on Sunday. My father had been a Lutheran but converted to Catholicism to marry my mom. But at this stage of his life he was still pretty much a Lutheran when it came to practicing the teachings of the Catholic Church. He rarely went to Mass with us except when he was seriously "in the doghouse."

I was now eight and getting ready to receive the Sacrament of First Holy Communion. Ordinarily you do that in your local parish church which for us was The Church of the Nativity. But my mother had an intense dislike for the pastor of that church, Monsignor Alberto Archese who each Sunday would announce from the pulpit, "This Mass is being offered for all those who put twenty-five cents in the first collection."

To my mother's way of thinking, that meant if you could only afford to put a dime in the collection basket, you wouldn't receive any of the graces from the Mass. She felt that was very wrong because twenty-five cents was a lot of money to some people back then. She used to call the Monsignor "nothing but a money-grubbing pastor who didn't care for the poor."

So we went to St. Sylvester's Church and used my grandmother's address to pretend we were members of that parish. And she enrolled us in the parish grammar school even though it was more than a mile away from our house.

For the first few years, mom would walk us to school everyday, pushing our baby sister in her carriage. She would also pick us up in the afternoon and walk us home. When Marilyn and I got older, we started walking by ourselves. There was an elevated train we could have taken but it cost a nickel each way and my mother said nickels, dimes and quarters all added up. We did ride the train on rainy and snowy days however

Since I wasn't celebrating the Sacrament of First Holy Communion until the end of May, 1941, I had more than five months to prepare. What I remember most was Sister Alice Marie talking a lot about mortal sin and damnation. In our classroom, the girls sat on one side and the boys on the other. It seemed like every time the Nun would discuss mortal sin which she said could send you into the fires of Hell forever, she usually stood on the boys' side of the room.

I remember the day Sister Alice Marie pointed to us boys and said if we looked at a girl and had an impure thought about her, we could go right to Hell for that. Tommy Harriety who sat behind me was our go-to guy when it came to sex. That was a subject few of us knew much about.

But Tommy did. He had been left back twice and had a lot of street smarts. He tapped me on the shoulder and whispered:

"If you're going to Hell for the thought, you might as well go all the way." Even with my naivety, it made sense. It also gave me my first really impure thought.

I'm sure Sister Alice Marie also talked about a loving and forgiving God who was always watching over us, but for some reason I didn't quite see it that way. I saw God as this great King with a long white beard sitting on His throne in Heaven with a big book opened on his lap. He would look down and catch me doing something wrong and write my name in His book in red ink. He was always watching me so I had better be careful. I don't know why, but looking back, that's how my young mind interpreted what the nuns were telling me. That's why I was afraid of God for a long, long time.

As a result, I focused more on my fear of God than on His love for me. But then, I didn't really understand "love" anyway. Once in awhile my mother would say she loved me, but I never really felt it. And, as I've said before, I never heard it from my father. He thought you expressed love by giving you things, like at Christmas or for your birthday. Or maybe, because of my low self-esteem, I didn't feel "loveable." I've come a long way on that subject since, but back then and for quite sometime it was a serious problem in my life. It influenced my feelings and sometimes my decisions ...concerning both God and other people.

One of the things that happened as a result of my hearing so much about sin—everything from telling lies to getting angry to missing Mass on Sunday—was that I began to judge other people, especially my parents and especially my father. As a result, I began to lose some respect for him because of the things he did or didn't do. I'm sure I was taught about goodness and virtue too, but sin seemed so much easier to see, even in myself. <u>What a terrible thing it is to be judgmental!</u>

Let me make something very clear, however. I don't blame the nuns or the teachings of the Catholic Church for what happened to me. I think there was a spiritual gear in my thinking machine that was either damaged or not working right for a rather long time. I thank God that later in life I got it fixed...or rather, a set of spiritual principles fixed it for me.

Following all the preparations for First Holy Communion and after learning most of the answers in the Catholic Catechism, I now faced another very scary hurdle—the Sacrament of Confession. That meant I had to walk into a small, dark room and tell all my sins truthfully to someone I didn't know who was sitting behind a thin white screen. Even at this stage of my young life, I was so used to keeping secrets or making things up that I often had trouble separating fact from fiction. I remember my knees literally knocking when Sister Alice Marie leaned over to me in the church pew and said it was my turn to go into the confessional.

It wasn't nearly as scary as I had imaged. I had memorized a few innocent lies and made up a story about getting mad at my sister and kicking her. That got me by. I received a few words of admonition from the priest and I think for my penance I had to say five "Our Fathers" and five "Hail Marys." I was still sweating when I walked out, but I was really relieved. The rest of the sacramental process was a cinch.

I remember well the day I received the Sacrament of First Holy Communion. It was on a Saturday, May 30, 1941. My mother bought me a white shirt, a white tie, and a new blue suit with long pants. No knickers. All the girls wore white dresses with white veils signifying "purity of the soul." The boys wore white ties, I guess to signify the same thing. My mom and dad were both there along with my two sisters, my grandmother, my Aunt Helen who was my mother's older sister, her son Albert, and a few other close friends and relatives.

My Aunt Helen, by the way, was as beautiful as my mother but had auburn hair and blue eyes. She was two years older and had been married to a fellow named Gus Gersbeck who became a very sick and very vicious heroin addict. Often when he was high, he'd go into a jealous rage and beat my aunt severely. She stayed with him for several years because she blamed herself for some reason and was ashamed to let anyone know what was going on.

Finally she couldn't take it any longer. She snuck out of the house one night taking their one-year-old son, Albert, and moved in with her mother and father, my grandparents. She got a job with the telephone company, raised her son and never looked back. She was probably the kindest lady I had ever known and I loved her dearly until the day she died.

The one thing I remember most about my First Holy Communion Day was Sister Alice Marie drumming into us that when the priest placed the Holy Eucharist, the Body of Jesus Christ in the form of a thin, round, white wafer on our tongue, we were not to chew it. She said that would be "sacrilegious." I didn't know what that meant exactly but it sounded bad. But that's all she said. She never gave us any specific instructions about what else to do. So I kept my mouth partially open to be on the safe side and kept swishing my spittle over my tongue until the wafer got so soft it just slid down my throat.

I tried to imagine that Jesus Christ, the Son of God, was now inside me. I know it sounds crazy, but I kept looking down at my stomach for some reason. I wanted to "feel" His presence. But I couldn't. It was something I would spend years seeking—to feel that I was in the Presence of God.

The next thing I was aware of, we were all standing and singing another hymn and marching together out of the church and into the arms of our parents and a whole bunch of cameras.

My dad was trying to keep yet another promise to my mother and was going through one of his drinking-less periods. He was also still making some extra money from working double shifts. So he had another big surprise for us. To celebrate this important day, he said he was taking everyone, including my grandmother, Aunt Helen and my cousin Albert, to one of the most famous restaurants in New York City at that time called Lundy's.

An historic seafood eatery, Lundy's overlooked Sheepshead Bay Harbor in Brooklyn where more than a hundred deep sea fishing boats would tie up at the docks every day with large catches of fresh fish. People would come from near and far to buy everything from flounder and fluke to striped bass and blue fish. Many would drop by Lundy's for lunch or dinner which was said in its heyday to be the largest restaurant in the United States. It reportedly could seat between five to six hundred patrons.

Located at 1901 Emmons Avenue, Brooklyn, it was officially opened in 1934 by a Jewish immigrant named Irving Lundy. He actually came to the United States from Russia as a teenager in 1905 and began selling clams and muscles out of a pushcart on the Brooklyn waterfront. Twenty seven-years later, he laid claim to one of the most successful eateries in the country. He truly lived the Great American Dream.

What I loved most about Lundy's were the large wicker baskets filled with small, round hot buttered biscuits. You could have all you wanted. My cousin Albert and I probably ate a basketful each along with a huge fish dinner. Albert was about eight years older than I but we got along really well and became much closer as the years went by. He was a handsome young man with a big brown wave hanging just above his forehead and was very protective of his mother. Albert also seemed to take life much too seriously.

We all had a wonderful time that day and I thanked my father for making it such a special occasion. I remember he rustled my hair again and said:

"That's because it was a special day. And I'm very proud of you for doing such a good job studying and learning all you did for your First Communion. I sure hope you do a better job in the God department than I do."

I'm sorry to say that only a few days later my father started on another drinking binge. Two weeks later my mother almost died.

She had been complaining about pains in her stomach but felt they weren't serious enough to see the doctor. And as I said, my father was now back to his heavy drinking which only made matters worse. Fortunately, our summer vacation from school had just started and Marilyn happened to be home the day my mother needed her the most. I was out playing "Kick the Can" with the guys. My sister was in her room when she heard mom shout to her from the kitchen. She ran out to see her bent over the kitchen sink in severe pain and screaming: "Call the doctor! Hurry! Call Dr. Altruda!"

Even at the age of ten, Marilyn was good at handling emergencies. She got our family doctor on the phone and told him what was happening. He could hear my mother screaming in pain. He said he would call an ambulance right away and would meet them at Saint Catherine's Hospital in Brooklyn. I arrived home just as two ambulance attendants were carrying my mother down the stairs on a chair. She was doubled over in a fetal position the pain was so great.

My sister went with my mother in the ambulance. Before they pulled away she shouted to me to take care of little Patty and to find dad and tell him to come to the hospital right away. I stood on the sidewalk and watched them go. I felt frightened and helpless.

I walked slowly back upstairs and into the kitchen where Patty who was three now was playing with some toys on the floor. There was a yellow phone hanging on the wall. I knew how to dial information so I asked for the phone number of The New York Journal-American newspaper. I called but no one in the press room had seen him in awhile.

His closest friend was a man named Dick Nolan who lived in Brooklyn. He was another real bad alcoholic. I dialed information again and then managed to get through to his wife, Mary. She said her husband was at work, although she didn't sound that sure about it. When I told her what had happened to my mother, she promised to make some phone calls to try and locate my father.

I thanked her and hung up. I remember sitting Patty in a chair at the kitchen table and giving her a glass of milk, some crackers and a coloring book. Then I went into my room. A few minutes later Patty came in with her coloring book, sat next to me on my bed and asked:

"Where did mommy go? Is she alright?"

I didn't know what to say I was so frightened myself watching as they took her away in that ambulance. I think all I said was:

"I'm sure she's going to be okay. And I'm sure daddy will be home soon. So why don't you color in your book for awhile, okay?"

We must have sat together on my bed for over an hour, maybe more. Then the phone rang. It was my Aunt Helen. She was at the hospital with Marilyn who had called her. She said she would be by to pick me and Patty up and take us to my grandmother's house. She said my mother was doing fine, but I didn't believe her.

I remember walking into the living room and looking out the front window. I think I was hoping to see my father come down the street. I pulled a chair up next to the window and sat there looking out until the sun set and the street lights came on. Patty came in and laid down on the floor beside me. She had stopped coloring and was playing with some of her dolls.

I was half dozing when I spotted my Aunt Helen's car pull to the curb. I grabbed my sister, ran downstairs, opened the door and hugged her. I asked how my mother was doing

"She had a very bad attack of appendicitis," she said pointing to her side. "That's where your appendix is. It burst open and caused an infection. But thank God Dr. Altruda was at the hospital when your mother arrived. He was able to treat it right away and saved her life. But she'll have to be in the hospital for at least a week or more."

"Can we visit her?" I asked.

"I'm sorry. You're both too young. But she's going to be alright, I promise."

Then we went back upstairs, got some clothes and toys and drove with my aunt to my grandmother's place.

I didn't care what anyone said, I knew it was my sister Marilyn who had saved my mother's life. I also knew that my mother almost died. Even though I was told she was recovering, that fear inside of me wouldn't go away.

Suddenly I began asking myself, where was my father when we all needed him? Why hadn't he been taking care of my mother when she was having all that pain. He should have taken her to the doctor. And now, why hasn't he come home or called her or gone to see her?

My father showed up at my grandmother's house two days later. He was quite drunk.

CHAPTER FOUR

Overnight the Whole World Changed

My father's periods of sobriety were getting shorter and shorter even when my mother came home from the hospital. She was still quite weak and I could tell he was trying to be there for her by not getting too terribly intoxicated. Still I could see what a struggle it was for him to control his obsession with alcohol.

My Aunt Helen knew what was going on and was very concerned. She would leave work at the telephone company at three o'clock and come by every afternoon to spend a few hours with my mother. She often brought dinner or would send Marilyn or me to the market for something for her to cook.

At the same time my father was doing his best to be home for dinner and would often bring something for all of us to eat. Between him and my aunt there were always plenty of leftovers for the next day. I think the confusion about dinner came because Aunt Helen was very upset with my father but wouldn't say anything in front of my mother. As much as I knew, she cared for my dad but couldn't understand why he was still drinking when he had a sick wife to care for as well as three small children. None of us could.

Also, since the doctor said my mom had to rest and not go anywhere for at least a month, I would often hear her pleading with my father to spend more time with Marilyn, Patty and me. She would beg him to take us places like to the park or the beach on weekends.

I've mentioned how often my dad would promise to do things with us and then not keep his promises. Sometimes when he sounded real sincere, I would believe him and brag to all my classmates that my father was taking me deep sea fishing or to see the Brooklyn Dodgers play baseball or to an amusement park. Then when we didn't go, I'd have to make up lies to tell my friends and classmates about what a great time I had going on all the rides or catching a ton of fish. Maybe that's another reason why I began to hate my father while learning how to be a good liar myself.

But my mother's pleading finally seemed to reach him. It was the summer of 1941 and he did take us to Rockaway Beach on a few weekends. He also took me twice to see the Dodgers play baseball at Ebbets Field in Brooklyn. I recall the first time we went they were playing the New York Giants. I don't recall the score but I remember the Dodgers won.

I couldn't believe it when I walked into that stadium and saw the glistening baseball diamond surrounded by brilliant green grass. It was like being in a different world. The Dodgers were having a pretty good season under their famous manager, Leo Durocher. I think they finished second in the National League that year.

My dad and I sat in the bleachers eating hot dogs. He drank beer and I drank coke. I remember I kept the programs to those games for a long time because some of the players in the starting lineup became big heroes of mine.

There was Dolph Camilli who played first base, the great Pee Wee Reese who played shortstop, Dixie Walker, the home-run hitting right fielder and Joe Medwick, the best left fielder in baseball at that time. Then there were starting pitchers like Tex Carlton and Freddie Fitzsimmons, and the tremendous relief pitcher, Hugh Casey.

I rooted for the Dodgers for years until their infamous owner, Walter J. O'Malley, smuggled them out of Brooklyn one night in 1958 and settled them all the way out in Los Angeles. I don't think Mr. O'Malley ever returned to Brooklyn because there was a price on his head and a lynch mob waiting to string him up.

My sister, Patty, had just turned four and always wanted to go to the beach with us. But my mother was concerned that my father wouldn't be able to keep an eye on all three of us. Patty would put up quite a fuss when she couldn't go.

My baby sister was growing up to be a beautiful girl just like Marilyn, with blue eyes and long auburn curls. But she also had a bit of a temper and a stubborn streak that would often get under my mother's skin. I knew if she kept it up she was definitely a candidate for the "rubber hose club."

By the way, this rubber hose I speak about was two-feet long and served as a behavorial weapon. My mother always kept it near at hand to threaten us into absolute obedience or to vent her rage when she suspected one of us of the slightest wrong doing—or when she was really angry at my father.

As for Patty going to the beach, Marilyn always had a special relationship with my kid sister despite their age difference. She promised my mother she would watch her so my mom gave in. My sisters spent most of those summer days at the beach building sand castles together near the water's edge and splashing me every time I came near them.

That was the year I learned how to swim. One day my father tossed me into a big wave and told me to move my arms and kick my legs. He was a great swimmer himself and before the day was over, I was building confidence in my "Australian crawl." I think I almost drowned a few times, but my father was right there to pull me up and encourage me to try again. I felt good when he patted me on the back and said he was proud of me even though I swallowed a gallon of salt water.

"Salt water is good for you," he used to say. "It cleans out your system and makes you healthy so long as you don't swallow any jelly fish along with it." Then he'd laugh and laugh and rustle my hair."

I never saw my father drink anything but soda on those weekends he was with us—at least not until we got home.

Rockaway Beach, which was a half hour drive from our place, was part of the Rockaway Peninsula located on the south shore of Long

Island, just east of New York City. The beautiful, white sandy coastline still hosts the largest urban beach in the United States, stretching for miles along the Atlantic Ocean.

In the early 1900's the then New York Woodhaven and Rockaway Railroad constructed a rail line across Jamaica Bay and Broad Channel and built a railroad terminal at the beach. It was the key that opened up the coastal community and the rest of the peninsula to the city's growing population. That railroad later became part of the Long Island Railroad and is now part of the New York Metropolitan Transit System.

Then in 1937, the Marine Parkway Bridge was built which opened the borough of Brooklyn to Reiss Park Beach and the Cross Bay Bridge was completed in 1939 in Broad Channel, Queens to provide access to Far Rockaway Beach and beyond. That's when the real exodus from the city to the Rockaways began

The wealthy no longer had a monopoly on the beachfront. Amusement parks, stores and resort hotels began to spring up, attracting people from all over to spend a day, a week or the whole summer there. Newly-paved streets soon became lined with small summer cottages that even recently-arrived immigrants could afford to rent. The whole area became part of America's melting pot where the Irish, Italian, Polish, Jewish, German and other immigrants learned how to mix while still keeping a small part of their own culture.

There was one cluster of streets and cottages that became known as "Irish town." It was famous for its smoky Irish pubs and noisy dance halls filled with pretty Irish lasses. It was where every young lad whether he was Irish, Italian, Pole or Jew learned how to sing Irish songs and dance Irish jigs. As I grew into young manhood it became one of my favorite haunts.

But at this stage of my life, my favorite spot aside from the beach itself was a famous amusement park called "Rockaway's Playland." Built in 1910, it quickly became a major attraction for people in the area and my family in particular. The most popular attraction was "The Atom Smasher Roller Coaster." There was also an Olympic-size swimming pool where many people went just to get the sand off so they wouldn't have to take a shower when they got home. The few times my mother went to the beach with us, she wouldn't let us go into that pool. She said it was just an over-sized bathtub for lazy, dirty people.

There was also a great Penny Arcade at Playland filled with terrific games like Poker Ball and Pinball machines where you could win tickets for prizes. Since my dad couldn't afford to let us play that many games, Marilyn and I used to save up our tickets, hoping we'd come back again and be able to get a bigger prize. Sometimes we had to wait for the following summer to roll around.

Almost every time we came home from the beach late in the afternoon, my father would drop us off and then head down the street to Monahan's Saloon. His parting words usually were:

"Tell Mom we all had a wonderful day and that I'll be home in a little while."

We rarely heard him come in. We were usually asleep by that time.

Before I knew it, mother was well. The summer had turned to fall and we were back in school again. I had also hit another milestone. I had another birthday on September 9.

While a lot of my friends didn't particularly care for school, I must admit I was beginning to enjoy my studies. We had a nun who taught the fourth and fifth grades whose name was Sister Agatha Marie. She put a great deal of emphasis on reading and writing. Since I was a dreamer who also liked to pretend, the books she gave me to read spurred my imagination. They made it easier for me to escape the reality I sometimes dreaded and find solace in the stories that soon became part of my own life. I remember the very caring nun once said to me:

"You know, William, they say that the world's best writers are the most avid readers. Maybe you've already found your vocation in life without realizing it. I encourage you to read every book in our library and if you need any help finding ones you might like, just ask."

I particularly enjoyed stories about heroes, like martyrs and Saints, explorers and Princes and even ordinary people who did extraordinary things. Looking back, it seemed whenever I would imagine being like one of them, my low self-esteem would dissipate—a little bit. Reading was definitely my great escape.

But at home, things were always on edge. My mother was constantly trying to find ways to make my father spend more time with us rather than with his pals in the saloons. She had gotten to know some of the wives of his drinking buddies and began inviting them and their husbands to our house on Saturday nights.

I got to know some of them too. The usual Saturday night crowd included Dick and Mary Nolan, Tom and Gladys Murphy, Bill and Francine Webber and Bob and Marian Sharkey. Every now and then another couple would show up, like Charlie and Debbie Wheeler. Charlie was the bartender at Monahan's and the father of Marilyn's friend, Nancy Wheeler.

My mom always had plenty to eat and the other wives brought side dishes. I think the ladies believed that old adage that if you eat a lot you won't get drunk. My father and his friends quickly disproved that. They always ate a lot but still got drunk at those gatherings and their conversations would get louder and louder.

That's when I began hearing about America going to war. It seemed to be their favorite topic and it frightened me. My dad always seemed to know a little more about what was happening than the others—especially about some German guy named Adolph Hitler who was at war with England and France. There was also some fellow named Benito Mussolini, a dictator who ruled Italy. He had teamed up with Hitler and their goal was to conquer the world. My father kept saying they were well on their way to doing that.

Few people in America knew anything about Adolph Hitler until he invaded the almost defenseless country of Poland on September 1, 1939. Before that, the ruthless ruler of the Nazi Empire had been an aimless drifter and failed artist before joining the German army at the outbreak of World War I. He won the Iron Cross for bravery which helped pave his way into politics at a time when a defeated Germany was in deep economic chaos. He and his Nazi comrades helped pull their country from the brink and before long Hitler became Germany's undisputed ruler.

The more my dad and his friends drank on those Saturday nights, the more heated the debate grew over whether or not the United States should enter the war to help our friends in Europe, especially in England. That country was begging President Roosevelt for assistance. But the

President was pursuing an isolationist policy. He was shipping them some arms but many of the maritime vessels were being torpedoed by Nazi U-boats. By now Hitler and his well-armed German army had taken over France and his Luftwaffe was bombing London and other British cities into submission.

My father was very sensitive about the war since his parents came from Germany. Actually they were born in Alsace Lorraine which was a coal mining region between France and Germany that both countries constantly fought over. It was inhabited by both French and German people and Grandpa and Grandma Borchert were fluent in both languages. However, when they came to America, Grandpa Borchert insisted they learn and speak English only which deprived me of learning French and German myself.

Bill Webber and my dad were vehement about the United States doing everything it could to save England and all of Europe in fact, even to the point of going to war. Perhaps they felt that way to a small degree because they were both of German descent and didn't want anyone to think they could possibly be "German sympathizers."

Tommy Murphy, Dick Nolan, Bob Sharkey and all the wives including my mother were dead set against the idea of America going to war. From what I learned, most of the country felt the same way at that time...until December 7th of 1941.

That was the morning the Japanese launched a surprise attack on the U. S. Naval Base at Pearl Harbor in Hawaii, leaving more than 2,400 American servicemen and civilians dead, 188 U.S. aircraft destroyed and 21 U.S. naval ships either sunk or damaged.

Sunday mornings were a time of leisure for many U.S. military personnel at Pearl Harbor. They were either asleep or in mess halls eating breakfast or getting ready for church. They were completely unaware that an attack was imminent.

The Empire of Japan had been in negotiations with the U.S. government concerning its expansionist policies but felt they were getting nowhere. So rather than give in to our country's demands, they chose to team up with Adolph Hitler and Benito Mussolini to destroy our nation. At least that was their aim.

The sneak attack on Pearl Harbor so outraged Americans that President Roosevelt immediately abandoned his policy of isolationism and declared war on Japan the very next day. This brought the United States of America officially into World War II and into conflict with Germany and Italy too.

While I didn't understand all that was going on back then, I do remember that particular Sunday afternoon when my entire family sat in the parlor listening to the President and other commentators on the radio, talking about how and why the Japanese attacked us. I think my mother was crying. I know she was frightened. And I know my dad was very angry. He kept saying he wished he had the chance to kill Hitler and the Emperor of Japan himself. I also recall he spent the rest of the day in Monahan's Saloon and came home very drunk that night.

On Monday, December 8, President Roosevelt appeared before Congress to ask for an official declaration of war against Japan. I've heard and read his famous remarks many times but still get impressed by those words that stirred Americans into action...especially my father:

"Yesterday, December 7th, 1941, a date which will live in infamy, the United States of America was suddenly and deliberately attacked by naval and air forces of the Empire of Japan.

"The United States was at peace with that nation, and, at the solicitation of Japan, was still in conversation with its government and its Emperor looking forward toward the maintenance of peace in the Pacific.

"As Commander-in-Chief of the Army and Navy, I have directed that all measures be taken for our defense, that always will our whole nation remember the character of the onslaught against us.

"No matter how long it will take us to overcome this premeditated invasion, the American people, in their righteous might, will win through to absolute victory.

"With confidence in our armed forces, with the unbounding determination of our people, we will gain the inevitable triumph, so help us God."

As I said, the President's speech really touched my father. Once again he cut back on his drinking and came home almost every night for dinner. All he seemed to talk about was the war. But every time he mentioned how much he looked forward to being drafted into the Army, he and my mother would have an argument. She wanted to know who would take care of her and the children if he went into the service.

Once President Roosevelt officially declared war on Germany and Japan, Congress passed the U.S. Selective Service Act. It called for men between the ages of eighteen and thirty seven to register for service in the armed forces. I think my dad was thirty three at the time.

One of the most controversial parts of the new law was that African-Americans were initially passed over for the draft because of racial assumptions about their abilities and the viability of a mixed-race military. But this changed in 1943 when they were called up and assigned to "labor units." All this finally changed for good as the war progressed and African-Americans went into combat, performing heroically.

When registration first began, there were more than thirty-five million men eligible for the draft. More than fifty percent were rejected the first year either for health reasons or illiteracy. Then there were the "conscientious objectors", those who could demonstrate "sincerity of belief in religious teachings combined with a profound moral aversion to war." Most of them were Quakers. A small number did fight in the conflict, but most had to perform alternate service in what were called Civilian Public Service Camps.

By war's end, approximately thirty-four million men had registered and ten million served in the military. Almost four hundred thousand were killed and over six hundred thousand wounded.

My father was more than patriotic. He was determined to do more for the war effort than simply volunteer as an air raid warden. He wanted to suit up and show up and fight for his country. In fact, every time he was home, drunk or sober, he had his ear tuned to the radio listening to the news about the war. He wanted to keep up with every battle that was fought, where it was fought and what was the outcome.

I remember one night at dinner my mother telling him about a phone call she received that day from her sister, our Aunt Helen. She said our cousin Albert had just joined the Navy. Even though he was only seventeen, he had talked his mother into signing the necessary enlistment papers. My father exploded.

"I don't get it! Here's my young nephew going off to war and I'm sitting around like some damn coward doing nothing!"

"Doing nothing?" my mother shouted back." What about supporting your family? Is that doing nothing?"

"There are a lot of married guys in the service. They just work things out. For example, Helen could move in here with you and the kids. She has a good job and you could get a part time one. Between that and all the government benefits, you'd be fine. If they don't draft me soon, I'll just go down and sign up myself."

Now it was my mother's turn to explode.

"You just want out of here so you can get drunk with a bunch of army buddies!" Then she lost control of her emotions, picked up a dish and threw it against the wall. "If you want to go, then go! Get out of here right now!"

She ran into her bedroom and slammed the door. My father grabbed his jacket from the kitchen rack and headed down the stairs. We all knew he'd wind up in Monahan's saloon and there would be another big argument when he came home. We weren't disappointed.

Yes, my father was eager to fight "those dirty Nazis" and "those lousy Nips." Over the years I've sometimes wondered if my father also suffered from low self-esteem as a young man like I did. Perhaps he didn't feel good about himself and thought that fighting for his country might change all that.

Anyway, things finally did calm down at home. I believe my mother came to realize that my father's desire to defend his country was sincere and that her opposition was based on fear. I think it frightened her that he might never come back from the war. That fear probably grew worse each time she heard on the radio or read in the newspaper about all the casualties piling up in Europe and the South Pacific. I could see it in her face when my father would come home and start looking through the mail for his draft notice

It all came to a head that spring when his good friend Bob Sharkey was drafted. He was younger than my dad and had no children. That really upset my father. First my cousin Albert joining the Navy and now his friend Bob was going into the Army.

My mom told me some years later that my father went to an Army recruiting office in the city the next day and tried to enlist. In fact, she said he demanded that they take him. My father discovered for the first time that the military wasn't drafting family men with more than two children. Seeing how dedicated he was, my mother said one of the recruiters tried to pacify him by saying that if the war got worse, they'd probably call him up. But that didn't satisfy him. He left very disappointed, got drunk and stayed drunk for three days.

As much as she tried to understand his disappointment, my mom was having more and more difficulty accepting his drinking. His anger at the world was making him a nasty drunk. He'd say terrible things and then try to apologize. Other times he'd claim he didn't remember because he was in a blackout.

I'll never forget one night when I heard them screaming at each other in the parlor. I also heard some things crashing to the floor. I leaped out of bed and ran in to see them actually brawling with each other and knocking over lamps and tables. Marilyn and Patty followed me. We all started crying and pleading with them to stop. My mother suddenly came to her senses when she saw us. She bent down and hugged us and apologized for what they were putting us through. My father was so drunk he simply slumped into a nearby chair.

Mom made Marilyn and me get dressed, wrapped Patty in a blanket and took us all over to my grandmother's house. While it wasn't the first time she did this, it certainly was a night I'll never forget. I don't remember what time it was when all this happened, but it was very dark and very chilly as we walked that mile and a half to City Line.

My dad came over to my grandmother's house the next day. I remember my Aunt Helen really told him off. He promised to go with my mother to see the priest and take a six month pledge not to drink. He swore this time he would keep it. Deep down I knew they really loved each other, so even terrible rifts couldn't keep them apart.

Still, I've wondered over years why good women like my mother and later my own wife stay with alcoholics who only cause them anxiety and pain. Maybe they have a sixth sense that tells them eventually everything will work out. Sometimes it does. Sometimes it doesn't. At this stage of my father's life, it wasn't working out. It was only getting worse.

I recall it was a nice sunny Saturday morning in late May or early June when I was out in the street playing stickball with the guys. I really loved that game which we played with a broomstick and a pink rubber ball we called a "spaldine." I used to brag I was "a two-sewer man" which meant I could hit the ball past two manhole covers or sewer lids that were spaced down the street. Some of the older kids could hit it three sewers. I never saw anyone hit it four sewers.

There were usually a bunch of other guys waiting around to play the winning team. There were also girls rooting for their favorite guys. When you sense some pretty girl is smiling at you, it can create a lot of pressure. That's why I always hated striking out. I'd feel like a loser and try to hide behind some bigger fellows.

Suddenly we all saw this taxi cab turn the corner and drive slowly down the street, apparently looking for an address. It forced us to move out of the way to let it pass. Then it stopped. The door opened and a man staggered out very drunk and very disheveled. He had a stupid, drunken smile on his face and was dribbling from his mouth. He tried to hold on to the cab door but slipped and fell into the street. He was my father.

As the cab driver came around to pick him up, I could hear some of the kids laughing. Those who knew my father appeared embarrassed for me at first. But they joined in the laughter too when the cab driver had a problem getting my drunken father to his feet and dragging him toward our front door.

It's difficult to describe my feelings as many of the kids stared at me while trying to cover up their laughter. I think I may have hoped that one of the manhole covers would have popped open so I could fall into the sewer and drown. The shame and humiliation were that excruciating. So I simply turned and ran. I didn't know where to go or what to do. I just ran.

Back then there was still a lot of "country" around our neighborhood...dairy farms, horse stables, large fruit and vegetables farms and a lot of open land all the way to Jamaica Bay. That was the first big inlet near us that was fed by the Atlantic Ocean. It was a great place to fish for flounders and eels and catch large Blue Claw crabs.

There was one main highway nearby called the Belt Parkway that connected New York City with Long Island. The fruit and vegetable farms

I spoke of started on the other side of that road and covered hundreds of acres. Most people referred to them as "The Japanese Nurseries" because they were owned by Japanese-Americans who settled there many years before. They also had acres of flower gardens where they grew the most beautiful roses and many other kinds of blooms.

Some of the older fellows used to work there in the summer time. You had to be fourteen to get your working papers back then so I didn't qualify. But I would enjoy visiting the farms with some friends. The owners were very kind and would give us radishes and carrots to bring home. I even got to meet a few of the pretty Japanese-America girls my own age who would smile silly smiles and then shyly dash away. I hadn't been to the nurseries now in over a year, mainly because my father had ordered me to stay away.

"I don't want you to go anywhere near those damn Japs!" was the way he put it.

The next thing I remember I was running across Belt Parkway and finding myself in a large, barren field that I was certain was part of the fruit and vegetable farms. I couldn't understand why there wasn't anything growing at that time of year.

Up ahead I saw some storage buildings and some vacant houses that belonged to the owners of the Japanese nurseries. Everything seemed to be empty and there was no one in sight. That's when I stopped running. I just stood there looking around.

What I was to learn later really shocked me even though I had heard my father and others talk about all the atrocities being committed by the Japanese during the war in the South Pacific. I guess I never equated that with the warm and friendly folks I had met and gotten to know at these farmlands.

Right after the attack on Pearl Harbor, anti-Japanese propaganda spread rapidly across the nation. Despite the lack of any concrete evidence, Japanese-Americans were suspected of remaining loyal to their ancestral land and thus a security risk to the United States.

Succumbing to bad advice and popular opinion, President Roosevelt signed an executive order in February, 1942 ordering the relocation of all Americans of Japanese ancestry to concentration camps in the interior part of the United States. While the order focused primarily on the large Japanese presence on the West Coast, I came to understand that some other large concentrations of Japanese-Americans were also included like those who owned the farms and flower gardens just across the parkway from us.

Evacuation orders were posted in Japanese-American communities giving instructions on how to comply with the executive order. Many families had to sell their homes, their stores and most of their assets at a fraction of their true value. Many were housed in temporary centers such as stables at local racetracks until the camps were completed in remote areas of seven western states.

The housing was Spartan, consisting mainly of tarpaper barracks. The camps were often too cold in the winter and too hot in the summer. The food was mass produced army-style grub. Eventually the military accepted a number of carefully investigated Japanese-Americans who wanted to get out of the camps by volunteering to fight for their country which was America in two all-Nisei army regiments. They went on to distinguish themselves in battle.

In 1988, Congress attempted to apologize for those harsh and unjustified actions taken during the war by awarding each surviving internee $20,000. But such a puny award didn't come close to salving all the hurt and bitterness caused by the President's executive order. The concentration camps that interned "American citizens" remained a dark mark on our country's record of respecting civil liberties and cultural differences.

I spent the rest of the day and early evening wandering around, looking into empty houses with broken glass windows and fruit and vegetable barns that still smelled of the produce they once stored. It was eerie and confusing.

Even though it was late May or early June, the night air got very chilly, especially with the wind blowing in from Jamaica Bay. Yet I didn't want to go home. I had "run away" a few times before when my mother's screaming or my father's drunkenness had gotten to me. But I usually returned in a few hours and most certainly before the street lights went on. We always had to be home before that occurred otherwise it was the rubber hose for sure.

I thought about some friends I might stay with. I knew they'd like to have me but I wasn't so sure about their parents. They would probably call my mom or dad and then I'd really get killed. I also thought about going to my Grandma McLintock's house but the same thing would happen. It was probably after ten o'clock by the time I realized I had no other place to go but back home.

It had been a long and very emotional day so by the time I opened my front door and got ready to climb the stairs I was completely exhausted and very hungry. I hadn't eaten anything since breakfast. I only hoped my mother would understand when I explained to her what had happened. Then I noticed she was standing at the top of the stairs. She had heard me open the door and was waiting for me with that rubber hose hidden behind her back. I got the first whack before I even reached the kitchen. I remember she kept screaming:

"How dare you stay out like this! You had me worried to death! I thought something happened to you! How dare you treat me like this! How dare you!"

And after every scream she'd slam me again with the rubber hose. I ran into my room. It was a dumb thing to do because I was now trapped. She kept hitting me on the arms and legs, even when I dropped to the floor and tried to crawl under my bed.

I remember my sister Marilyn yelling at my mother to stop. She was crying as she tried to grab my mother's arm. That's when she got whacked too. My mother seemed to be out of control. Finally she stopped and glared at me saying:

"Don't you ever do that to me again! It's bad enough what I have to go through with your father! Don't you ever do that again!"

Then she turned around and walked back into the kitchen. Marilyn looked at me with tears running down her face. She just shook her head and went into her room. I sat on my bed trying to understand what had just happened. My arms and legs were stinging with pain. I thought my mother would have at least let me explain. I thought she would feel sorry for me when I told her about all the kids laughing and poking fun. But she never gave me the chance. I wondered how people could be so unfair, so mean and cruel, especially your own mother.

When I closed my door, got undressed and went to bed, I never even thought about my father, where he might be or what he might be doing. I really didn't care. And I was sure he didn't care about me and what had happened that day. It took me a long time to go to sleep that night, even when I tried dreaming and pretending.

When you think things can't get any worse, they often do. That September, Uncle Henny, my father's oldest brother, was killed in a tragic car wreck. The police said they found an empty bottle of bourbon in the front seat. The doctor at the hospital said my uncle was totally intoxicated at the time of his death. I don't know if any of that registered with my father or not...I mean, that it was booze that killed his older brother.

Uncle Henny was the wealthy one in the family, very well respected until his success went to his head. He and his wife, my other Aunt Katherine spelled with a "K," lived in a lovely big house in Glendale, Queens, which was a very upscale neighborhood at the time. They had one son, Henry, who was another one of my heroes. He was a real big guy about six years older than I and was the star fullback for St. John's High School football team, a prominent school in the area. He was also his father's pride and joy.

When I say all that money went to my uncle's head, that's based on the stories I heard about him while growing up. He wasn't the handsomest of men, but Uncle Henny's money helped him attract a pretty blond girlfriend. At least that's what Aunt Katherine charged him with when she divorced him.

He moved into a stylish apartment in the city with his young girlfriend who loved to throw big parties for her friends. My uncle enjoyed going to the racetrack and playing cards for high stakes. He was also a very big drinker, mainly bourbon on the rocks. But the biggest problem I heard about was that he trusted the three men who managed his sheet metal plants. He trusted them too much.

It seemed like everything came apart at the same time. His business ran out of cash, his girlfriend walked out on him and his son, Henry, who already had a scholarship to play football at Notre Dame, died of a ruptured spleen when he was injured playing in a championship football game. His funeral was one of the saddest I ever remember attending. I think half of the student body at St. John's was there including the football team with each member wearing a school jersey.

They say Uncle Henny went into such a deep depression that he locked himself in his apartment for days. When he finally ran out of bourbon, he went out to get another case. He smashed his car headlong into a pole going eighty miles an hour.

My Aunt Katherine arranged for a one-day wake followed by a quick burial the next morning in Evergreen Cemetery in Brooklyn. I remember I hardly recognized her she looked so pale and gaunt. Then I realized she was still mourning the loss of her son. I'm sure she had mixed feelings about her late ex-husband.

I think my father was very upset because more people didn't attend his brother's funeral. He always believed his older brother's braggadocio, that he knew everybody in town including all the big shot politicians and businessmen. But the funeral parlor wasn't even half-filled.

In the end, it seemed all that Uncle Henny's death meant to my father was another excuse to go on another self-pity bender. And that he did. He got into another car wreck which turned out to be a minor fender-bender. But I heard the fellow he hit wanted the police to arrest him for being drunk and abusive. The cops let him off with a speeding ticket.

As I've said, when you think things can't get any worse, they often do. Two weeks before Christmas, I set the house on fire.

CHAPTER FIVE

Joy in The Midst of Gloom

Webster's Dictionary defines the word "appeasement" as a way to bring about a state of peace, to allay unsettlement, to create calm and to pacify. It's a word that can be applied to a number of situations and actions like warfare, difficult negotiations, tough business deals or strained relationships.

In my father's case, it was the latter situation that explained why he and his friend, Charley the vegetable man, had just finished painting my mother's kitchen. For months she had been complaining about the awful yellow color that covered everything but the ceiling. That was white and peeling. So, after another drunken spree followed by another big argument, my dad found a way to crawl out of the doghouse one more time. He made the kitchen look clean and bright for the coming Christmas holidays by applying two coats of sparkling white paint.

But he made one mistake. He left the half empty paint cans in the hallway outside the kitchen door along with the paint brushes sitting in a can of turpentine

All those who paint know that turpentine, which is used less often these days, was once an essential cleaning agent for paint brushes since most paints were oil-based, not water-based as most are today. Turpentine is also one of the most flammable liquids you can find. I didn't know that. I had to discover it for myself.

It was Saturday afternoon a few weeks before Christmas. My mother was out shopping with my sisters. My father was catching up on his sleep. I had been doing some reading in my room. My stomach started to growl so I went into the kitchen to get something to eat. The smell of paint still filled the room. I glanced through one of the glass panes in the kitchen door and saw the paint and the brushes sitting in the can of turpentine.

Why did I do it? That was the first question the Fire Marshall asked me. How he knew I did it in the first place shocked me at the time. Now I know an experienced fire investigator can quickly spot a guilty person when their whole body is shaking and their face is filled with fear. To this day I honestly don't know why I did such a stupid thing.

There was a book of matches on the kitchen table next to a pack of my father's cigarettes. I took them and walked out into the hallway. I knelt down next to the paint and removed a paint brush from the can of turpentine. Maybe I wanted to see if the paint brush would light up and become a torch. I struck a match. The next thing I know the paint cans, the turpentine and the brushes were all ablaze.

Talk about panic! I ran back into the kitchen and filled a glass with water. When I poured it on the flames they only got worse. I remember running into my father's bedroom and waking him up shouting, "Dad! Get up! The hallway's on fire!"

My father leaped out of bed. He was in his underwear. He charged into the hall. By now the curtain on the kitchen door was also ablaze. So he kicked the burning cans down the stairs. The problem was, the live Christmas tree he had bought the day before was standing in the downstairs hall, next to the front entrance. That caught fire too. I just stood there paralyzed with fear.

My dad ran back into the kitchen, grabbed the phone and called the police and fire departments. It was amazing how quickly they arrived. Meanwhile, he doused the burning curtain on the kitchen door, took a pail from under the kitchen sink and began throwing buckets of water down the stairway which was now also on fire. I think that's what saved the day along with the fact that the hallway walls and ceiling were made of heavy plaster instead of wood.

By the time the firemen put the fire out, the entire entrance hallway and stairs were blackened by smoke as was my mother's newly-painted kitchen and part of their bedroom. Several steps on the stairway had been chopped away by the firefighters so that you could see into the grocery store below which received significant water damage. I just sat in my room shaking to pieces, knowing I was in very serious trouble. Then the Fire Marshall walked in with my dad who was now wearing a pair of pants. His face and arms were covered with soot.

"It had to be that electrical outlet in the hallway," I heard my father say to the fire official. "It probably short-circuited and caused a spark. It was my fault for putting those paint brushes and turpentine right next to it."

"No," the stocky, ruddy-faced official replied rather calmly. "There's no possible way the fire could have started like that." Then I spotted his all-knowing eyes staring down at me as he said, "But perhaps your son can tell us how it started."

There's no way to describe all the frightening emotions that suddenly shot through my entire body. I knew I was trapped…found out…nailed to the floor. In nano-seconds a series of questions zipped through my brain…what would happen if I confessed…is there any possible way to deny it…does he really know that I did it? But it also took just that long to realize I had absolutely no defense. So I just lowered my head and burst into tears.

"I'll leave the boy in your hands," the Fire Marshall said to my father. Then he turned and walked slowly from the room. When I look back now, I'm convinced my father knew I was the culprit all along and was trying to protect me. But he had no chance of convincing an experienced arson expert.

My dad never said a word to me. He just stood there for another moment before walking out and closing the door behind him. Again, when I think about it, what was there he could have said or done? Sure, he could have yelled at me or hit me. In fact, that's what I expected. Maybe he understood that I was already punishing myself enough for doing such a stupid thing and hoped the enormous fear and anxiety I was going through would teach me a lesson. And maybe, just maybe, he felt a bit guilty himself for all he had been putting me through. While the damage was considerable, it could have been a whole lot worse.

As for my mother, her reaction was what I had expected. She got absolutely hysterical. But I can understand that now. By the time she arrived home from shopping all the fire trucks had gone. But there was a police car and the Fire Marshall's car still parked across the street and some busybodies staring at the blackened front door.

Also, a few of my father's friends from Monahan's were there helping to repair the hallway steps the firemen had chopped up. Those fellows were like most of the drunks I've met in my life...good guys on the outside trying hard to become so on the inside.

I can still hear my mother's voice as she climbed the soot-covered stairway and saw her once newly-painted kitchen charred from all the smoke. "Oh my God!" she kept shouting. "Oh my God!"

No, she didn't hit me with the rubber hose. Somehow my father convinced her not to follow her normal instincts. But when she did calm down enough to come into my bedroom and face me, she gave me a long, loud and angry scolding through tears of deep frustration. I remember the gist of what she said:

"Here it is a few weeks before Christmas and you do something like this. As if things aren't bad enough. Do you have any idea what it's going to cost us to fix this place up? And where's the money going to come from?

"I thought you'd be the last one to do something stupid like this. What if you had burned the whole house down? Did you ever think of that? How much more trouble do I have to go through?

"You're not going anywhere for a month...not with your friends ...nowhere. And you'll help with the dishes and cleaning the house. And no more radio shows until I think you've learned your lesson. Do you understand?"

I simply nodded my head, praying the verbal flogging was almost over. It was. "And clean up your room!" she shouted before turning around and angrily stomping out. Compared to the rubber hose, I felt like I was getting off pretty easy, at least for the first few weeks or so. Then each day began to feel like a year.

Again my father's pals from Monahan's helped him clean the place up in a matter of days. They also helped repaint the hallway, the kitchen and my parents' bedroom and this time left nothing behind that could be ignited. But it took my mother much longer to calm down and put the incident behind her.

I think she was the kind of person back then who always looked at the negative side of things. At dinner she kept saying that the fire could have burned down the entire building. She wouldn't look at the positive side or at least voice it—that fortunately the damage was easily repairable and that things were back to normal, or whatever normal was at our house rather quickly.

We did have a pretty good Christmas that year. Dad didn't drink very much or fall into the Christmas tree like he did the year before. And it seemed that he and my mother had become a lot closer and more loving once more. We visited a lot of friends and relatives and had people over to visit us. It struck me that the fire might have had an impression on my father as much as it had on me, for it seemed to be keeping him on his good behavior.

Another reason that thought occurred to me was his sudden decision to enroll in a special school to study the technology of air conditioning. I don't remember how it all came about but I do recall hearing him talking with my mother from time to time about finding a new occupation. He would say things like:

"Our union contract isn't up for negotiations until next year. That means we won't be getting a pay increase until then and nobody knows how much it will be. If we're not offered enough we could be going out on strike and that could mean weeks without any money coming in."

"The other problem is, everybody at the paper drinks. You know that. There's five saloons within two blocks and Moochie's bar is right across the street. I'm always under pressure to join the guys for a drink every time we get a break between editions. That's why I'm starting to look for a different kind of job, one that pays a lot more money and is not surrounded by saloons. That would be better all around, don't you think?"

I remember how my mother put her arms around my dad and held him tight. Naturally she agreed with his observations. Also he was currently going through one of his longest "almost sober" periods and she hoped it would last forever. She had been at her wits end trying to find ways to slow him down or get him to stop and now once again she saw hope on the horizon. I always thought it was amazing how she was able to forgive and forget the past. But then maybe she didn't. Maybe it was just that hope always seems to spring eternal.

At dinner one evening my father mentioned that an electrical engineer he knew at the paper told him he was leaving to go into a relatively new field called air conditioning. He suggested my father look into it.

While air conditioning might have been considered a new field in the early 1940's, it certainly wasn't a new concept. Actually, the first modern electrical air conditioning unit had been invented way back in 1902 by a man named Willis Carrier from Buffalo, New York. The introduction of residential air conditioning, however, didn't come along until the 1930's. I remembered seeing it on exhibit when my Aunt Maggie took me to The 1939 New York World's Fair.

Two things happened that greatly slowed down the industry's development. First was The Great Depression when few could afford such a luxury, including businesses. Then came the start of World War II and the greatly increased need for steel and electrical components to build equipment for combat—ships, planes, tanks, jeeps and related technical support systems like radar and sonar. It was only after the war that the air conditioning industry took off and played a vital role in spurring the nation's economy.

Even though it was 1944 and no one knew when the war might end, my father saw it as an opportunity to get in on the ground floor. He believed it was a business that had huge future potential. At least that's what he had heard when checking with other engineers.

So he enrolled in a one-year program that would teach him both the fundamentals and advanced knowledge of the technology. My father's plan was to keep his job as a pressman until he had graduated and found a job in the air conditioning industry. His dream was to someday have his own air conditioning business.

My dad once told me he had a lot of excellent opportunities over the years to improve himself...to move ahead...to give his wife and family a better life. But booze took them all away. For example, he often wondered how far he might have gone as a band singer and vocalist had it not been for his drinking. He had a number of good job offers he blew when he showed up tipsy for interviews. He drank his way out of the possibility of becoming a pressroom foreman. And now here was a chance to get involved in an industry that seemed ready to explode.

The night course my father took was in the city. His class started at six in the evening. He finished at the newspaper at five and it was only a twenty minute subway ride to school. He made it easily the first month or two. My mom kept saying how proud she was of him. But then he started giving in to the pressure from his drinking buddies. He began dropping by Moochie's "just for a few beers." He started arriving late for class. Then he missed a few classes. He managed to hang on until shortly after Thanksgiving Day.

But something else happened around the same time that helped grease my dad's inevitable downward slide. His father passed away. Grandma Borchert found him slumped over in an armchair next to the parlor window in their second floor apartment.

Retired now, he had gained so much weight that he couldn't walk very well. So he just sat by the window drinking and waving to people as they walked down the street. There was a half finished quart of Rye whisky on the floor between his legs when he took his last breath. That's how he had lived the last two years of his life, sitting by the parlor window drinking as he watched the world pass him by.

Marilyn and I always enjoyed visiting our father's parents before they sold their bakery shop. So did my baby sister, Patty. She loved their ginger snap cookies, Marilyn liked their German strudel pastry and I could eat their Black Forest Cake all day long.

My grandfather, a pudgy white-haired man about five feet six with a thick German accent, had been a baker back in Alsace Lorraine where he met and married my grandmother. She wasn't even five feet tall but always wore a bright smile on her handsome wrinkled face. When she spoke English, it always seemed to come out as a mixture of French and German. It didn't take them long to open their own bakery in Ridgewood shortly after they arrived in America.

Despite the fact that Grandpa Borchert also became an alcoholic, his bakery was very successful and helped support eight children, three daughters and five sons. It's strange how the disease of alcoholism affects families. Four of the five boys, including my dad, became alcoholics just like their father. None of the daughters ever had a problem, just like their mother.

Grandma Borchert was very happy that both Marilyn and I attended the funeral. She said grandpa loved us very much and used to talk about us all the time. I remember how surprised I was to see how much fatter he had become. I heard someone say he had swollen up from drinking too much alcohol. It looked like the undertaker had to stuff him into the coffin with a shoe horn. Another thing I remember is all the talk at the wake about poor Uncle Henny and poor "little Henry." I thought it was strange that most people still referred to my cousin as "little Henry" when he had been such a big guy.

The one other thing I remember is how cold it was that October day when they buried my grandpa in Evergreen Cemetery, not too far from Uncle Henny's and "little Henry's" graves. I could see that my dad was upset again because there weren't many people at the funeral. He got even more upset when he saw all the empty chairs at the luncheon for the mourners.

As I said, my father stayed relatively sober until just after Thanksgiving Day. My mother had decided to celebrate the holiday at our place. She cooked a huge turkey, put an extra leaf in the kitchen table to make more room and invited her mother and sister. Dad decided to invite his mother too which angered his sisters who always expected her to be with them on holidays.

When she saw all the food on our kitchen table that day, I recall my Aunt Helen asking my mother:

"Where did you get all the ration coupons to buy all this food, especially that big turkey?"

"I've been saving up all my red stamps and green tokens just to make this a very special day," my mother smiled. "Also, Gladys Murphy and Debbie Wheeler had some ration books they weren't planning to use and

my mother-in-law sent me some too. That's why we invited her."
Everyone laughed including Grandma Borchert.

"Well what am I, chopped liver," my aunt pouted. "You could have asked
me too"

"I will, when Christmas rolls around," my mom laughed again.

I think my Aunt Helen was simply pointing out how difficult it was at
that time to have a nice spread when almost everything from soup to nuts
was being rationed.

With the war raging in both Europe and the South Pacific and
hundreds of thousands of American troops requiring huge amounts of food
and materials, the home front was being asked to conserve on practically
everything in their lives. However, when voluntary conservation didn't
appear to be working very well, the U.S. government's Office of Price
Administration (OPA) was created in May of 1942 to launch a strict price
control and rationing program.

The effort was initiated for two primary reasons: to control supply and
demand at home and to prevent the wealthy from purchasing whatever
amounts of commodities they wished and storing them away.

War ration books and tokens were issued to each American family,
dictating how much gasoline, tires, sugar, milk, meat, butter, flour, silk,
shoes, nylons and other types of clothing one person could buy. Across the
country, some eight thousand rationing boards were opened to administer
those restrictions.

By the end of 1942, half of U.S. drivers were issued an "A" sticker to
paste on the front windshields of their cars and a mileage ration book
which allowed them to buy four gallons of fuel per week. This was for
owners whose car use was deemed "nonessential." It practically eliminated
family pleasure trips in order to save for necessary jaunts and emergency
use. The "Victory Speed Limit" was set at thirty five miles per hour and car
pooling was encouraged.

A green "B" sticker was for drivers whose work was deemed essential,
such as those working in defense plants. They could purchase eight gallons
of gas per week. Next were red "C" stickers for doctors, ministers, mail
carriers and railroad workers. Truckers supplying the population with a

variety of goods had a "T" sticker for unlimited amounts of fuel. Recycling also came into being under the government's direction and encouragement. This provided more materials for the war effort such as steel, aluminum and rubber. "Victory Gardens" also sprung up and by 1945 were producing more than forty percent of America's vegetables.

It was nice having Grandma Borchert and everyone else with us that Thanksgiving Day because of the special, unexpected announcement my mom was to make just before we started eating. It took everyone by surprise, including my father—I think. At least it looked that way.

After asking everyone to sit, my mom went and stood next to my father who was seated at the head of the table getting ready to carve the turkey. She appeared quite nervous, yanking at her apron strings. She coughed once or twice and said:

"I wanted today to be a very special occasion because...well, because I have something very special to tell everybody."

She seemed to blush slightly as she put her hand on her stomach.

"I have some very important news. I just found out about it the other day. I'm going to have another baby. Isn't it wonderful?"

It was wonderful. It was really joyful news in the middle of all the gloom that had been surrounding our family, from my father's terrible benders to the house fire to my grandpa's recent passing. Still, it was probably a good thing no one had started eating yet because my Grandmother McLintock and my Aunt Helen looked like they might have choked on their food.

I recall neither of them appearing very happy at first, but then quickly forcing a smile and congratulating my mother. Marilyn and I kept staring at each other. We were both stunned. I don't recall how my little sister, Patty, reacted since she was only five.

My father, who was still holding the carving knife in his hand, dropped it and leaped up. He pulled my mother close to him and kissed her. They hugged for a long time. Grandma Borchert sat there smiling and clapping her hands. I don't think she was really aware of all the troubles our family had been going through as a result of her son's alcoholism.

The meal was absolutely delicious, especially the mashed potatoes, turkey gravy, white meat and cranberry sauce. That I do remember very well. The rest of the day was filled with a lot of general family gossip. My mother kept telling everyone how much she was looking forward to going with my father to the Pressman Union's annual Thanksgiving Dinner and Dance that coming weekend and telling all their friends the good news.

While my father was still pursuing a career in the field of air conditioning, he began hearing rumors that he was being considered for a foreman's position that was opening up at The New York Times. He had been doing some extra shift work there and had become friends with the retiring foreman at the paper. His drinking pal, Dick Nolan, said he first heard the rumor "through the grapevine" and then asked Ed Hickey, the President of The Pressman's Union, if it were true. Dick and the union official knew each other quite well. He said the union president would "neither confirm nor deny" the story.

From what I learned later, my father was also very friendly with Ed Hickey who, as union chief, would recommend press room foreman candidates to the various newspapers and his word carried a lot of weight. So my dad surmised that if Hickey would "neither confirm nor deny" the rumor, then there had to be something to it.

That Saturday night when he took my mom to the Pressman's Thanksgiving Dinner and Dance at Werderman's Hall on the city's West Side, he promised her and himself he would be on his best behavior. The problem is, if you're a drunk, it's difficult to keep such promises when the booze is flowing like Niagara Falls.

I know from my own personal experience that there was never any shortage of whisky at most union rackets or social functions. That night there were bottles of Scotch and Rye on every table and Bourbon and other drinks available upon request. Also, my dad was surrounded by all his drinking buddies who always took advantage of free booze.

Until the day he passed away, my father was convinced that Ed Hickey had his eye on him that night, sizing him up for that managerial position. But a press room foreman's job doesn't just require knowledge and experience. It also calls for self-discipline and a friendly but somewhat distant relationship with those under your supervision. You couldn't be everybody's drinking buddy.

As hard as he tried, my father was not able to hold up under the imagined scrutiny he felt that night. He needed to relieve the pressure. So he got smashed and blew another great opportunity to improve his life and that of his family. He not only embarrassed my mother by getting sloppy drunk and singing off-key with the small band, but his behavior also shocked Ed Hickey who was a pretty heavy hitter himself.

The final straw that wiped out another great job opportunity and almost killed my father at the same time was when he tried to stop my mother from leaving the dinner dance. She was embarrassed and angry about his behavior. As she rushed toward the stairs leading to the street, my father reached out to grab her arm. He lost his balance and tumbled down fifteen marble steps. He was unconscious when they put him into an ambulance.

My father told me some years later that when he finally came to at New York's Bellevue Hospital, the Emergency Room doctor said he was astonished he had no broken bones. He only had lacerations on his head and arms. The physician was even more shocked by my father's comment:

"Thank God I was drunk because if I wasn't I would have been uptight and might have seriously hurt myself."'

My father said the doctor frowned in disbelief and replied: "If you weren't drunk in the first place, you probably wouldn't have fallen down the damn stairs!"

Isn't it strange how so many alcoholics give booze the credit for keeping them alive when, in truth, John Barleycorn kills millions of drunks every year.

With another opportunity to advance in life becoming one more drunken memory, my father's downward slide began to pick up more speed. For awhile my mother seemed to walk around in a trance. The new hope she once had was now turning quickly to despair. Then, despite her pregnant condition, she began screaming again and threatening to leave. And as the drinking and the screaming increased, so did its effects on the whole family.

My sister Patty had just started school and she didn't like it one bit. My mother brought her for the first week but since she was now expecting another baby, she wasn't in any condition to keep taking that long trip. Marilyn had already graduated and was in high school so the onus fell on me.

Patty had gotten even more stubborn. She'd walk so slowly I actually had to pull her along. Then she would stop and stamp her feet. She frequently made me late for class. And then she would often complain at school that she was sick and I would have to take her home early and miss some classes.

One day when I complained to my mother about the problems I was having with my kid sister, my mom came down on me rather harshly.

"How much do I ask you to do around here?" she shouted. "Hardly anything! So when I ask you to take your little sister to school for me and look after her, why can't you simply do it without complaining?

"Can't you see all the problems I have already—problems with your father, problems with your older sister, problems with having another baby. Do you have to add to them? So I don't want to hear you whining anymore about your little sister. Just go do what you're told!"

So I decided to confide in my older sister only to find that Marilyn, who was fourteen at the time, had her own problems with my mother.

"I wanted to date some boys who were asking me to go to the movies," she told me. "I tried to talk to mom but all she did was yell at me, saying I was too young and that I shouldn't trust boys. So I went to dad. He tried to talk to mom for me but all it did was start another big argument.

"So that's why I'm sneaking around. All I'm doing is going to the movies with a bunch of boys and girls or sitting on stoops at my friends' houses talking. But if mom finds out there are boys around, she'll kill me. She's already called me a slut. I don't see what I'm doing wrong. What else am I supposed to do?"

So I gritted my teeth and put up with Patty's problems. What helped was getting lost in books again and daydreaming. They both became my favorite pastimes.

One day Sister Agatha Marie gave me a book called WHEN THE SORGHUM WAS HIGH. It was about a Maryknoll missionary priest named Father Gerard A. Donovan who went to China in the late 1930's to convert people to Catholicism.

On October 6, 1937 he was kidnapped by Chinese bandits and taken from his mission in Manchukuo to their hideout in the mountains. The bandits hated "the new preachers coming to our land" and demanded $50,000 in ransom which the young missionary order had difficulty raising quickly. In a matter of days the bandits killed Father Donovan.

Since I was a hero worshipper, the story of his martyrdom really impressed me. He was one more person I put on a pedestal. I felt this was the kind of guy I would like to be, strong, bold and courageous, someone who sticks up for what he really believes. I remember Sister Agatha saying to me at the time:

"If the story of Father Donovan impressed you so much, William, then perhaps it's God whispering in your ear that you may have a vocation to become a missionary priest just like him."

I didn't know what to say to her. That thought had never occurred to me even though I had a great deal of respect for priests and nuns. Being someone who always considered himself more of a sinner than a saint, I knew it took a great deal of courage and self-discipline to be holy. I felt that was beyond my reach.

At the same time, I remember how intrigued I was at the thought of being a heroic missionary in some far off land. It was something that fueled my imagination and expanded my daydreaming. Meanwhile Sister Agatha began supplying me with more information about Father Donovan and his missionary order.

What I discovered was back in June of 1911 when the Maryknoll Missionary Order was founded in Ossining, New York, there were more than seventeen thousand Catholic priests serving the laity in America. But there were only fourteen American priests serving in missionary work around the world. For some reason, that statistic seemed to challenge something inside of me.

I went on to learn that at the end of World War I, three newly-ordained Maryknoll priests were sent to China to set up Catholic missions in that Asian country. Before long there were Maryknoll priests and brothers working in foreign lands around the globe—from China to Japan and from Africa to South America, converting people to Christianity and setting up schools and orphanages to care for poor and needy children.

Even though I was only eleven, I began to seriously consider the idea of becoming a priest, a Maryknoll missionary priest. Looking back, I think that idea was most likely prompted by three things: my hero worship of Father Gerard Donovan, Sister Agatha Marie telling me that the Maryknoll order accepted candidates at the age of thirteen, and the fact that practically everything going on at home upset me and I was looking for a way out.

There may have been one other reason I was attracted to the priesthood—my ego. Since I had low self-esteem, I was always looking for attention, ways for people to think well of me. Back then, priests, nuns and seminarians were practically idolized by their Catholic relatives and friends.

The thought did occur to me that I might receive the same kind of treatment—especially from my mother. I was sure my father would be a different story. Even though he was drunk most of the time now, he had caught on to my lies, exaggerations and imaginings. He would probably just brush off this latest idea of mine as "another pipe dream."

It's strange that whenever I think about the reasons I finally did go off to a Maryknoll seminary, "serving God" was never at the top of my list. I'm sure it was somewhere on my list, but apparently not that high up. I didn't say a word to anyone right away about what I was thinking except to Sister Agatha Marie. Even though she was convinced by now that I had a vocation to the priesthood, she felt it was a little too early to begin the process of contacting the Maryknoll order. Still, she wanted to talk with my parents. I dissuaded her by saying I would do it myself when I felt ready. She agreed.

By late spring of 1945 my mother was already six months pregnant and the great news coming from the war front in Europe was bolstering her spirits. The Axis was rapidly coming apart. Italian partisans had captured the dictator Benito Mussolini on April 27, brutally beat him and strung him up to die in front of thousands of patriots clamoring for his execution.

Three days later, on April 30, Adolph Hitler committed suicide in his bunker beneath the streets of Berlin where the last battle of the war was being waged. On May 7, the German High Command surrendered unconditionally. By then the Allied Army had already uncovered Hitler's gruesome secret—death camps that had inhumanely gassed more than six million Jews. That shocking holocaust event remains something the whole world will never forget.

Naturally, my dad celebrated the end of the war in Europe by going on another bender. I think he still had deep regrets over never having had the opportunity to fight for his country. He was now drinking so much that my mother began sending Marilyn or me over to Monahan's Bar and Grill to bring him home for dinner. Sometimes he would come with us, sometimes he wouldn't. Either way, there was usually another brawl when he did arrive home generally in a stupor.

The days seemed to drag on. Eventually summertime rolled around again and we were on vacation. I came home late one afternoon to wash up for supper. It was August 6, 1945 because I remember the radio was blasting away with exciting news about the war in the Pacific. My mother, who was now nine months pregnant, kept telling me she heard a newscaster say that America had just dropped something called an Atom Bomb on Japan, killing hundreds of thousands of people in a city named Hiroshima. She also heard President Harry Truman say he hoped it would quickly end the war against Japan.

On August 9, another one of those fearsome bombs was dropped on Nagasaki, leveling the entire Japanese city, killing thousands of people. Finally on August 14, 1945, with great reluctance, the Emperor of Japan accepted the terms of unconditional surrender. Attempting to "save face," he told his people:

"It is according to the dictates of time and fate that we have resolved to pave the way for a grand peace for all generations to come, by enduring the unendurable and suffering the insufferable."

That was the same day my Aunt Helen had to rush my mother to St. Catherine's Hospital where my baby brother was born early in the afternoon of August 14. My father couldn't be found anywhere. He finally showed up at the hospital that evening, very drunk and still celebrating. I learned that my mother was so ashamed by the fact that nothing had changed she began to weep.

My father kept shouting that they should call the baby "Vincent Joseph" to go along with the fact that he was born on "VJ Day"—"Victory

Over Japan." He even claimed that when he saw my new baby brother in the nursery, he had veins on his forehead in the shape of a "V." That observation turned out to be false.

When my mother told him that wouldn't be their baby's name under any circumstances, I learned later that my dad became rather angry. That was the way booze was now affecting him. His personality would change from nice to nasty and with it his words and actions. Nurses had to call a security guard who gave him the choice of calming down or leaving the hospital. Fortunately Aunt Helen showed up with my grandmother. After seeing my mother and the baby, they drove my father home.

My parents christened my little brother on a Sunday afternoon in September in St. Sylvester's Church, two weeks after my twelfth birthday. My mother named him Robert Frederick after both of his grandfathers. After all the fuss over "VJ Day," my dad was pleased with her decision. At the time, however, he was so deep in the doghouse that he had little or nothing to say about it anyway.

The christening party began at approximately four o'clock in the refurbished basement of Monahan's Saloon. My mom wanted a small party at our apartment but both she and my dad realized they had to invite more people than their place could accommodate. Most of our relatives showed up along with many of my mother's friends and my father's drinking buddies and their wives.

Since the war was now over and rationing had ended, there was plenty to eat and drink. I found out later that my father had to borrow money from a loan company to pay for the party. It was just one more time he had to lean on usurious lenders.

I remember my sisters and I went home early with my mother who became concerned that all the cigarette smoke would have a bad affect on little Robert. Back then practically everyone smoked, not knowing the dangers as we do now. Many people stayed late at the party. I don't remember what time my father arrived home or how drunk he was.

The rest of the year was like riding on a terribly bumpy rollercoaster. While Marilyn and I enjoyed playing with our baby brother who we called Bobby, I don't know how much joy he gave my mother. She loved him to death of course, but he was also one more responsibility she had in the middle of the continuing chaos.

Thanksgiving Day was awful. Christmas Eve my father came home so drunk that he fell into the Christmas tree again. But as I've said, when you think things can't get any worse, they generally do.

The second week of January, 1946, my Uncle Freddie committed suicide.

CHAPTER SIX

Escaping the Chaos

There's no way to know why anyone would want to take their own life, even when they try to explain it in a suicide note. Despite all the psychological, emotional, financial and relationship situations that may be involved, it's still the dumbest thing anyone can do because suicide is usually a permanent solution to a temporary problem.

Uncle Freddie didn't leave a note. However, I recall my Aunt Catherine telling my parents once that if she had been paying closer attention, she probably could have seen his intentions written all over their bedroom wall. That's where her husband had been spending most of his time after losing his job because of one too many alcohol-related incidents. He was either alone in his bedroom or sulking in his finished basement where he continued to drink a whole lot of beer. He gradually went into a deep, deep depression.

Since he was practically broke and Aunt Catherine now had to work to support the family, she didn't know where he was getting the money for all the beer. She later learned her oldest son, Freddie, Jr. was supplying his father with six-packs.. At the wake he kept blaming himself for his father's demise.

By the time Uncle Freddie killed himself, he had borrowed from everyone he knew, including my father who was deeply in debt himself to finance companies and loan sharks. Still, he lent his favorite brother three hundred dollars which was money he had to borrow himself and money he knew he was never going to get back.

From what I understood, it was probably around five in the morning when Uncle Freddie snuck out the back door of his house and into his garage carrying a vacuum cleaner hose in his hands. He made sure all the garage doors were tightly shut before attaching one end of the vacuum cleaner hose to the tailpipe of his car. He put the other end through the back window and rolled the widow closed. Then he got into the car, started the engine, sat back and closed his eyes He never opened them again.

Even medical examiners don't know exactly how long it might take for a person to asphyxiate himself under such conditions. They can only guesstimate. All anyone really knows is that when Aunt Catherine left her house to drive herself to work that morning around eight o'clock, she found her husband dead in the front seat of the car and the garage filled with noxious fumes. She was still trembling from shock at my uncle's wake.

It was another very sad funeral with few mourners outside of the immediate family. Once again, instead of my father seeing and benefitting from the obvious—that two of his brothers had now died from states of hopelessness fueled by alcoholism—he allowed himself to plunge even further into his own state of despair. That's because he had no idea he was totally powerless over alcohol and that his life had become unmanageable.

I remember at the wake hearing my Aunt Catherine talking with my parents as tears streamed down her cheeks.

"I just can't understand why he did it," she kept say over and over again. "We weren't going to lose the house or anything. I was making enough money to buy groceries and pay the mortgage. And Freddie and Bobby are both working and were chipping in."

"I should have called him more," my father said as though trying to accept some of the blame for what happened. "I should have kept in touch."

"He wouldn't have answered your calls anyway," Aunt Catherine replied. "After he lost his job, he just buried himself in the basement with his beer. I couldn't get him out of there. None of us could."

My mother just stood there shaking her head. I've often wondered if she was thinking about the possibility of my father doing the same thing. She had already seen so many tragedies caused by drinking that just the possibility of it must have frightened her.

I remember not long after Uncle Freddie's funeral, my mother sent me over to Monahan's saloon again to bring my father home. I found him in one of his "crying jags." He put his arm around my shoulder, lifted his glass of beer from the bar and said to those around him:

"Look. This here's my boy, my oldest son, Billy. He's a great kid. I got two beautiful girls and a baby boy at home. I've got everything to live for...and I'm letting this stuff kill me. I must be crazy."

Then he leaned close and whispered: "Tell your mother I'll be home in about an hour."

It was getting more difficult for me to fall asleep at night waiting for my father to come home and knowing the calamity that would usually take place—the screaming and hollering, the carving knife coming out of the kitchen draw, the chase around the house, then going to grandmother's place. Marilyn and Patty told me they felt the same way. All little Bobby did was wake up and cry.

That night my father staggered in around midnight. My mother must have been in a deep sleep because I didn't hear a sound coming from their bedroom. I probably waited almost ten minutes before finally putting my head down on my pillow. I started dreaming about Maryknoll and I fell fast asleep.

Sister Agatha Marie had just given me the name of Maryknoll's Vocational Director at their major seminary in Ossining, New York and suggested that I contact him. That's when I realized it was about time I sat down with my parents to tell them about my aspirations.

I decided to tell my mother first. While, as I've said, my father was onto some of my "bad habits" like lying and exaggerating, my mother seemed to sense that these "innocent impulses" came from all the books I was reading, stories that filled me with great imaginings. So I knew it would be easier to reveal to her the rather enormous decision I was about to make. But I needed to find the right time to tell her.

We had just gotten home from Sunday Mass and I could see she was in one of her better moods. My father was working one of those extra shifts at another newspaper—or at least that's what he said—so he wasn't home. Marilyn and Patty were in their room and little Bobby was asleep in his crib. I asked my mother if I could speak with her in the parlor. I saw her face fill with concern.

"I've been meaning to tell you about this for a long time," I started very nervously as we sat together on the parlor couch. "You know Sister Agatha Marie. Well, she said I shouldn't wait any longer to tell you."

"Did you do something wrong I don't know about?" my mother asked, immediately jumping to the negative. "Are you in trouble? What is it?"

"No," I said with a smile, trying to dispel her anxiety. "No, it's nothing like that. It's something good...something I really want to do. But I need your permission."

"My permission?" she said with a deep frown running across her forehead.

"I...I want to become a priest. A missionary priest. At a place called Maryknoll."

Suddenly my mother's eyes filled with tears. "A priest!" she murmured. "A priest! I can't believe it."

"I've been thinking about it for a long time," I continued. "Sister Agatha gave me the name of a missionary I should contact at Maryknoll. He's in Ossining, New York and I'd like to go see him."

"Are you sure about this?" my mother asked, now with a broad smile on her face. "You're still so young."

"Sister said I could go into the seminary next year if I wanted to, right after my graduation," I said. "I was hoping that would be alright with you ...and dad."

Her eyes filled with tears. She reached out and hugged me until I could hardly breathe. "A priest!" she kept saying. "My son a priest. I can't believe it."

All of a sudden my possible vocation to the priesthood became the one bright spot in my mother's life. It was something she could brag about to all the neighbors and particularly to all our relatives. It was something that made her feel God was blessing our family and that everything was going to be alright.

Without realizing it, I had opened for my mother the floodgates of hope and joy. So naturally she was fully supportive when I told her I wanted to contact Father John C. Murrett, Maryknoll's Vocation Director. She immediately gave me her approval to visit him in the coming spring.

It was strange how I suddenly felt so grown up and proud that I was making my mom so happy. But then as I thought about it, I realized how scared I was having to approach my father on the subject. Fortunately I didn't have to right away. My mother did it for me. I don't remember whether he was sober or not at the time, but his reaction was essentially what I had expected.

"There's plenty of time to think about this," he said. "We'll see when the time comes."

While that was all he had to say to me that particular evening, I heard him arguing with my mother about it a few nights later.

"It's just another one of his pipe dreams," he told her. "Don't you go banking on it or getting your hopes up. He'll get over it just like he did with all his other fantasies. Just you wait and see."

But I wasn't over it by the time April of 1946 came around. I had been corresponding with Father Murrett. He had sent me several copies of a magazine called THE FIELD AFAR published by the Maryknoll Order. It was all about the courageous things their missionaries were doing in foreign countries, many that had names I could hardly pronounce. It continued to stir my imagination and heroic desires.

Then came that Saturday in late April when I found myself on a New York Central Railroad train moving along the Hudson River from Grand Central Station in Manhattan to the small upstate community of Ossining, New York. At twelve years old, my parents, including my father for his own reasons, had confidence in me to travel such a long distance alone. My mother, of course, was sure that God was riding with me. She was also the one who talked my father into coughing up the money for the trip.

I've traveled up and down the Hudson River by train many times since, but that first excursion left me awed. To see that great expanse of water dotted with small private boats and large cargo ships was breathtaking. And when I saw the West Point Military Academy far in the distance looming high atop the river's cliffs, I thought about my dad and his deep disappointment about not being able to join the Army and fight in the war. I knew it was something he still used as an excuse to drink.

Father Murrett met me at the railroad station. I couldn't get over the kind look on his slightly wrinkled face and his warm smile that exposed some brownish teeth, the result of many years in China where it was apparently hard to find a good dentist. He had graying hair and was much older than my father. But he talked to me like I was an adult, like he had known me all his life. He told me how much he appreciated my coming and said he had an exciting tour planned.

"I must say I'm very impressed you made this trip all by yourself," he smiled, putting his arm around my shoulder. "That shows you have what it takes to be a good missionary—independence and spunk. You'll see that today when you meet some of my fellow priests who have been all over the world."

I must admit I was a bit overcome at first just being there at Maryknoll and seeing the huge major seminary buildings and bell tower designed in Asian architecture. But Father Murrett's warm welcome helped me to relax very quickly.

Since it was just past noon, the first place he took me was to the large dining hall at the major seminary. I didn't feel awkward at all when he introduced me to a whole lot of priests and seminarians. I felt comfortable and grown up. Over lunch he and a few other priests told me all about the many years they had spent on the missions in the Orient and on the continent of Africa.

"The Chinese language can be quite difficult to learn," one of the elderly missionaries now retired explained to me. "The Chinese people speak different dialects in the various cities and provinces throughout the country. I had to learn the dialects spoken in my mission area and also study the culture so that I wouldn't offend anyone. But when you're there for awhile, the language and the culture all become second nature."

"But the people are so warm and friendly," my host Father Murrett remarked, "that they forgive the mistakes you're bound to make, for awhile at least. They are more interested in learning about God and how He wants them to live rather than in any weaknesses you may have. They make you feel very special even though you're not. They understand we are all simply God's servants."

Father Murrett said he loved his work in China and was disappointed at first when he was called back to America. He had spent more than thirty years there doing what he was ordained to do—spread the Gospel of Jesus Christ. Then he smiled and told me how much he also enjoyed doing what he was doing now—encouraging young men like me to follow Christ, and to follow him as a Maryknoll missionary priest.

Later as we walked around the impressive grounds, my new-found missionary friend suddenly stopped, bent over and plucked a small flower from the soil. He handed it to me.

"It's the first crocus of spring," he remarked as if we had found something very special. "It's said to bring one great blessings. Here, put it between the pages of one of your books and keep it as a memory of your first visit to Maryknoll. Then someday when you're in China or on some other mission, you can take it out and relive this day."

I kept that crocus until it completely dried up, shredded and blew away. That happened at a time when I really needed a great blessing and none seemed to be forthcoming.

He then showed me this large enclosed field which he said was used for "Departure Ceremonies." He explained that Maryknoll missioners, those newly-ordained and those who had been teaching in various seminaries, would gather here with their families to celebrate their departure for foreign lands. Since the Order had many missions in Asia, a large golden Chinese gong hanging from a post was struck twelve times at these ceremonies to honor those who would soon be leaving..

As we walked through the marble corridors of that awesome place, looking into classrooms and study halls, Father Murrett explained that it would take me twelve years to be ordained a priest. That would include four years of high school, four years of college, one year of meditative preparation at a special place in Bedford, Massachusetts, and three years of sub-Deaconate and Deaconate studies in Ossining.

He said all this education would be completed at Maryknoll seminaries in California, Illinois, Pennsylvania, Massachusetts and New York. He explained that should Maryknoll accept me as a candidate for the priesthood following my graduation, I would begin my studies in September of 1947 at a preparatory seminary in Clarks Summit, Pennsylvania called "The Venard."

My heart was really pumping by the time we made our last stop, a visit to the quiet and impressive seminary Chapel. After saying a prayer, Father Murrett took me below to show me the tombs of Father Frederic Price and Father John Walsh, the founders of Maryknoll and heroic men who had done something truly momentous...something that tapped into every fantasy I ever had.

On the way back to the train station, the Vocation Director pointed to some high walls in the distance and told me it was a famous prison called Sing Sing Penitentiary. I said I heard the name on a radio show called "Gangbusters." It was the place where the police sent real bad guys "up the river." He smiled and said.

"Thank goodness you're going down the river. And when you get home, be sure to thank your parents for allowing you to visit with me today and see what I hope might become God's destination for you." Then we shook hands and I boarded the train.

I found it a strange dichotomy that a missionary seminary would be sitting atop a tall hill looking down at an infamous prison along the river. I found it even stranger that some years later I would be back at Sing Sing as a newspaper reporter covering the execution of a ruthless killer.

I didn't need to take a train home that afternoon. I could have flown all the way by myself I was so high. I made another visit to Ossining that August. I remember feeling so sure that this was the place I wanted to be and told Father Murrett so. He kept saying I should pray every day for God's guidance.

It was after eight o'clock when I got home that evening. My mother was in the bathroom giving my baby brother a bath. My father was sitting in the parlor waiting for me. He was almost sober.

"You're really serious about this," he said as I stood in front of him.

"Yes I am," I replied.

"And you expect me to go along with it even though you're just a kid."

"I think I'm old enough to know my own mind."

"Maybe your mother thinks so, but I don't. I think you should finish high school before you decide."

"But I'll be going to high school in the seminary. What's the difference?"

"You have all the answers, don't you?" he said with just a touch of anger in his voice. I didn't respond. After a moment he got up and looked at me very seriously.

"I still don't agree," he said, "but I don't have much to say about things around here these days. It seems you've made your mother very happy so maybe that's a good thing. But it will probably break her heart if you decide to leave the seminary. Think about that."

Then he walked into the kitchen, grabbed his jacket and left. As I stood there I became aware that there was only one thing I wanted more than entering the seminary and that was leaving this house.

Things weren't getting any better or changing much except for the fact that my father had found a new drinking companion, my cousin Albert. He had been honorably discharged from the Navy for more than six months and was trying to get his feet back on the ground.

As a veteran, Albert was part of what was then called "the Fifty-Two Twenty Club." The U.S. government was paying all recently discharged service men and service women twenty dollars a week for a year to help them get settled into civilian life. Since the token payment wasn't enough to live on, my cousin asked my father if he could help him find a job. But nothing was happening because Albert was spending too much time with my dad in bars "discussing his prospects."

What I remember most about that time, besides my Aunt Helen raising hell that her son was coming home drunk too often, were the war stories my cousin would tell us whenever he would come to the house. I knew he wasn't bragging and wasn't looking to be patted on the back. He just wanted us to know that war was a terrible thing.

After training at The Great Lakes Naval Base in northern Michigan, my cousin said he was assigned to the newly-built light cruiser, the USS San Juan. Following a brief shakedown cruise, the ship departed for the

South Pacific in June of 1942. It escorted a large group of troop carriers heading for the Solomon Islands and action against the Japanese. The USS San Juan quickly became part of a carrier task force that supported the bloody invasions of the Japanese-held islands of Guadalcanal, Tulagi, Iwo Jima, Guam and the Marhsall Islands where thousands of American soldiers were killed and many more wounded.

While providing gunfire support for American troops landing on the beaches of Iwo Jima, the San Juan came under a fierce attack by Japanese fighter planes. My cousin said his anti-aircraft battery began running low on ammunition so he and another gunnery mate were sent to the stern for more shells. As they were returning, a Japanese plane strafed their gun position, killing the three remaining members of the anti-aircraft battery. As Albert said, fortunately his "number" wasn't up that day.

At another savage battle for the Santa Cruz Islands, while the Japanese were making their last bombing run on the U.S. Navy task force, one bomb passed through the San Juan's stern, flooding many compartments below and damaging her rudder. Albert and several of his fellow sailors were thrown twenty feet in the air by the explosion but no one was seriously injured. A dozen other sailors, however, were killed including two of my cousin's best friends. The ship limped into Sydney, Australia and spent four weeks receiving permanent repairs. Albert was a different, more serious person when he finally came home.

That drinking relationship between him and my dad didn't last long. It came to a rather abrupt halt when Aunt Helen teamed up with my mom to put a stop to it. I think the real reason it ended was because my cousin wasn't an alcoholic and he hated the hangovers. As for my father, being with Albert only deepened his regrets about not having gotten into battle.

While my relationship with my mother had significantly improved since I revealed my spiritual aspirations, my sister's relationship with her continued to deteriorate. Marilyn was fifteen now and my mother was finally letting her go out on an occasional date, but not without serious restrictions. My sister felt that because of my father's drinking, my mother didn't trust men in general. As Marilyn once described it to me:

"First, I had to tell her all about the guy so that she could approve of him. If she doubted me one bit, she'd check around. If she heard anything she didn't like, I'd have to cancel the date and then get slapped for lying.

"Mom wanted all of my boyfriends to come from good Catholic families. I was only allowed to go to the local movie house or to a neighborhood party at the home of someone my mother knew. And I had to be home no later than nine o'clock."

But that wasn't the least of it as my sister recalled.

"Whenever I'd come home a few minutes late, mom would be hanging out the parlor window yelling at me for disobeying her. She made such a fuss that the poor guy I was with would get scared to death. He'd turn around and run off and never ask me out again.

"I remember this one date I had with a really handsome boy named Bill Barry. All the girls were after him. He had his driver's license and was allowed to borrow his father's car. I think he liked to show off. Mom didn't like the idea of me being in a car with any boy but since she knew the Barry family, she let me go out on a date with him.

"We had so much fun at the party we went to that we stayed too long. We were an hour late getting home. Since I wanted to see Bill Barry again, I asked him to drop me off a block away from the house. I didn't explain why but I knew he would incur my mother's wrath if she saw me getting out of his car. But he was too much of a gentleman and wouldn't do it. He had to drop me right at the front door.

"As usual, mom was leaning out of the parlor window. I knew what was coming just as soon as this handsome guy helped me out of the car. She started screaming at me for being so late, and then began yelling at him too. He got so scared that he jumped back into his car and screeched away. I never had another date with Bill Barry."

My sister Patty was growing up fast too. She was now in the third grade and still a pain-in-the neck to drag to school everyday. But since most of the nuns had now heard about my intention to enter Maryknoll, I had to act like a loving brother instead of the teed-off guy I was. But most of them knew about the difficulties I had with my sister and would pat me on the head once in awhile for my alleged patience.

The bumpy road at home continued to get a little bumpier as the year rolled along. There were some good days, especially that summer when some of Marilyn's growing list of boyfriends who had cars would take Patty and me along with them to Rockaway Beach. My mother thought we were taking the bus. But many days were filled with tension or were just plain bad. Mom would have to fight with my father to get us money for the beach or for a movie. I don't think she had any idea how deeply in debt he really was.

We had Thanksgiving Day dinner that year at my Grandmother McLintock's place. Albert had his latest flame with him, a pretty young woman named Anne. I could tell my Aunt Helen really liked her. My cousin also had found a very good job as an electrician-in-training for New York City's major power company, Consolidated Edison. My father ate too little and drank too much and fell asleep on the parlor couch.

We celebrated Christmas at home if you could call it a celebration. My father never made it home for dinner on Christmas Eve but finally showed up later with a pathetic looking tree. Then he turned around and walked out when he and my mother began arguing over all the tree ornaments and decorations he had broken the year before. Marilyn and I did the best we could with what we had. Once the lights and tinsel were on, the tree it didn't look half bad.

The only one who still believed in Santa Claus was Patty. And if she really did, she was probably wondering whether or not he would arrive that night with all the chaos in the house. My baby brother Bobby wasn't as concerned about Santa as he was about a diaper change and another bottle. I really don't know how my mother did it, but there were presents for all of us under that half-decorated, skinny old tree that Christmas morning.

It was almost a year to the day that I first visited Father Murrett at Maryknoll's major seminary in Ossining when I received my official notice of acceptance. I was invited to be a freshman student at the Missionary Order's preparatory seminary in Clarks Summit, Pennsylvania which was just outside of Scranton.

When my father read the letter, he was finally convinced it wasn't just another one of my "pipe dreams," not at the present time at least. While I could tell he was still a bit skeptical about the whole idea, I'm sure he was happy that my acceptance letter confirmed that Maryknoll would be paying for my entire four-year high school education. That included food and housing costs and everything except my clothes, personal effects and travel.

It was a big financial burden lifted off his back since going to a good Catholic high school in the New York area would have been very expensive. I probably would have wound up in a public high school. I could see the relief in his eyes, almost an expression that he was pleased with me. Of course my mother was ecstatic.

To celebrate my acceptance to the seminary—and perhaps the money I would be saving him—my father promised to take us all to the fabulous amusement park at Coney Island for the Fourth of July holiday weekend. Believe it or not, he kept his promise despite having a terrible hangover.

I had never been to the world famous resort before and neither had my sisters. We left Bobby with Aunt Helen. Patty, who loved to ride on Merry-Go-Rounds, had heard from one of her friends that the amusement park had one of the best carousels in the country. She was very excited.

Coney Island actually had once been a barrier island that gradually formed a connection to the mainland of southwestern Brooklyn through tidal currents and landfill. Over the years it became part of a string of Brooklyn beaches starting with Sea Gate to the west and Brighton Beach and Manhattan Beach to the east.

In the late eighteen hundreds when developers wanted to build a boardwalk, bath houses, clam bars and family amusements along that strip of the Atlantic Ocean, there was an outcry from conservationists to preserve it as a natural park. But the New York City power structure and their money won out and development took off.

By the time the "Roaring Twenties" roared into New York following World War I, Coney Island had become the largest amusement resort in the United States. It attracted millions of visitors every year. The Great Depression greatly depressed its attraction but the end of World War II quickly reignited its popularity.

The resort first became famous for The Wonder Wheel, the biggest Ferris wheel in the world which opened in 1920. Shortly after that The

Horse Race at Steeple Park attracted long lines of thrill-seekers. Then came The Cyclone Roller Coaster built in 1927 which remains the oldest wooden coaster still in operation. Another big attraction was The Parachute Jump which had first been erected in Flushing Meadows Park to excite the millions of people attending The 1939 New York City Worlds Fair.

I had first seen that ride when attending the Fair some years before with my Aunt Maggie. As I said, when the World's Fair ended, the one hundred and ninety foot high Parachute Jump was moved to the Coney Island resort area where it remains today.

I really got to know the Parachute Jump later on as a newspaper reporter. When the ride would breakdown, people would be left hanging helplessly high in the air, sometimes in a rainstorm for an entire day. I would interview them for a story when they were finally brought down— that is, if they were in any mood or condition to be interviewed.

I don't mean to get ahead of myself, but I also used to write stories about Coney Island's famous Polar Bear Club, the oldest winter bathing organization in the United States founded by the noted naturalist Bernard McFadden in 1903. Every New Year's Day visitors from around the country would join up with members of the club to partake in an annual swim in the freezing cold waters of the Atlantic Ocean. There were generally four to five hundred swimmers admired by eight to ten thousand onlookers. It still goes on today only there are now usually several thousand Polar Bear swimmers.

The Atlantic Ocean was a heck of a lot warmer that Fourth of July holiday we enjoyed with my mom and dad at Coney Island. And even though the air temperature was probably close to ninety, there was a very pleasant breeze blowing in from the ocean.

While the amusement park was crowded due to the holiday celebration, we all had a great time. I didn't see my father drink anything but a lot of soda. Of course I wouldn't have been surprised if he had been spiking it with something else since he looked so relaxed and laughed a lot. He let us go on all the rides. My mother probably wondered how he could afford it after arguing all the time over money.

I think that was especially true when, at the end of the day, he took us to another well-known spot in Coney Island, Nathan's restaurant. It featured the world famous Nathan's hot dogs and dad told us we could eat till our heart's content as the old cliché goes.

It's this kind of behavior that can really confuse and bewilder the families of alcoholics, experiencing such ups and the downs, the good moods and the bad, the lavish spending and the deep debts. Every time there's hope, it's smashed by despair. It drives the spouse and the children to desperation. And the truth is, most can only hang on for so long before sheer anger and resentment set in and the family begins to come apart.

But this particular July fourth was one of those "up" days. We thoroughly enjoyed eating at Nathan's which I learned began as a nickel hot dog stand in Coney Island back in 1916 and today is a nationwide chain of fast-foot restaurants.

Its founder, Nathan Handwerker and his wife, Ida, came to America from Poland. He took a job as a cook at a large, well-known food establishment called Feltman's German Garden which was also in Brooklyn. Within no time he was being applauded for his attention to every dish that was served.

Two of the singing waiters at Feltman's, Eddie Cantor and Jimmy Durante who went on to become stars of radio, movies and the Broadway stage, took a liking to Nathan and encouraged him to start his own business. So he had his wife, Ida, create a tasty hot dog recipe, then managed to borrow three hundred dollars and opened a stand near the boardwalk in the heart of Coney Island. Feltman's was charging ten cents for its hot dogs. Nathan undercut them by five cents and his business took off.

After all the fun at the amusement park, I was starving. I must have had at least three hot dogs and a big bag of those great Nathan's French fries. By the time we got home I was very tired and thought I'd fall right to sleep, especially since my parents hadn't argued all day and they seemed to be in harmony that night. But the excitement that was dancing in my head about going off to Maryknoll kept me awake for hours.

As I recall it was late August of 1947, just two weeks before my fourteenth birthday, when we left by car for Clarks Summit, Pennsylvania. It was around mid-morning. It was an exciting but very quiet ride through the beautiful countryside. My parents seemed as if they didn't know what to say to me or to each other. And I didn't know what to say to them. It was like none of us really believed what was happening—their son on his way to begin the long journey to become a Catholic missionary priest.

Before leaving, Marilyn and Patty both hugged and kissed me goodbye and were crying as I got into dad's car. A few of our neighbors stood on the sidewalk smiling and waving at me. I must admit I felt a little special and enjoyed the attention.

I had already said my farewells to both my grandmothers and some of my aunts, especially my favorite one, Aunt Helen, and my cousin Albert. I knew he had come home from the war with a deep faith in God after seeing so many terrible things happen. He told me once that it was God who saved his life. But I don't remember him going to church very much. Perhaps that's why he took me aside that day and said:

"I know everybody's excited about you going into the seminary to become a priest, but are you sure it's really want you want to do?"

"I'm sure," I replied.

"No girls. No dancing. No fun. No screwing around. It doesn't seem normal to me giving all that up," he remarked. "Why would any guy want to do that?"

"It's hard to explain," I said. "I just feel it's what God wants me to do right now."

Then he shook my hand and added, "You know you can always change your mind. Nothing is forever."

For some reason Albert's comments seemed to stick in my head and would pop up from time to time as the weeks, months and years went by.

There were a number of cars in the parking area at The Venard seminary when we arrived around two o'clock that afternoon. It had only been a four hour drive including a stop for lunch in Clarks Summit, only a short distance from our final destination. I remember my father glancing at me a few times with moist eyes. I kept wondering why since he never told me how he really felt about my going away—at least not in a serious way. My mother kept straightening the jacket of the new black suit she had just bought for me.

The Rector of the seminary, Father William North, was standing on wide cement steps leading to an impressive entrance greeting everyone. He was a tall, heavy-set man with a big friendly smile and receding gray hair. There were two other priests with him whom I came to know very well, Father Elwood Dowd, the Prefect of Discipline, and Father Paul Farnum who taught the freshman class Latin and geography. Both men had spent a number of years as missionaries to China.

I gazed up to see this large, imposing gray building with an awesome Chinese-style tower much like the one I saw at the Maryknoll seminary in Ossining. It encompassed two huge shiny iron bells that pealed out at different times each day. They alerted everyone, especially the seminarians, to the start and finish of various duties and functions such as morning and evening prayers, meals and study periods.

Erected in 1913, the stately place was called "The Venard Preparatory Seminary" in honor of Saint Theophane Venard, a member of the Paris Foreign Missionary Society. He was a Catholic martyr who was canonized in 1988. Following his ordination to the priesthood, Theophane Venard established a Catholic mission in West Tonkin, Vietnam in 1859. Shortly after, the Mandarin who ruled the city passed a law forbidding any proselytizing. The young missionary refused to deny his faith so after torture and imprisonment he was beheaded on February 2, 1861.

I was soon to find that Father North was a great Rector and a very understanding man. He chattered pleasantly with my parents for a few minutes, welcomed me warmly, and then turned us over to some senior classmen who showed us around.

The wide halls and tall ceilings of The Venard reminded me of my first visit to Maryknoll's major seminary in Ossining. The floors there were also made of glistening maroon tile and the walls of white dimpled plaster.

There were two floors for classrooms and study halls and two floors for dormitories and private rooms for the priests who taught or had other special duties. Downstairs was a library that adjoined a large dining hall and a kitchen where a small cadre of Maryknoll Sisters did the cooking for the priests and seminarians. On the main level was the Chapel, one of the most beautiful you would ever want to see with an eight-foot high cross of Jesus Christ crucified hanging above the altar.

The grounds immediately surrounding the seminary contained two baseball fields, a football field, four handball courts, two tennis courts, a very large swimming pool and a small lake which froze in the winter just in time for the hockey season. The remaining acreage was devoted to large groves of fruit trees and sprawling farmlands to grow corn and a wide variety of other vegetables.

My parents and I were amazed to see such a self-sustaining campus, especially one with such great athletic facilities since this was a community dedicated to the spiritual life. I'll never forget what Father North told my mom and dad when they expressed their surprise before they left. He said The Venard was there to treat the whole person—the mind, the body and the soul—because it takes the honing of all three to make a good missionary priest.

Naturally my mother was crying when she hugged me and kissed me goodbye.

"I'll visit you every month, I promise," she wept."And I'll send you whatever you need. Just let me know. I love you so much and I'm very proud of you. I don't know how else to say it."

Then she hugged me and kissed me again. My father simply put his arm around me, squeezed me and said:

"You take care of yourself ...and be sure and say a prayer for me now and then."

They both got into the car and drove slowly away. My mother kept waving to me out the window until their car finally disappeared in the distance.

Deep inside I felt very grateful that they had driven me instead of sending me by bus as some other parents had done with their sons. But little did I know it would be the last time I would see my father at The Venard. Over the next four years, each time my mother would visit she would come by bus. And she would always have a different excuse for my dad.

Perhaps that's why I always felt a bit resentful toward him when I'd come home for six weeks during the summer. Or maybe my resentments still came from his continuing drunken behavior which had not abated one bit.

My first night at the seminary I had to be in my upper bunk in the freshman dormitory by nine o'clock. That was part of the strict rules we new arrivals had been given by our Prefect of Discipline, Father Elwood, at dinner that evening. And I had to be up at four thirty the next morning when the tower bell pealed. I barely made it to the Chapel by five.

I remember it was so quiet that first night I had difficulty going to sleep. Maybe that's why my cousin Albert's question kept popping up in my mind:

"Are you sure it's really what you want to do?"

Finally the crickets outside my window stopped making such a racket and I slowly drifted off to sleep.

CHAPTER SEVEN

What Will I Tell My Mother?

My mother came to visit me that Columbus Day and the Saturday after Thanksgiving. Both times she took a Greyhound Bus to Scranton and a taxi to Clarks Summit. I don't know what it cost but I knew she really couldn't afford it.

She said my father decided to work some extra shifts to make some extra money which was why he couldn't make the trip. I knew that wasn't the truth. As I've said before, my mother was a very bad liar. She didn't want to talk about my father or what was going on at home. She only wanted to know how I was doing and what it was like being in the seminary after three months.

"I'm still trying to figure out the rules and regulations," I laughed. "Like making sure my bed is made every morning before going to Chapel for example. And what is the quickest way to get to my study hall after dinner every night."

"Study hall?" she said seeming startled. "You mean you have to go to school at night too?"

"And on Saturday mornings" I said shocking her even more. "And then there are my manual labor chores like cleaning bathrooms, waxing the hallways, washing the windows, mowing the lawns."

"Do you have any time to pray?" she finally smiled.

My mom was probably expecting me to talk more about spiritual things. Instead, I think I made it sound like I was in some concentration camp rather than in a seminary.

When my mother visited me again the week before Christmas, she brought along some very nice presents—mostly candy and cookies—which I had to share with everyone else according to the rules. Once more she didn't want to talk about my father except to say that he had gotten the gout and was unable to travel very far except to his job. She said it without looking me in the eye.

I remember telling her she didn't have to come every month, not because I didn't want to see her but because it was a long costly trip and I was doing fine. I promised I would write more often. She started to cry and asked if I was really okay. When I assured her I was, she said rather reluctantly that perhaps she'd come every other month if I really didn't mind.

When she began to visit every three months, I realized there was more trouble at home than I wanted to think about. Still, whenever my mother would come, she never wanted to talk about anything but how happy I was making her and how all her friends and neighbors were always asking about me and keeping me in their prayers. It was like they already had me ordained.

When I arrived home the beginning of July, 1948 for my six-week summer vacation, Marilyn filled me in on all that was happening. It was worse than I thought. My father had stopped bringing his paycheck home so my mother was now taking the train into the city every Friday to get it from him. Sometimes she would have to go from bar to bar to find him and then embarrass him in front of his drinking pals to get his money.

Quite often he would have cashed his paycheck at Moochies and spent it there and at other joints on the lower East Side. If he was on a real bender, he would have to borrow more money from loan sharks to take care of the family. My sister told me about one particular incident that made me wonder whether I was needed more at home than at The Venard.

The parlor furniture my parents had been dragging around every time they moved was rather old and somewhat tattered by now. Marilyn said mom wanted to fix the place up a bit for my homecoming. She saw some nice, inexpensive furniture advertised in the newspaper she could buy with no money down and only a few dollars in time payments each month. So she had it delivered and had the old furniture hauled away.

Dad had a fit when he came home half-drunk that night and saw it. My sister said he started yelling that my mother had no right to buy something they couldn't afford. He demanded she send it right back, that the old furniture was good enough and that he had no money to pay for any crappy new furniture. She yelled back that she was keeping it. That's when the fight began.

"Dad lifted one of the chairs and tried to throw it through the parlor window, breaking the pane of glass," Marilyn told me. "But it wouldn't fit through the window so he started tossing the seat cushions down into the street. Mom grabbed his arms and tried pulling the cushions away from him.

"They both lost their balance and fell on the floor. He landed on top of her. So she began slapping him.. He went to slap her back but stopped. I don't think I ever saw daddy hit mom under any circumstances, did you?"

I shook my head. She continued to tell me what happened.

"He got up yelling and cursing. Then he staggered away, got his jacket and went over to Monahan's as usual. Mom and I went to the broken window and looked out to see where the cushions had landed. There was a small crowd of people looking up at us. Mom was really embarrassed. Two ladies had the seat cushions in their hands. Mom asked me to run down and get them. I was embarrassed too."

What could I say...that maybe I could help somehow now that I was home for awhile. I knew I couldn't. Besides, I didn't like myself at that moment for what I was really thinking—that I couldn't wait to be out of here again in just six weeks.

Marilyn said our cousin Albert came over the next day to fix the window pane. He had gotten married to his flame Anne in June and was living not far away. I regretted not being there for their wedding but sent them both a set of Maryknoll Rosary Beads which I paid for from the five dollar bills my aunts were sending me on occasion. My cousin was now a full fledged electrician for Consolidated Edison, working nights which is why he was able to help my mother out during the day.

As if the fight over the furniture wasn't enough, my sister told me she had another bad run-in with my father at Albert's wedding. That surprised me because, despite his drinking, my sister had always been closer to my dad than my mother. In fact, I remember my father would often run interference for her whenever she'd get into trouble over something minor or when she wanted to do something or go somewhere my mother wouldn't approve. He rarely won the day for her, but he always tried valiantly.

So it didn't take me very long to discover that my father's drinking and bad behavior were far worse than when I had left.

As for Albert's wedding, my sister said she was sitting next to my dad because my mother didn't want to. My mother was talking with people at another table. Apparently my father was not only drinking a lot but also smoking rather heavily. Marilyn said the smoke began disturbing others at the table including her when the food was being served. It was so bad in fact she said one of the ladies seated nearby commented to my father very politely:

"Would you mind not smoking while we're eating? It's bothering us."

My father glared at her and replied rather nastily:

"Who the hell are you to be telling me I can't smoke at my nephew's wedding? If I want to smoke, I'll smoke!"

Marilyn said she was so shocked and embarrassed by his attitude that she didn't know what to do. Then she noticed my father's open pack of cigarettes on the table right next to his drink. Angered by his behavior, she picked up the pack of cigarettes and shoved them right into his highball glass saying quite loudly:

"That lady is right. You shouldn't be smoking while everyone is eating!"

Then all hell broke loose. She said my father jumped up and shouted at her:

"I'm your father! You don't talk to me like that in front of all these people! Do you hear me? You don't talk to your father like that!"

By now my mother heard what was going on. She came over and dragged my father away before things got any worse. Marilyn said she had to go outside to calm down. She didn't want to come back to the wedding, but did so only not to offend Albert. That night when she got home, my father apologized. He said he didn't know why he had acted that way and would try to be a better father in the future. That was simply one more promise he didn't keep.

But it wasn't only my father who didn't always tell the truth and had his mood swings. My mother had her slips too, probably because she thought she had to lie and cover up for my father quite often. She was afraid of what might happen otherwise.

For example, I noticed that summer she was still making excuses for him when he was too drunk or hung over to go to work or to make an important appointment. She felt she had to save his job or there would be no money at all. Where would it come from? What could she earn? And who would take care of the baby all day?

Still, my mother must have felt terribly embarrassed every time she would call the newspaper and tell another tall tale. She probably knew that the pressroom foreman on the other end no longer believed her, certainly not after hearing the same kind of untruths from other frightened and despairing wives in the same circumstances.

But my mom's fibs were nothing like the innumerable lies my father told her over the years, like the solemn oaths that he was finished with drinking forever; that if she'd only give him another chance he wouldn't let her down; that if she left him he'd have no reason to live. I'm sure she wanted to believe him every single time, perhaps because she sensed that deep down inside he was telling her the truth. But it was the truth as he saw it and usually his "truth" turned out to be one more terrible lie every time he'd get drunk again.

And after every lie or broken promise, I would hear my mother ask him the same questions over and over again:

"If you really love me and the children, why do you do the things you do? How can you be so kind and loving one day and so mean and cruel the next? How can you let me live like this, never knowing where the next dollar is coming from or when the next phone call I get is from the police telling me they found you dead somewhere? Why can't you just stop drinking? Other men do. Why can't you?"

Someday my mother would learn the answers to those questions and they would change her entire life. But for now, she continued to struggle just to find a little hope. I was going on fifteen now and was struggling to find my own answers. But when you're that age, despite your surroundings, hope always does seem to spring eternal.

Wherever I went that summer outside of my home, my spirit seemed to be lifted by almost everyone I met. Even Father John St. John, the pastor of St. Sylvestor's Church helped me a great deal. I was told when I left The Venard for vacation I had report to my pastor every week and let him know what I was doing, where I was going and the friends with whom I was associating.

"Our spiritual life doesn't stop just because we're on vacation," he told me the first time I saw him. "In fact, we have to be more focused on spiritual things during idle times when our minds and souls have a tendency to drift. This is particularly true during the summer which opens us up to many temptations.

"When we go to the beach, for example, there are many pretty girls in skimpy bathing suits who like to flirt. And our old friends enjoy going to places we shouldn't be frequenting any longer. Even hanging around on street corners where there's usually a lot of cursing and guys telling filthy stories isn't suitable now that you're in the seminary.

"All I'm saying is, the Devil doesn't want you serving God. He wants to talk you out of your vocation. Be aware of that and don't let him do it."

At first I felt like I was being put into a straightjacket until Father St. John explained it's the way priests and seminarians learn how to stay on the straight and narrow and live the kind of spiritual life most people find difficult. At first his comments and advice made me feel good inside, but gradually I began to find these weekly sessions somewhat burdensome. I told myself it was all part of what I had chosen and that I would continue on until I chose to do something else. However, at that time, the idea of being a heroic missionary priest was still burning brightly inside.

It was also burning brightly in the homes of my grandmothers, some aunts and uncles and some good friends my parents and I went to visit during those six weeks I was home. I could tell by the way we were greeted. It was usually on Sundays when my father did his best to lessen his input. I would often leave with several five dollar bills in my pocket and a Rosary or two.

The only place I felt my relationships were a bit strained or uncomfortable was among the kids I grew up with. While they still played stickball and other street games on occasion, they were now more into girls and trash talk like Father St. John warned me about. When I'd come around, they wouldn't know what to say except "How ya doin, Billy?" or "How you like being away at that place?" The girls said even less. I had a sense they thought just smiling at me might be a sin. It was crazy and I didn't know how to break the ice.

One day I decided to take a walk around the neighborhood. While I had been away only a short while, I felt like getting reacquainted with my growing up years. Also, since I hadn't spent much time with my sister Patty who was going on ten, I asked if she'd like to come along. She seemed eager to be in my company for a change.

As we strolled through the familiar streets, some people we'd pass would smile and wave. A few even approached me and asked how I enjoyed studying to be a priest. I realized that my mother's prideful gossip had reached beyond the confines of her close friends and family. Patty noticed it too. She turned to me and said:

"You get a lot of attention, don't you? I don't get any. Even Bobby gets more attention than me."

I was taken aback by her remark and replied:

"I don't think that's true, Patty. Mom and dad love you. Marilyn and I love you. So do a lot of people."

She looked down at the ground and said: "No, not a lot of people. The only attention I get is at school because I'm not doing that good."

We stopped at the neighborhood playground where we sat on a bench and talked for almost an hour. The more my sister told me about not having many friends or going many places, the more I realized how selfish I had been not paying that much attention to her during those years I had to drag her to school.

"I'm sorry I used to get so mad at you when we'd go to school together," I said. "I guess I wasn't a very understanding brother."

"You were okay," she smiled. "I was the pain. I always hated school. I still do."

"You're so pretty and you're smart," I smiled back, trying to encourage her. "You should make more friends at school then you'd find it a lot more fun. And start doing things that you enjoy like I did. I used to read a lot of books. Still do."

"But I'm not smart like you. And I don't like to read." Then she touched my hand and said very softly, "I sure wish you were home. Maybe things wouldn't be so bad."

"Why don't we write letters to each other," I suggested. "And don't tell me you don't like to write too."

"I don't," she grinned. "But okay. I'll write to you if you promise to write back."

"I will," I said, and kissed her on the cheek.

On our way home, I took her into Dr. Stein's Pharmacy and sat at the soda fountain. I used one of my five dollar bills to buy my sister a big ice cream soda with whipped cream and a cherry on top while I had a chocolate milkshake. It still didn't wash away my feelings that I was a very selfish brother. I told myself I would do better in the future.

Before I left that summer to go back to the seminary, I talked to my sister Marilyn about Patty. I asked her to give Patty more attention and help her in every way she could. But I knew it would be difficult. There was more than seven years of separation between them and Marilyn's own cup was brimming over with expanding social activities. I returned to The Venard really concerned about my kid sister.

It was my sophomore year when I really began to enjoy seminary life and all the activities it had to offer including sports and certain manual labor chores.

One afternoon I was speaking with Brother Fred, a lean, rugged looking man in his early fifties who was in charge of all the farming and livestock activities at The Venard. He was a man of few words but used them well. I happened to mention that I once lived near large vegetable farms and nurseries that were owned by Japanese-Americans and how sad it was they had their lands and their homes taken away from them at the start of World War II.

"I remember hearing something about that," he replied. "It just didn't seem right. But if you're interested in farming, I could use a good hand. Here at The Venard we plant in the spring and harvest in the fall, everything from apples, peaches and pears to corn, carrots and potatoes. In between we raise and kill chickens, slaughter hogs and cattle and keep everybody's bellies full. Do you think you could handle all that my friend?"

"I'd sure love to give it a try," I replied enthusiastically.

When Brother Fred saw how eager I was, he went directly to Father Edward Desmond who assigned all manual labor chores and requested my assistance. That's how, over the next three years, I learned the fine art of planting and harvesting crops to the bloody art of killing chickens and butchering hogs.

While Brother Fred was more of a serious man, his hardy right arm, a big, muscular Irishman from County Cork named Brother Francis Xavier, was just the opposite. He had thick, black curly hair, friendly chiseled features and was warm and welcoming. That made it easy for us to become fast friends. Brother Xavier immediately saw I had the stomach for butchering three and four hundred pound hogs. He showed me how to knock them unconscious with a sledge hammer, cut their jugular with a sharp knife, haul them into a tub filled with boiling hot ashes, then shave and dissect them, trimming out the bacon, ribs and hams.

It may all sound a bit gross, but it was the way The Venard fed almost three hundred hungry priests, seminarians, brothers and sisters. I must admit, however, that I wasn't as good at killing chickens with a hatchet. In fact, I often proved that chickens can literally run around with their heads half chopped off.

In the fall we put most of the fruits and vegetables we harvested into wooden crates and stored them in a large underground dirt cellar dug into the side of a hill. And in the winter, I engaged in my favorite pastimes with my favorite crew—the Maple Syrup Squad.

There were six seminarians including me that would tap several hundred maple trees when late November rolled round. We'd string gallon-size empty juice cans over metal taps to catch the sugary sap that would slowly drip from the trunk of the tree. Then once a week, usually on a

Saturday morning, I'd take the seminary's jeep—Brother Xavier had taught me how to drive it—attach a cart with four huge metal milk containers, and set off to collect the sap.

Most of us would cheat and drink a little of the cold, delicious sugary liquid right out of the cans. But there was always plenty for the end product. Once the milk containers were filled to the brim, we'd haul them up to the seminary kitchen and empty them into two huge silver cauldrons. The Maryknoll Sisters would then boil the sap down into the greatest tasting maple syrup you could lay your tongue on. I can still taste it to this very day.

Since I had contributed several articles to the seminary's monthly magazine called THE VENARDER during my first year, I was invited to join the staff. One of the articles was about the Japanese-Americans losing everything which still bothered me a great deal.

While I always loved to read, I now discovered how much I also enjoyed writing. It was a way to take my imaginings and put them on paper even if it was only to enhance an article about the new missionary on the staff teaching Greek or the finals of the handball tournament.

I don't know if it was the work I was doing or it was a job no one else wanted, but I was promoted to Editor of the magazine by year's end. I served in that position until I graduated, mainly because it was something I really enjoyed. And since I was writing and editing stories that ran the gamut from sports to people profiles to exciting missionary tales, I got to know everyone at school and they got to know me. That added significantly to my comfort and ease and the feeling that this was my real home, a place where anger and resentment and family troubles were no longer part of my life. And I didn't feel guilty about that at all.

But I did stay in touch with my mother and my sisters, mainly Patty. We wrote frequently and became closer than we had ever been. I wrote my father one letter to let him know I had won a spot as a pitcher on our varsity baseball team and was the starting center on our basketball team. I had grown to well over six feet by this time which was relatively tall for a young kid back then. He never wrote back. So rather than waste my time and getting angry, I never wrote him again.

On special occasions, Father North, our Rector, would declare a "Free Day" when all classes would be cancelled and all the seminarians were allowed to take long hikes or trips to Clarks Summit and Scranton if you could afford the taxi fare. I had developed a number of close friends by now, three in particular—Walter Barrett, Dennis Hanley and Al Molesphini. I remember how we pooled our resources that day and took a cab to Scranton to see a musical vaudeville show at the city's well-known State Theatre.

We had heard about the show from Father Farnum, our English teacher who loved musical theatre. He said the vaudeville show starred George M. Cohan, Jr. and was in very good taste and very moral. He was right about the moral thing, but from what we saw and what I learned later, Junior was no match for his late father.

The original George M. Cohan composed, produced and starred in more than three dozen Broadway musicals in the 1920's and 1930's and published more than three hundred songs. He was perhaps best known for his renditions of "Yankee Doodle Dandy" and "Give My Regards to Broadway." And during World War I, he propped up the American troops with standards like "Over There" and "You're a Grand Old Flag." He was a really big Broadway star whose statue is prominently displayed in New York City's Times Square.

His son did a fair job singing some of those same old songs that day and the chorus behind him did even better. Also, he was quite interesting when talking about his father's remarkable exploits. But looking back, I don't think the show was worth the money we paid although none of us said that to Father Farnum. We simply thanked him and let it go at that. We had dinner at an inexpensive cafeteria and came back to the seminary broke. But it was an enjoyable "Free Day."

When I came home the following summer of 1949, I was surprised at how much my little brother Bobby had grown until I realized he was already three. Patty, who was now eleven, was still struggling at school and Marilyn had more boyfriends than the hogs back at The Venard had flies. That's because she was about to turn eighteen and had more freedom to date. There was one guy she seemed kind of serious about, a nice looking fellow named Eddie Dean. I met him briefly one night when he came to pick her up. He was very friendly toward me but I remember how nervous he seemed around my mother.

Aside from that, not much else had changed. Things with my father were just as bad as ever.

I remember my pastor, Father St. John, asking me how things were at home during our first chat that summer. He was well aware of the problems. It was the first time I admitted to him or to anyone for that matter how much I disliked my father. I may have even used the word "hate" because I saw a stunned look on his usually peaceful countenance.

"I know how you must feel growing up in that kind of situation," he said, "but we must remember that Jesus Christ didn't go around hating people, especially sinners. Jesus loved them despite their weaknesses. And since you and I are trying to be like Christ, we must follow his example."

For a minute I thought this priest was joking. If he knew my father he wouldn't say something so ridiculous. And besides, Jesus Christ is God. How can I possibly do the same kinds of things God does. Am I really supposed to love a man who does nothing but hurt people and tear his family apart? It was as though Father St. John read my mind. He remarked:

"I know that sounds almost impossible right now, William, but we're only asked to try. And since you're studying for the priesthood, you have a sacred responsibility to be as Christ-like as possible even if you find it difficult at times."

I was a liar growing up but I didn't want to be a liar anymore. But that's exactly how I felt when I promised my pastor I would follow his advice and try to be more Christ-like. Heck, I didn't even know what that meant and as far as I was concerned it sure didn't apply where my father was concerned.

As I was leaving, my pastor asked if I had been to visit Sister Agatha Marie recently. He knew how close we had been and the role she played in my entering the seminary.

"She's been quite ill. She has a very bad heart," he said. "But she's still at the convent and I'm sure would be delighted to see you."

He was right. When I went to see her the very next day, Sister Agatha's face seemed to light up the moment I entered the small sunroom where she was seated reading her prayer book. She looked very frail.

"William!" she smiled. "I hardly recognize you. My, how tall you've gotten."

"It's good to see you, Sister," I said as I handed her a small statue of Saint Theophane Venard which I had kept on my dresser at home. "I thought you might like to have a statue of the saint our seminary is named after."

"How generous you are. That's why I'm sure you will make a wonderful priest." Then she looked deeply into my eyes and asked, "Are you happy, William? Are you pleased to be studying for the priesthood?"

For some strange reason I hesitated when she asked me that. I had such great respect for this lady who had always been so kind and loving to me that I knew I had to tell her the absolute truth. I couldn't lie to her like I felt I had to Father St. John. After a moment I recall saying:

"I don't think I would be as happy at any other place right now then the Venard, Sister Agatha."

"I'm glad to hear that," she smiled.

Why I had struggled to answer her question honestly in the first place, I'm sure I didn't really know at the time. I do now. There had always been some doubt in my mind, fostered perhaps by my father's skepticism and my cousin Albert's remarks. But since I was out of my house and enjoying my life so much—mainly the sports, the studies and the farm chores— those doubts never came into focus.

Also, even when home, I was spending a great deal of my time away from the house getting re-acquainted with friends in the neighborhood, taking Patty different places, visiting with Albert and other relatives and reading some good books at the library. My absence began to bother my mother for some reason. Then one morning she grabbed me as I was leaving and asked why I seemed so anxious to get back to the seminary. I don't remember her exact words, but they were something like:

"This is still your home and you should try and be happy here the short time that you're back with us. I know your father's drinking still bothers you. It bothers all of us. But we are your parents and you can spend at least as much time with us as you do with everybody else while you're on vacation."

She was right, but I didn't want to admit it. In fact, I didn't even want to discuss it. I sensed it was her way of trying to keep the family together instead of watching it fall apart. I think I simply apologized and said I'd try to do better. But inside, I wanted to bolt out the door and grab the next bus back to Clark Summit.

Then I realized my actions were hurting her so I decided to stay home a little more. There were some nights when I'd sit in the parlor with both my parents and tell them about the missionary priests I had gotten to know, the stories I heard about their conversions and exciting activities in places like Tanganyika, Africa, Hong Kong and Shanghai, China and the enjoyable work I was doing on the seminary' farm.

I would always see my father struggling to control his drinking while I was home. As he sat in the parlor listening to my yarns, he would start to doze off. My mother would jab him gently in the ribs with her elbow, trying not to show her anger. She would keep saying...tell us more about this or tell us more about that. I wondered whether she was seriously interested in my stories or was simply gathering information to pass along to her friends and neighbors. I think it might have been both.

I was back at The Venard less than a month when I received a letter from my mother that really stunned me. She said my sister Marilyn had eloped to Elkton, Maryland with Eddie Dean. I later learned that Elkton was called "the elopement capital of America." My mother said she was heart-broken because she had wanted to give my sister a big wedding when she got married.

Sorry to say but I recall my first thought was that my sister had finally found her own way of getting out of the house. I think my second thought was, I hope she loves Eddie and they get married in the Catholic Church. They did, in St. Theresa's Church in Rego Park, New York on October 14 of 1949.

I believe it was around the middle of my third year when the reality of being a priest and serving God in a very special way began to sink into my psyche. I think it actually started around five o'clock one morning as I knelt in our beautiful Chapel staring up at the eight-foot high cross of Jesus Christ crucified hanging above the altar. There was nothing different about this particular morning and there was nothing special bothering me at the time. Also, I always enjoyed the time I spent in the Chapel. It gave me a feeling of peace and serenity.

Tall, white candles flickered in the darkness as Father North led us in prayer. All the priests, brothers, seminarians and sisters had their heads bowed and from what I could observe were in deep, spiritual meditation. I was meditating about Brutus, the four hundred pound hog Brother Xavier and I were going to slaughter that afternoon. I had watched him grow from a piglet and was hoping I wouldn't get too sentimental when I dropped the sledge hammer down on his noggin.

Suddenly it struck me—hey, what's going on? Here you are in the Presence of God and your mind's someplace else. Why aren't you meditating on spiritual things like everyone here in the Chapel? Then came the biggie. Why can't you "feel" like God is right here with you? Isn't that how it's supposed to be?

That train of thought was broken by someone ringing the altar bell and Father North rising to begin the Mass. I opened my Missal and read aloud with everyone the special prayers for the day written in Latin. I tried to force myself to pay close attention to what I was reading because I didn't like the way I felt at that moment.

As I said, when I look back now, I can clearly see that this was reality finally starting to set in. Even though I tried not to think about it too much, I soon came to realize that practically everything I was involved in at the seminary seemed more important to me than my spiritual life. I don't know how, but Father Thomas Slattery, my Spiritual Director, came to notice it too. Before leaving on vacation, he called me into his office for a talk. It was brief. He left me with two questions to ponder over the next six weeks I would be at home:

"Why do you want to be a priest and, how much are you working on your relationship with God?

Father Slattery must have been in touch with my pastor because Father St. John asked me the exact same questions when I went to see him for my weekly review. I recall admitting how much I enjoyed my work on the farm, being part of The Maple Syrup Squad and engaging in sports. I quoted our Rector, Father North, who said all those things were part of making a good missionary priest.

My pastor didn't want to debate with me. Like my spiritual director, he only wanted to emphasize that I had to keep the real focus on serving God and to do that, I needed to develop a close, personal relationship with Him.

Decisions can be difficult when you have to make them by yourself. But decisions can be easier when someone else makes them for you. That's what happened the year I graduated from The Venard. Father Slattery made the decision for me. However, I did something that made it relatively easy for him to make that decision.

We had a great basketball team my senior year if I must say so myself. My friend Dennis Hanley, a skinny little guy about five feet seven was our lead guard. He had a terrific two-hand set-shot and could sink it almost every time he shook free. My friend Walter Barrett, who I remained close to until the day he died, was a powerful forward. He was square-jawed with a crew cut and his broad shoulders would scatter the opposition every time he drove to the basket for a layup. As the six foot two center, I was a pretty fair rebounder with a good hook shot that could put points on the board.

We were coached by a terrific fellow named Frank "Ace" Murray who had been a big star for St. Francis College's basketball team in New York City before entering Maryknoll to study for the priesthood. He was a Deacon at the time which meant he was in his last two years of study before ordination. He had been sent to The Venard for one of those years to teach philosophy and theology to us seniors.

"Ace," which is what we all called him, was a task-master as a coach and ruthless on the basketball court. For him, it was almost win at any cost. He toughened me up and turned me into a bully every time we played a game.

We were in a county basketball league and tied for first place with our biggest rival, Scranton Prep. That was the largest Catholic high school in the area and its teams would win in almost every sport every year.

The championship game was played in our gym on a Sunday afternoon and it drew quite a crowd. Not only were most of the priests, brothers and seminarians on hand but a goodly number of the Maryknoll Sisters as well. Many parents and some teachers from Scranton Prep drove in to root for their team which was naturally favored to win.

There were mostly big, muscular coal miners' sons on our opponent's roster. Ace told us we had to be tough and not let them push us around.

There were two referees for the game. One was the athletic director at Scranton Prep and the other was our own Father Raymond "Drainpipe" O'Donahugh who claimed he had once been a basketball star himself. He was well over six feet tall and very skinny which is why we was tagged him with the monicker "Drainpipe." He smiled when we'd call him that but he didn't care for it one single bit.

It was a tight game from the outset. The lead went back and forth until late in the fourth quarter when Dennis Hanley hit a couple of set shots which put us out in front by four points. But fighting on the inside for rebounds and trying to defend against my broad-shouldered opponent caused me to chalk up four personal fouls. One more and I'd be out of the game. Ace kept shouting to be careful, but the bully instinct he had ignited inside of me was on fire.

Driving down the lane for a layup, I was sure I had avoided my defender who stood directly in front of me. As the ball dropped into the basket, I heard Father O'Donahugh blow his whistle and point at me with seeming delight in his eyes. Maybe I had called him "Drainpipe" one too many times and he was getting even.

"That's a charge!" he shouted. "You're out of the game!"

I literally saw red. I was positive I hadn't charged into my man, that I hadn't committed a foul. In a flash I was also convinced Father O'Donahugh was trying to show special consideration to the visiting team, that he felt being nice was more important than us winning. I was also certain that he knew it wasn't a foul but didn't care. It's strange what the mind can conjure up in a matter of seconds but that's exactly what I recall happened to me that afternoon at The Venard Preparatory Seminary in Clarks Summit, Pennsylvania.

I suddenly turned, ran toward the priest and stuck my finger in his face. I yelled that he was wrong and he knew it. "Drainpipe" was stunned, but then yelled back:

"I told you, you're out of the game!"

Why I did it I still don't know. It was like why did I set my house on fire? I couldn't answer that question either. I just reached out and punched the unsuspecting priest square on the jaw. As he staggered backward, lost his balance and fell down, I could hear everyone in the gym breathe in simultaneously from shock and then just stand there in total silence holding their breath.

Ace came running onto the floor and helped the other referee get Father O'Donahugh to his feet. Then he grabbed me angrily by the arm and told me to head for the locker room. I remember feeling everyone's eyes on me. I was certain the roof would be caving in on top of me at any moment.

We lost the game by five points. No one said a word to me about the incident at dinner that night except Walter Barrett. He whispered, "I would've done the same thing." I guess everyone knew that the final verdict and punishment would be handed down by our Rector who I'm sure was embarrassed by the whole shocking incident. The verdict would come after breakfast the next morning.

It's very strange what can run through your mind during extremely tense times. It may sound crazy but for a very brief moment I hoped Father North didn't have his version of my mother's rubber hose. I was positive that I was on my way out of The Venard, that you can't scandalize Catholics visiting a seminary as well as priests, brothers, sisters and your fellow students without the ultimate punishment—the electric chair or something close to it. So I was totally shocked by what Father North had to say.

As soon as I entered his office, he could see the fear in my eyes and the trembling in my hands. He knew the pain and anxiety I had been going through since the full impact of my actions had hit home. This kind and gentle man knew I had to be put back together rather than be taken apart any further. That's why he was in charge of a seminary filled with young men—very young men.

He came around his desk, pointed to a chair and sat down across from me. I can recall the first thing he said to me that morning:

"Relax, William. I'm not going to make things any worse for you than they already are. I'm not going to hang you from the bell tower."

His warm and understanding smile did help me ease up as much as possible under the circumstances. He then went on to say something like:

"I don't believe that one incident, as serious as it was, should eradicate all the good things you have done in the past. At the same time, we can't simply ignore it since too many people were quite scandalized by your actions.

"However, the young seminarian I saw out there on that basketball court yesterday was a young man filled with zeal. He wanted to do everything he could to win that game for his team. Now if that young man could only harness that zeal for the right purposes—like serving God and his fellow man—he could someday make a fine missionary priest. Don't you agree?"

"I guess so, Father," I uttered, almost completely stunned by his going in a direction I never expected. I was waiting to be hung from the bell tower.

"So I've decided to give you a second chance. But I'm putting you on probation for two months. No Free Days. You will have extra study halls...no rec hall on Saturday afternoon...and you'll help clean up the kitchen on weekends."

Then he stood up. I followed suit. He put his hand on my shoulder.

"I'll be watching you like a hawk," he concluded, "and I expect nothing like this will ever happen again."

"It won't," I murmured.

"Oh, if you haven't apologized to Father O'Donahugh by now," he added, "I advise you to do so. And I would also advise that you stop calling him Drainpipe."

I left the Rector's office that morning very happy but very confused. Some friends told me he didn't throw me out because he was a great sports enthusiast and needed me to play hockey that winter and pitch for the baseball team in the spring. While there may have been a wee bit of truth to that, I wanted to believe that Father North simply saw more good in me than I saw in myself.

That wasn't confirmed one way or the other, however, when I met with Father Slattery to discuss the matter. I think he was surprised I hadn't been given my walking papers but wasn't inclined to overrule his boss—not yet anyway. He simply urged me to focus on my spiritual life during the time I had left in my final year, asking God for his guidance to help me reach a firm and honest decision concerning the priesthood.

About three weeks before I was to graduate, Father Slattery sat down with me one last time. I was still equivocating but my spiritual director wasn't. He said he had been watching me closely since the fall and admired my dedication to every work and study assignment I had been given. He said he wished he had seen as much dedication to my spiritual life.

"William," he said warmly but very seriously, "I think some day you will make a really wonderful father, but I don't think it will be here at Maryknoll. That's why I advise that you leave us but never forget what you have learned here. Take it with you and you will be a better man for it."

There was only one question that continued to haunt me as I rode the bus back to New York that warm morning in late June of 1951:

"How do I tell my mother that after four years, I am leaving the seminary for good? How do I tell her that I was not becoming a Maryknoll missionary priest?"

CHAPTER EIGHT

What Should She Tell the Neighbors?

Four years away from home can leave you a stranger in your own neighborhood. That it did.

Four years in a seminary can lead people to believe you've been touched by God's grace to be a priest. That was no longer true.

Four years of living a rather independent life despite some rules and regulations can make it difficult to live again with people who think you are dependent upon them. My goal was to change that as quickly as possible.

At eighteen, I had to now figure out what I was going to do with the rest of my life. First I had to get my present life in order. To begin that process, I had to let my parents know I had decided not to become a priest.

I felt my father would have no trouble swallowing the news. I think he always believed it was just a matter of time before I awakened from my "pipe dream" and crashed back down to earth. Despite being a drunk, he still had a great deal of perception, particularly when it came to me. From the way things turned out, he had been closer to the truth than I was and for some reason I resented that.

As for my mother, telling her the news would be an entirely different story. By now what may have been an "heroic dream" for me which was more of an apt description of my desire at the time, it had become a reality for her. My mother's dream of one day seeing her son standing on the altar saying Mass had become tattooed on her mind, her heart and her soul. It was what gave her hope and joy and a special reputation in the neighborhood when everything else around her was falling apart.

I was home almost a week trying to figure out how to raise the subject when she did it for me. Over breakfast one morning, she simply asked where I would be going next. Where was Maryknoll sending me to continue my studies for the priesthood?

"I hope it's not too far away," she smiled. "You know how much I love to come and visit you."

Her brow furrowed when she saw the look on my face. She immediately knew there was something wrong.

"I've been planning to talk to you about that, mom," I replied. Even I could hear the trepidation in my voice.

"What's wrong?" she asked as though expecting me to tell her the Pope himself had just ostracized me from the Catholic Church.

"Please don't get upset," I pleaded, "but I've decided not to go back to the seminary."

"You what! I don't believe it. What did you do? You were there four years. Why won't they let you come back?" Her eyes were now filling with tears.

"Because I've decided not to become a priest," I said very quietly.

She lowered her head and began to cry harder. I don't believe I could have hurt her more if I had hit her with her own rubber hose or put a bullet right through her heart. Her face turned white as the tears continued rolling down her cheeks. It bothered me that my mother thought I had done something wrong, that I had committed some great sin and was being booted from the Catholic Faith. I tried to explain that it was my own decision, a decision I made after talking with my spiritual director. She just kept crying.

That's when I realized there was no way I could get her to understand why I left, why I decided the priesthood was not my calling. Then, after a very long moment, my mother looked at me and said something I will never forget.

"What am I going to tell the neighbors?"

My father was in one of his quiet moods when he came home that night half in his cups. I didn't even want to speak to him but I knew he'd be getting my mother's version of the story. So I told him about my decision. Perhaps I expected him to say "I told you so," but he didn't. He simply said:

"Well, now that the cat's out of the bag you can get on with your life. I don't know what I can do but if you see any way I can help you, let me know."

The days that followed were terribly uncomfortable for my mother and me. My sister Patty was delighted I was back at home but she couldn't say so out loud. Little Bobby was almost six now and we were practically strangers. But now we would have a chance to get to know each other. As for Marilyn, she was only concerned about my welfare and my future. She was also looking forward to my getting to know her husband Eddie better and their new baby girl, Eileen.

Then something totally unexpected happened, something that gratefully lightened the atmosphere at home to some degree. My father hit "the numbers."

There was an illegal gambling racket in the city back then called "the numbers game." Today it's called "Lotto" and it's legal because the city or state takes most of the money. My father had been playing it through a bookie. You simply selected a number you liked, put a few dollars down on it, and hoped to Providence you'd win. Twice a week some unknown source would pull a number from a hat and the winner would walk away with big odds. My dad hit for one thousand dollars.

Naturally he spent some of it "buying the bar" at Moochies and some of it paying down his debts with the loan sharks. But he also brought home five hundred dollars to put down on a new car.

His old Ford Coupe was on its last legs so he took my mother with him to the new Kaiser-Frazer dealership in City Line. With a down payment of a few hundred dollars, they bought the first new car they ever owned.

It was a 1951 four cylinder dark blue "Henry J." It was named after Henry J. Kaiser, the chairman of the board of The Kaiser-Frazer Corporation. I thought stupidly at the time that my father bought it because his middle name was "Henry." The two-door sedan was great on gas and easy to handle. Since my mother had finally gotten her driver's license a few months earlier, she seemed very happy, at least happier than she had been in awhile.

I remember having lunch one day with my cousin Albert. He wasn't surprised about my leaving the seminary even though he said it did upset my Grandmother McLintock and others in the family who worshipped the clergy. He said my Aunt Helen was disappointed too, mainly because my leaving upset my mother.

That was the day Albert handed me a cigarette, an unfiltered Lucky Strike, a habit he had picked up in the Navy. He lit it for me and told me to inhale. After coughing my lungs out, I smoked most of the cigarette, got dizzy and almost threw up my lunch. But I went on from there to eventually become a four-pack-a-day Lucky Strike smoker until I almost died from nicotine poisoning twenty five years later.

When I asked my cousin about his job, he told me it wasn't a place I would want to work and said nothing more. I soon learned he was stuck in a position he didn't like despite the good money he was making. But he never did anything about it and became a very unhappy man. But Albert did tell me my father belonged to what was called a "father and son Union." He said this meant the sons of pressmen could get a Union card, learn the trade and follow in their father's footsteps if they so desired.

I didn't say it then, but I knew that wasn't my desire. However, it did spark an idea that became more exciting the more I thought about it.

Every time my father managed to come home for dinner, he always had a copy of the newspaper with him, The New York Journal-America with its big red banner headline. I started reading it, from the front page news stories to the sports pages to the great syndicated columnists that appeared in the editorial section. I believe that's what got my juices flowing and rekindled my desire to write.

One night I reminded my dad about his offer to help me find a job if he could. I must confess that deep inside I felt he owed me something for all the hurt and embarrassment he had caused, hurt I could still feel every time I'd see him drunk again. I asked if he knew anyone at the newspaper who could get me an interview for a job in the editorial department.

It took a few weeks. Actually I thought my father had forgotten our conversation. Then he asked me to meet him at work one afternoon because there was someone he wanted me to see. That person was Al Marder, a bald fellow in his early fifties with dark circles under his eyes and a very sad look on his pale, stubbled face. Al was in charge of the "copy boys."

I'll never forget walking into the city room that day and hearing the loud din of typewriters clacking away, the rumble of news wires spurting out information from around the world and the shrill voices of writers, editors and newspaper make-up men shouting to hear each other over all the noise. They were exchanging ideas about breaking stories and how they should be played in terms of column width and length in the news pages they were getting ready to publish. It was the most exciting scene I had ever witnessed and I knew instantly, just as I did once back at The Venard, that this was a place I really wanted to be.

The New York Journal-American was actually the flagship of the Hearst organization headed by the famous and infamous William Randolph Hearst. He founded the newspaper way back in 1896 as The Evening Journal and then acquired The New York American in 1901. He eventually merged the two newspapers in 1937 creating The New York Journal-American. It went on to become the largest evening newspaper in the world.

It boasted highly popular columnists like Westbrook Pegler, Dorothy Kilgallen, Jimmy Cannon, Jack O'Brien and fashion editor Robin Chandler Duke. The newspaper also introduced the nation's first full daily comic strip page as well as the renowned cartoonist Rube Goldberg.

"If you like a lot of noise and confusion, you're in the right place," Al Marder shouted at me. "But it quiets down for a short time between editions."

My father had to get back to work so he wished me luck, shook Al's hand and left.

"He's a nice man, your father," the chief of the copy boys smiled. "He's always trying to do favors for people."

That was a side of my father I didn't really know. But my main interest at that moment was finding out whether or not there was a spot open for me on the copy boy staff. So I listened as Al continued to talk very loudly.

"I should tell you right up front that copy boys are nothing but a bunch of glorified errand boys. We take the copy from rewritemen to the city desk and the make-up desk. We grab the news bulletins and wire stories from the Associated Press and United Press teletype machines and run them to the news desk. And we keep everyone supplied with carbon paper for copies and information from the morgue when necessary. The morgue's where we keep all the background information on everybody and everything.

"The rest of the job is getting coffee and sandwiches for the editorial staff. And you do all that for the extravagant sum of twenty four dollars and fifty cents a week."

"But you also get to learn how a major daily newspaper operates," I said.

"And a long shot chance of becoming a newspaper reporter," Al replied. "The really good, hard-working copy boys get looked at first—that's after they've been around here a few years."

The balding man who hadn't hit the big time himself yet saw the eagerness on my face and hired me on the spot. I don't know why but perhaps he liked the idea of my father being a pressman for the newspaper. Or perhaps there was a favor involved. Or it could have been he just needed another copy boy. It really didn't matter. All I know is that my father helped open the door to a career I came to love. Looking back, he gave me the opportunity to go as far in the media business as my talents would take me. And I believe to this day that I could have gone very far had I kept my powder dry.

Now that I was earning a paycheck, even though it was quite small, it was enough to cover some college credits. So I decided to enroll in night school at St. John's University which was located in downtown Brooklyn. I already had almost two years of college credits from the extra work I had done at The Venard where I had received a really great education. I continued to major in English while also taking courses in philosophy and ethics.

It was my ethics class, believe it or not, that paved the way for me to become a newspaper reporter at the ripe young age of eighteen and a half.

There was a major scandal going on at the time involving the Mayor of New York City and some if his cohorts that had just been unearthed by the Federal Bureau of Investigation. It was the fall of 1951, a few months after I had enrolled at St. John's. It was alleged that Mayor William J. O'Dwyer had been receiving millions in graft from city developers who needed building permits. The mayor's closest pal, Fire Commissioner James J. Moran, was accused of being the bag man who collected all the dough.

The federal prosecutors in the case couldn't pin anything on the mayor but they had plenty of witnesses to testify against the fire commissioner. He was indicted on fifteen counts of grand larceny. He managed to post bail while awaiting trial.

One night at the university I noticed this white-haired man with a red, blotchy face sitting near the back of the room in one of my classes—my ethics class. I did the usual double-take that occurs when something totally unexpected happens. I had been seeing that same face on the front page of my newspaper for days. He was James J. Moran, the indicted Fire Commissioner of New York City.

I think the double-take also happened because I immediately saw the absurdity and hypocrisy involved. Here was a man who forced hapless developers to hand over millions now deciding to catch up on his "ethics" while waiting to be hauled before a jury of his peers.

I knew our first edition was put to bed by nine a.m. so I made sure I was in the city room before eight the next morning. Mr. Eddie Mahar, a ruggedly handsome man with thick eyebrows and graying hair who many believed was the best City Editor in a town of nineteen newspapers, was already at his desk. He was debating quite loudly with his two assistant city editors what news stories would be on the front page and which would be the headline story of the day.

I approached Bobby Spellman who ran the switchboard at the city desk and asked if I could speak to Mr. Mahar. Being so busy, Bobby initially pushed me aside, saying it was the wrong time. But I wouldn't budge. I was standing less than five feet away from the City Editor when I said loud enough for all to hear:

"But I have a front page story, Bobby! It could be the headline story!"

With that, Eddie Mahar spun around, lowered his silver-framed eyeglasses, glared at me and shouted:

"What the fuck are you talking about, kid? And who are you? Can't you see we're busy trying to put out a newspaper?"

Spellman butted in saying, "He's one of our new copy boys, Eddie."

But I wouldn't be ignored.

"James J. Moran, the Fire Chief, is in my ethics class at St. John's University," I said even louder. "Don't you think that's a great story, Mr. Mahar? A crooked city official studying ethics at St. John's University?"

He yanked his glasses off and grabbed my arm.

"Are you bullshitting me or what?" he barked. "How do you know that?"

"I told you, he's in my class," I replied, now half scared to death by his threatening presence. "He's in my ethics class at St. John's University. That's where I go to night school. I saw him there last night."

Mahar turned and shouted to Sam Day, the Managing Editor, who was standing behind his desk about twenty feet away. Sam was in his late sixties with shocking white hair and well over six feet four.

"Hey, Sam! I'm holding up the front page. We just got a tip on a great story about that fucking fire commissioner studying ethics at St. John's University. Isn't that hot shit! Just need five minutes to check it out!"

Then he turned to me again and said: "Thanks, kid. I'll see you later."

As I moved slowly away from the city desk, I heard Bobby Spellman ask the operator to get him St. John's University on the phone. For a brief moment I was angry that they didn't take my word, that they didn't trust me. That's how naïve I was. But just as quickly I realized that every news story had to be checked and double checked to make sure of its accuracy.

The big red-banner headline for the first edition read:

INDICTED FIRE COMMISSIONER STUDYING
ETHICS AT ST. JOHN'S UNIVERSITY

When the final edition was put to bed, Al Marder told me the City Editor wanted to see me right away. The whole city room had been buzzing all day about "the story that new kid Borchert just broke." Some of the copy boys who had been there for several years hoping to become reporters were staring at me with envy—some with anger. I could understand. We were all competing for that same reportorial prize and the brand new kid on the block was now leading the pack.

This time Eddie Mahar was warm and friendly although his words were just as vulgar and profane as they had been earlier. I once told a friend of mine who was also a former newsman that Eddie Mahar was the only person I had ever met who could string together seventeen profane words and make a perfect English sentence.

He told me I had "a nose for news" and that he was making me a "fucking police reporter." I'd be covering the Brooklyn police beat. He said I was replacing "an old bull shitter" by the name of Johnny Crosby who was retiring. Johnny had been handling the lobster shift at Brooklyn Police Headquarters—midnight until eight a.m.—for the past twenty years.

Al Marder, Bobby Spellman and most of the rewrite guys I had gotten to know came over to congratulate me as well as the Managing Editor, Sam Day, who I always respected for his great news judgment. Only two of the eight other copy boys, Stan Baer and Gus Engleman, wished me luck. They were both in their late twenties and were promoted a few years later.

Trying not to show my complete ignorance, I asked the City Editor what was expected of me. What kind of stories was he was looking for and how did I go about getting them? He smiled because he knew I was totally wet behind the ears. So I stopped talking before he could really see how totally ignorant I was. He made it easy.

"There are nineteen newspapers in this city, young man," he said. "Go over to Brooklyn Police Headquarters and make friends with the other reporters. They'll be glad to show you the ropes. After that, you're a smart kid so I expect you to beat them to the fucking story every chance you get."

For some reason I was eager to tell my dad the good news, perhaps because I felt he did me a big favor opening the door. I went downstairs to the press room but there were only a few guys around cleaning the presses. So reluctantly I headed for Moochie's Bar and Grill. My father was surprised when I walked in. Since I had been so busy with work and school and he was so busy boozing, I rarely saw him, even at home. When I told him I had just been made a police reporter, he looked at me somewhat skeptically.

"No, it's true, Dad," I said, feeling offended. I knew what was going through his mind. After all, not only did he still have doubts about my veracity which bothered me a great deal, but he also had been around the newspaper business a long time. Despite his drinking, he knew that most reporters were older, more seasoned professionals, not eighteen-year-olds fresh out of a seminary.

"I broke a big story today, the headline story about the Fire Commissioner studying ethics at St. Johns where I go. That's why the City Editor promoted me," I continued enthusiastically. "He said I had a nose for news. If you don't believe me, you can always check with Al Marder."

"I don't have to check with anybody," he finally replied. "If you say it's true, it's true. Would you like a beer to celebrate?"

The thought of drinking the stuff that brought nothing but trouble and confusion into my life and into the lives of my whole family had been the furthest thing from my mind. Now here it was being offered to me as a token of celebration, something that should go hand-in-hand with the good things in life, like promotions and sudden prestige. I had never put booze into that category but my father had been doing it all his life. For many people, it was the social thing to do—but not if you're an alcoholic.

"No thanks, Dad," I said almost automatically. "I'll have a coke."

I then asked if I should wait for him so we could take the train home together. He suggested instead that I hurry home myself and give my mother the good news. He said he'd be home later. He was—much, much later.

The period of the 1950's was an interesting time to be a newspaper reporter in New York City. First, many considered it the heyday of journalism with nineteen newspapers and the emergence of in-depth electronic media news, both on radio and TV. Despite the problem of hauling huge studio cameras to outdoor crime scenes and other events, television news was rapidly emerging from its infancy.

On the socio-economic front, while more and more skyscrapers were rising to create a whole new horizon, the city was also experiencing what became known as "white flight." That phrase was coined to describe people fleeing changing neighborhoods in all five boroughs and heading for the suburbs because of the growing crime rate and the increasing cost of the welfare burden. Brooklyn was significantly affected as hordes of the white middle class left to find better schools for their children and more peaceful neighborhoods where they could grow up safely.

As a result, places like Brooklyn's Bedford-Stuyvescent area and the Prospect Park region began to erode into ghettos filled with rundown tenements and gang violence. And, while no one would admit it at the time, the city's newspapers, including The New York Journal-American, got tired of filling their news pages with "black crime stories." Reporters would be asked by the editor when calling in a story, "What color is it?" That led to fewer and fewer stories involving the minority population finding their way into the pages of the city's newspapers.

That's the atmosphere I found myself in when I walked into Brooklyn Police Headquarters in Park Slope shortly before midnight on a very chilly Monday in December of 1951. I had already checked in with the Night City Editor Art McClure in Manhattan from the "press shack" to let him know I was there ready for work. The press shack was actually a long room above a Greek diner directly across the street from police headquarters. Reporters from most of the newspapers who worked out of the shack had a small desk, a chair, a telephone and a telephone book. Those were the tools of the trade.

There were no reporters around when I arrived so I went over to headquarters and spoke to the lieutenant on the booking desk. I asked where I might find some of them. He pointed to a saloon across the way on Flatbush Avenue called the Edison Bar. He said I might find some of the reporters in there or in the five other saloons within a two-block area. He was wrong. I found all the reporters in the Edison Bar. At least it seemed like it.

It was a very noisy joint so I had to ask the bartender twice—he was a former catcher for the New York Giants baseball team by the way—if he knew a reporter he could introduce me to. He did. That's how I met Charlie Feeney of the New York Daily Mirror. He was in his late fifties, overweight, with bloodshot eyes and a loud, happy laugh. I couldn't tell at first whether his laugh was genuine or the result of the straight shots with beer chasers he was knocking down.

I didn't realize that Charlie, who always wore a beaten-up gray fedora indoors or out, knew I was coming. So did most of the other reporters that covered the Brooklyn beat. They heard some kid was replacing their buddy Johnny Crosby. In those days, even though there was a great deal of competition to get an exclusive story, the newspaper business was like one big club. Everybody seemed to know everything about everybody else.

Before I had a chance to ask The Daily Mirror reporter how he went about covering the news in Brooklyn, how he got leads on stories, how he found out what crimes were being reported in various precincts, he asked me what I wanted to drink.

"I'll have a coke," I said nonchalantly.

He let go with that loud, happy laugh and replied:

"The hell you will." Then he yelled to the bartender, "Hey, Harry. Give my young friend here a shot and a beer."

The enemy was at the gate once more, only now it was dressed in a very enticing getup. It was presenting itself as part of the surroundings, as part of the camaraderie, almost as if it were simply another tool of the trade. You might say I was too weak and immature to withstand its formidable presence and say no…that I couldn't stand up to the peer pressure. Someone told me some years later I couldn't because I was essentially an alcoholic in waiting.

Charlie kept prodding me. "Come on, kid, drink up. It'll make a man out of you."

Suddenly I felt insulted. Who the hell does this guy think he is saying something like that, I thought. I'm just as much a man as he is, maybe better. I'm a newspaper reporter just like him and I'm only nineteen. By the time I'm his age I'll be the Managing Editor. So I picked up the shot glass and said:

"Here's to you, Charlie."

I had seen my father down many a shot and beer, so I knew how to handle it. I lifted the shot glass to my lips and let the magic elixir flow down my throat. I started coughing so hard it almost flowed right back up. So I quickly downed it with the beer.

"That's the problem with all that Coca Cola shit you been drinking," I remember Charlie saying with another big laugh. "It weakens the goddamn palette for the whisky to slide down right. Let's have another."

The next one went down easier. My new friend then told me about checking the police teletype machine behind the front desk at Brooklyn headquarters for crimes committed throughout the borough and calling the local precincts if some of the reports appeared interesting. He said it was good to get to know the detectives at the busiest precincts because they could give you tips on breaking stories.

Then he introduced me to Joey George of the New York Daily News who also bought me a shot and a beer.

"I'd suggest you carry a small notebook you can fit into your pocket," the short, lean man also in his fifties with a pock-marked face advised. "And make sure you have a few pencils and plenty of loose change for phone calls when you're out at a crime scene. You never know how long you'll be stuck there.

"By the way," he added, wiping his running nose with a dirty handkerchief "if you don't have a car, you better get to know the city's subway and bus systems like the palm of your hand. You don't want to waste time getting to breaking stories or to the police precincts around town."

I met five more reporters at the Edison Bar that night. I learned a lot, had a total of six shots and six beers and didn't pay for a single one. Looking back, I believe they were all having fun with the new kid, seeing how well I could hold my liquor. I didn't get sick or fall down like they may have expected. I was proud of myself. I remember heading back to the press shack feeling a little dizzy. But I also felt like I always wanted to feel and never did until now—comfortable, grown up and in charge. The booze even made me believe I was now a veteran newsman.

I was back in the Edison Bar the very next night having a few shots and beers in order to get ready to go to work.

There were times when I've wondered if that's how my dad started, getting enticed into drinking by some friends or co-workers who thought it was a necessary ritual, an important part of their relationships, an important part of the way they operated and did business, an important part of how they felt about themselves and others around them. That's what happened to me that first night. And my solemn oath that I would never become anything like my father was flushed right down the toilet. I was already on my way and had no idea.

When you're young, healthy and in fairly decent shape, you can handle booze for a while. So, despite drinking a little too much on occasion, I began to make great strides in my chosen profession. Strange as it may seem, I often felt like alcohol was oiling the hinges on the doors that were being opened.

I began to think the magic elixir was helping to make me a better reporter, a better writer, a better dancer, a better ladies man and that it was aiding me to expand my horizons and really enjoy life. It took away my feelings of low self-esteem and added a great deal of bravado in its place. Without realizing it, I was beginning to think like my father, that booze was his buddy, that it had saved his life the night he fell down those fifteen marble steps at Werderman's Hall. That's how insidious it can be right from the start.

Since my ego was now in full stride, fanning my goal to become the best reporter on the staff, I began covering practically every incident coming across the police teletype. It all seemed important news to me—murders, rapes, robberies, gang fights. Art McClure was quick to tell me in a very polite but emphatic way that most of the stories I was calling in were "the wrong color."

"I appreciate how hard you're working, Bill," I recall him saying to me on the phone one night. "You're calling in stories three or four times a night. Johnny Crosby maybe called in one story three or four times a week.

"But you've got to be more choosey in what you cover. There's so many crime stories in some of those Brooklyn ghettos and we can't print them all. You know what I'm saying. Start looking other places for better stories."

So, instead of trying to buck the system, I regret to say I joined it. Actually I didn't see any other course. I began looking harder for incidents that had unusual angles—and were "the right color."

For example, there was the story about a character I literally created called The Santa Claus Bandit. Since it was only weeks away from Christmas, the Night City Editor ran two of the four news articles I developed right on the front page of the first edition. He told me to keep up the good work.

It all started with a series of holdups at jewelry stores, liquor stores, pawn shops and appliance stores in Brooklyn's Seventy Eighth Precinct.

The thief was said by some witnesses to be wearing a red cap with a white tassel on top and what looked like a fake white beard. I never asked his color. Using my imagination which was always working overtime, I tied all four crimes to the same guy and nicknamed him The Santa Claus Bandit. The detectives laughed and went along with it, saying it was very appropriate for the season.

Then came a stroke of good luck. The bandit was captured holding up a jewelry store a week before Christmas. The police found his apartment filled with jewelry, cases of booze and all kinds of clothes and pawn shop items. I said in the story that this was a Santa Claus who liked to take presents rather than give them. McClure played it up on the front page along with a picture of a real Santa Claus—well, as real as Santa can be. The bandit turned out to be black but I never mentioned it.

The advice that Charley Feeney and Joey George had given me about making connections with detectives was still bouncing around in my skull when I met a Captain Louis Goldberg who headed the Brooklyn Morals Squad at a crime scene one night. He and his men investigated everything from illegal gambling to porn. I knew he'd be a great contact. However, he seemed overly friendly and asked for my phone number at the press shack. Before I knew it I was getting tips from him about planned raids on mob crap games, illegal bingo games and raids on houses of prostitution.

A number of my fellow reporters started getting miffed over my scoops. They were receiving calls from their editors asking why they didn't know about all the police raids appearing in the Journal-American. I remember Harold Phalen, a reporter for The Brooklyn Eagle, looked into it. Someone he knew on Captain Goldberg's staff told him his boss "had the hots" for some young reporter and was tipping him off.

One night when I was at the shack with a bunch of other reporters, Phalen broke the news.

"It seems like Captain Goldberg has a would-be lover in our midst," he grinned, looking almost directly at me. "I'm not going to guess who's kissing his fat ass for exclusive stories but I'd suggest he stop before his relationship with good old homo Louie gets too serious—and we get too pissed off."

I think everyone there knew who it was but felt that Phalen's warning would suffice. It did. While I was really embarrassed by the insinuation, the truth was I had never heard any rumors that the chief of the morals squad was homosexual. So I stopped answering the Captain's phone calls and everything returned to normal.

Between work and partying, I was starting to run late for some of my classes at St. John's night school. Then I began missing some of them. In June of 1952, I dropped out altogether and never went back. I've been told I have more than enough credits, both from college and life experience, to graduate, but I still regret not having finished my formal college education.

It was mainly the partying that was the culprit. Since I was still on the starting rung of the reporters' pay ladder, I wasn't making enough money to attend college, get my own apartment and have a good old time too. Of course back then, it wasn't unusual for young men to live at home until they married or at least became involved in a serious relationship. And neither my mother nor my father was putting any pressure on me to move out, not at the moment anyway.

I was eager to fit in so I became a regular fixture at the five beer joints that surrounded police headquarters, including the Edison Bar. I'd sleep it off at home from eleven a.m. until around six p.m. Sometimes I'd have dinner with my mother, Patty and Bobby or, as I was gradually doing, follow in my father's footsteps and make some excuse that I had to be somewhere else.

That somewhere else was either with a bunch of new drinking buddies at a dance hall in Sunnyside, Queens where many gorgeous airline stewardesses resided, or at a vaudeville show in Hoboken, New Jersey. That's where I first saw comedians George Bums and Gracie Allen. While I didn't have a car, it was easy to get to those places by bus or train.

In the summer I was a regular at the White House which was a bar on the boardwalk at Rockaway Beach. It was a popular hangout for guys and gals my age. I was now part of a friendly foursome-Donald, Arnold, Ernie and myself, four young horny guys who usually drank too much to score. Donald had an old Model T Ford which got us around but didn't attract many girls. Still, between the White House, the crowded sandy beaches and rowdy Irishtown, you could always find plenty of girls to date. And I dated some very nice young ladies, but again, I usually drank too much.

Over the next three years, in spite of all the partying, I advanced rather rapidly at the newspaper. I went from covering the Brooklyn police beat to covering the Manhattan beat and then onto criminal courts. That's when one of the Assistant City Editors, a guy named Joe McGovern, gave me the chance to write some of my own stories. He believed in helping guys like me get ahead.

My stories involved both the rich and the poor who committed all kinds of mayhem and were being judged by a jury of their peers. Some of the trials were better than four-star movies which made it easy to create some interesting copy.

That's also how Eddie Mahar first took notice of my writing ability. He began bringing me into the city room to work with McGovern on special assignments. Joe, who was a handsome and highly-decorated Marine Corps hero in his late thirties, was also a very heavy drinker. Maybe that's why we became such real close friends.

I remember one of the first big assignments he gave me was to write a major feature story about the Korean prisoners of war returning home in terrible condition after years in North Korean concentration camps. I remember Joe telling me:

"Those POWs have been through hell. Some of them may not want to open up. Then talk to their wives, even their kids. Play up the family angle—what was it like when their husband or father was in a prison camp. How long was he gone? How do they feel now that he's home? Has he changed much? Let's see how good you are at getting into their heads."

Apparently I wasn't too bad because the story got kudos not only from Joe but from Mahar and Sam Day as well. They played it up big on the front page.

I interviewed the POWs and their families at St. Albans Naval Hospital where the servicemen had been sent for rehabilitation. While touched by their harrowing tales, I was also taken by the fact that I was back in St. Albans, Queens where my late Uncle Freddie committed suicide in his home there some years before. Both of those terrible incidents stayed with me for days.

The next feature story Joe had me write was about a heroic, fast-thinking captain of a large airline cargo plane that was flying from San Francisco to Tokyo, Japan. Just past the point of no return, the plane lost two engines and the captain and his crew were perilously close to crashing into the Pacific Ocean. He ordered his crew to quickly throw all the cargo overboard to lighten the aircraft and they managed to make it safely to their final destination. Believe it or not, one of the copy editors put a headline on the story that read:

HEROIC PILOT DROPS LOAD OVER THE PACIFIC.

The headline was changed for the second edition.

I didn't know it at the time, but Eddie Mahar was grooming me for bigger things. He not only liked my work, but liked me personally. Even though he cursed like a trooper, the City Editor also practiced the same religion I did and admired the fact that I had spent four years in a seminary. He was a prominent member of the city's Catholic laity, the former President of the Catholic Institute of the Press and a close friend of New York City's Catholic Church leader at that time, Francis Cardinal Spellman

On occasion he would have McGovern send me off to cover special events or some off-beat story he might like to play on the front page. The first such assignment seemed rather weird at first. I was to cover and write a feature story about famous bandleader, Tommy Dorsey, who had just died and was being waked at the upscale Campbell's Funeral Home in midtown Manhattan. Instead of it being weird, the wake turned out to be very interesting and exciting—that is, as exciting as a funeral can be. I recall Mahar saying to me:

"Don't get too damn impressed by all those fucking celebrities who will probably be there just for show. Remember, they shit just like you do. In fact, some of them are bigger assholes than you.

"And by the way, see if you can find out if some of them really liked Dorsey or not. I heard lots of people hated the bastard's guts. There's nothing like shaking up a good funeral if you can do it."

By the time I arrived, movie stars and celebrities packed the place beginning with Frank Sinatra who had exploded onto the scene as Dorsey's lead vocalist. This was in the "swing era" when there were many great orchestras including Benny Goodman, Glenn Miller, Kay Kaiser, Cab Callaway and Harry James.

Others attending the funeral included Lana Turner, Ava Gardner, Mickey Rooney, Bing Crosby, Bob Hope, the nation's leading lady golfer, Babe Diedrickson and her husband, wrestling champion George Zeke Zaharius.

Among the well-known musicians and singers were Louis Armstrong, Vaughn Monroe, Peggy Lee, Lena Horne and Dick Haymes who had also sung with Tommy Dorsey before making it big in the movies. Even though I was star-struck at first, I managed to elicit a comment or two from most of the mourners about the band leader's impact on their lives. They all said they loved him which negated my City Editor's "inside information."

Dick Haymes was especially friendly and invited me for a drink at a bar across the way once I had finished my interviews. One part of our conversation that night as we sat together drinking Scotch and soda sticks out clearly in my mind. He was answering one of my questions about how he liked the press.

"Since you asked, I'll tell you." Haymes said. "I think the press is simply a necessary evil in my business. Sure we need you fellows to get better known, to promote our shows and to keep us in the limelight. But we don't really like it when you become a threat."

"A threat? What do you mean by that?" I asked, enjoying his frankness.

"You want to get into our bedrooms, crawl up our pants leg or into the panties of our pretty ladies. Too often you accept gossip as fact. That's where I draw the line because you only shine the spotlight on our screw-ups, the things that make headlines for you—divorces, family squabbles, drunken brawls, broken relationships. When it happens to ordinary people, no one pays attention. When it happens to any of us, it makes headlines."

"You mean like with you and Rita Hayworth? I asked rather squeamishly, adding "I meant your beautiful wife."

"That's what I mean about believing all that gossip. We're very happily married. I've had no affairs and neither did she. In fact, she'd be with me right now except she's starring in a big new movie being shot in Spain."

"Sorry, but I guess I just proved your point, didn't I?"

We had a few more drinks and parted on good terms. Actually I left to write my story. He stayed to have a few more drinks.

During our conversation, the singer happened to mention that he usually stayed at The Biltmore Hotel whenever he came to New York, mainly because he liked the hotel's well-known Biltmore Bar. For some reason I remembered that about a year later when a rumor hit that Rita Hayworth was divorcing him. The actress's decision was important because Dick Haymes was Argentinian and a divorce could cause him to lose his green card in the U.S.

Joe McGovern asked me to check on the validity of the story. I managed to reach the singer at the Biltmore and he was kind enough to give me another interview. Once again he denied the rumor which actually turned out to be true. Rita left him for an Arabian Prince by the name of Ali Kahn who was worth billions. So gossip can sometimes turn out to be fact.

Once again one of the Journal-American's headline writers was either drunk or having fun when he penned the big, red headline for the first edition that announced:

RITA STILL LOVES HER DICK

It was re-written for the second edition.

I don't know why, but it seemed as if booze was beginning to surround me wherever I went, even involving itself in the stories I was writing. For example, my next special assignment concerned the late great actress Diana Barrymore. She and her rich, famous husband had just been arrested the second time for public intoxication.

They had been fighting and creating all kinds of havoc in their fancy penthouse apartment in artsy Greenwich Village. Neighbors were constantly calling the police. The building manager told me Diana was a bigger drunk than her once famous actor-father, John Barrymore, who died of alcoholism.

While I got kudos once again for the story from both McGovern and Mahar, it seemed to once again prove the point singer Dick Haymes made to me at the bar that night—that the press loves to shine the spotlight on troubled relationship to create front page news. But I didn't dwell on that. I was now beginning to get By-Lines for my stories—"Written By William G. Borchert." Boy did that go to my head. I wanted the whole world to know what a big shot I was becoming, especially my father.

I assume that most sons or daughters for that matter want to have a relationship with their fathers even when there have been problems or bad blood between them. But it's not a one-way street. If there's no positive response, they often give up—sometimes permanently.

While my resentments about the past ran deep, I was hoping that now, with us working for the same newspaper, we might be able to find some common ground on which to build a better or at least a different kind of friendly relationship.

Since I was coming into the city room some days to write my special assignment stories, I would drop by the pressroom. But my father was always working so hard in order to keep his job he had little time to see me except between editions. That's when I'd occasionally bump into him in Moochie's.

He was starting to see my By-Line stories and would brag to all his buddies about me. But I wasn't quite sure how comfortable he was watching me drink, especially when I was downing shots and beers. I'd notice a concerned look on his face. However, I remember one day when we were at the bar together, he turned to some of his pals and said:

"Ain't it great. My son here writes the damn paper and I print it. They couldn't get along without us."

Everyone laughed as he patted me on the back. It had been a long time since I had seen my father so proud of me and it felt good. But then I also remember the day he grabbed my arm as I was about to knock down another shot and said:

"I'd go a little easier if I were you."

For some reason I reacted very angrily. "I'm not you!" I replied. "I know how to drink! You don't!" Then I turned around and left the bar.

I was making enough money now to buy myself a car. So I did—a brand new 1954 powder blue Chevy Bel Air convertible. It had a white top and white bucket seats. If there ever was a chick magnet, this was it. My buddies Arnold and Ernie forsook Donald's Model T Ford and only wanted to drive around in my convertible. So did everybody at the White House Bar in Rockaway Beach. I had to brush the girls off like flies. Of course, that's just my big ego talking.

Having a car also enabled me to get around more easily on my job. There were no more subways, buses, elevator trains, taxi cabs or hitching rides. I could now drive myself to cover special assignments or to crime scenes, fires and other locations where stories were breaking. Little did I realize, however, that drinking and driving could prove to be a dangerous and sometimes lethal combination. Like it was with so many other things in my life, I had to discover that for myself.

I believe it was a rainy Friday night in October of 1954, only a few months after I bought the car, when that discovery occurred. I was partying at a wild and crazy bar named "Tutti's" when I got a call from the Night City Desk which had six phone numbers where they might reach me—five bars and my home. I was told that the Brooklyn Navy Yard was in flames, that ships were exploding, and they wanted me to get right down there and cover the story.

Frank Tutti, the bar owner, was kind enough to send me off with a large container of rye and soda and a pat on the back for his favorite big shot reporter. I hopped into my powder blue convertible and sped away filled with pride and excitement—and too much booze. I tuned the radio to my favorite music station and began sipping from the container as I swerved in and out of traffic, skidding a few times on the wet roads.

To make time, I decided to drive underneath an elevator train line. As I hummed along with a great Frank Sinatra song, I forgot all about the fact that at Bergen Street the elevated line went back underground and became a subway. I saw the large blinking red light on the cement barrier that held the Dead End sign too late. I smashed into it head-on at seventy miles an hour.

I remember coming to in the Emergency Room at Jewish Hospital, a place I had often been before when covering shootings, rapes and murders in Brooklyn. Now I found myself among the bleeding mob of patients.

The gray-haired doctor staring down at me said I had six broken ribs, a fractured left arm and a fractured jaw. He said my teeth had come through my lower lip when my face hit the steering wheel and that I had bitten off the tip of my tongue when my teeth clashed down on it. Other than that I was fine.

When the doctor and his crew were taking me to the operating room, I have a vague recollection that I asked him how badly my new car was damaged. I think he just smiled and shook his head in disbelief.

After a week in the hospital, my mother brought me home and nursed me back to health. Our relationship had greatly improved by now. She waited until I was feeling much better before she told me how concerned she was about me.

"The doctor told me how much you had to drink the night of the accident," I recall her saying. "It reminded me of the accidents your father's had when he was drunk. I don't know if you remember the one that almost killed you and the whole family.

"Please don't become like your father, Billy. Please. You're doing so well now and I'm very proud of you. But drinking will only ruin everything."

Did I listen? Of course not. What do mothers know? They just worry too much. In fact, I listened so much that the following Saturday afternoon a bunch of my drinking buddies came by to see how I was doing and I was right back into it.

It's well known that alcoholics love to visit the sick and bury the dead since there's generally a bottle of booze around on those occasions. My father didn't disappoint them. However, as the bottle of rye was being passed around, my dad grabbed it and wouldn't fill my glass. I remember him saying:

"You shouldn't be drinking any of this hard stuff with that wired up jaw. But I have something else that might help ease your pain."

He walked over to a closet, took out a bottle of Christian Brothers sherry wine and filled my glass to the brim. While I didn't enjoy the heavy sweet taste, I did enjoy the warmth of the sherry as it ran slowly through the small gap between my teeth and down my throat.

Now, if you sip enough Christian Brothers sherry wine through a wired up jaw, you can get pretty drunk—and pretty sick from the heavy sweetness. And if you ever tried puking through a wired up jaw, it isn't very pleasant. In fact, I thought I was going to choke to death.

I made two important decisions that afternoon as a result of that terrible episode. First, there would be no more partying until my jaw healed. Second, I would never again drink Christian Brothers sherry wine. Whenever I tell that story, I always make a point of saying that in my struggle to throw up through that wired up jaw, the big pieces shot out of my ears.

As for my overall healing, that took a few months. My spirits got a real big boost when I learned my convertible had not been totaled and was able to be completely repaired. The auto body shop told me that the undercarriage of convertibles is heavily weighted to make up for the difference in not having a top. They said the strength in the frame probably saved my life.

Any sane individual would have learned their lesson from such a near-death experience. But as I've said, the disease of alcoholism is threefold—physical, mental and spiritual. That mental part got me into six more drinking-related car accidents, none as serious but they could have been.

By the time the Christmas holidays rolled around, I was back at work and back on the party circuit. That terrible accident was but a distant memory. Perhaps in my subconscious I thought I was invincible. At least that was the way I started drinking again, giving no thought to any other possible consequences.

Then shortly after New Year's Day, I woke up one morning to find myself engaged. I was twenty-one years old, having the time of my life, and the last thing in the world I wanted was to be married. Yet here I was engaged.

I know it sounds nuts but to this very day I still can't remember how, when or where it happened. Her name was Pat just like my younger sister. Her brother, Allan, was a good friend of mine and I do recall he introduced us at a dance hall one night. The next thing I knew we were engaged. That's when something in my brain told me I was drinking far too much and far too often

My mother liked Pat a lot. Either that or she believed marriage would settle me down and I wouldn't drink so much. To make things worse, I learned that Pat's father, a police captain in the borough of the Bronx, had put twenty-five hundred dollars down on a hall for our wedding reception without discussing it with anyone. I had a hunch he wanted his daughter out of his house too. My biggest concern was that he carried a big gun.

While my fiancee was a very nice girl and quite attractive, I knew I didn't love her, as if I knew much about love anyway at that time in my life. It was just one more tangled mess I had gotten myself into by not knowing how to say no. At least that was the excuse I used along with having had too much to drink. But how do you get out of a situation like that? I wasn't very proud of the way it happened, but I was relieved that it did.

One of Pat's girlfriends was getting married in New Jersey. The wedding was at one o'clock on a cold Saturday afternoon in February of 1955. I had been on night side rewrite that Friday, writing stories for the first edition and a feature for the Sunday paper. Since she had a car, I asked her to pick me up at work around eleven that morning. She made me promise not to drink until we got to the wedding.

I left the city room around ten and headed for Moochie's to keep warm. I intended to only have a few shots. By the time Pat arrived, I was more than warm. I was already quite tipsy. She was very angry.

When I climbed into the passenger side, I noticed Pat had a girlfriend with her sitting in the back seat. Her name was Frances. We had never met, but during the drive to Saddle River, New Jersey, we got to know each other quite well. She was a gorgeous creature who was also engaged, only her boyfriend was in the Army and stationed in Germany. I guess that's why I thought she looked lonely and decided to befriend her.

At the wedding, I discovered that Frances liked to drink the way I liked to drink so we both got loaded. I recall at one point my fiancée pulling me aside as I came off the dance floor with Frances and saying very angrily:

"You're making a fool out of me! You promised you wouldn't drink so much and look at you. And the way you're carrying on with Frances is embarrassing. Are you doing it intentionally?"

Looking back now, I think I was. That's probably why I kept on drinking, because it was bothering her so much. And I used to claim my drinking never hurt anyone but myself. How dishonest drunks can be.

I must have gone into a blackout at some point which is when you continue to operate but don't remember later or even the next day what you've done. What I do remember is coming out of that blackout on another dance floor, only this one was in a German cabaret miles away in Ridgewood, Queens. It wasn't far from where my father's parents once had their German bakery.

How I got there I still don't know. I was in the middle of the floor once again with Frances, dancing up a storm to the music of a German "umpah band." Pat sat glaring at us from a nearby table filled with people we had been with at the New Jersey wedding.

Suddenly Frances, who was obviously as drunk as I was, went wild, taking off her red satin jacket and flinging it up into the air. So I took off my dark blue jacket and flung it up into the air. Now a crowd started to circle around us, clapping their hands to the music as well as to our twirling, crazy routine. Next I saw Frances's blouse go flying so I let my shirt and tie go chasing after it. Now the crowd was really into it and so were we. Frances lowered her skirt and let it fall to the floor which was followed by my trousers.

As she danced around in her slip and me in my tee shirt and blue shorts, the crowd kept clapping so loudly it almost drowned out the German umpah band. Suddenly the engagement ring I had given Pat which had been a family heirloom came flying over the raucous mob. It landed near my feet. Frances must have noticed it too because she picked up her clothes and wobbled to the Ladies Room to get dressed. I picked up the ring and my clothes and staggered to the Men's Room to do the same. That's when the band stopped playing and the crowd dispersed.

I threw some cold water on my face. I think the surprise of what had just happened was starting to sober me up. But I don't think it was until I had my pants and shirt back on and was tying my tie in the mirror that I came to realize I was no longer engaged to be married.

At first I had very mixed emotions. I knew l owed Pat an apology for the stupid, drunken, hurtful way I had been acting all day. She was a very decent person and didn't deserve it. But then I thought quite selfishly that if I apologize right away, she might forgive me and take the ring back. As things stood, I told myself I was off the hook and wanted to stay off the hook. If ever there was a totally self-centered, insensitive person talking to himself at that moment, I was looking at him in the dingy bathroom mirror.

After finishing dressing, I felt I needed to be in the company of some understanding friends. Since it wasn't even nine O'clock in the evening, I snuck out a side door and grabbed a taxi to one of my favorite haunts in Richmond Hill, Queens. It was called Gallagher's Tavern. Some of the close friends I had grown up with hung out there because of the dance hall in the back that attracted a lot of pretty girls.

Some of the guys at the bar yelled at me as soon as I walked in:

"Hey Billy boy! What are you doing out by yourself? Ain't you still getting hitched?"

Others hollered: "Does Pat know you're sneaking around on her? Buy us a beer and we won't tell on you." Everyone laughed until I stupidly took the engagement ring out of my pocket, held it up and bragged:

"I'm a free man again and I'm going to stay that way for a long, long time."

After having a few drinks with my cohorts, I headed for the dance hall in the back. As badly as I felt about my actions that led to a broken engagement, I also couldn't help feeling a sense of relief that it was over. As for my ex-fiancee, I believed in the adage that time heals all wounds. Or perhaps I used that adage to help me not dislike myself too much for the kind of hurtful person I was quickly becoming.

The only real worry I had left concerned her father and the money he had put down on the catering hall for our wedding. I hoped he would get it back. I was very much relieved when I heard he did. But I wasn't surprised. He was a police captain.

There were two young ladies sitting at a table near the dance floor with a friend of mine. Both of the ladies were real winners. The jukebox was playing one of my favorite songs, "It's Cherry Pink and Apple Blossom White." I walked over to the table, pointed at the two beauties and said:

"Eenie, meenie, mighty mo..."

The gorgeous, auburn haired lady won. Her named was Bernadette. We danced together until midnight. Three and a half weeks later we danced off to Elkton, Maryland, the elopement capital of America, and got married. It was March 16, 1955.

CHAPTER NINE

Great Opportunities Come and Go

W e dated almost every night until we eloped. I just had to be near her. I couldn't think about anyone or anything else when she was out of my sight. I never felt like that about anyone before, certainly not about Pat or any of the many lovely young ladies I had gone out with over the past three years.

As I've said, I probably didn't know much about love at that time in my life, but this had to be the closest thing to it, that's for sure.

Her name was Bernadette Forcina. She came up to my shoulder and had the most expressive brown eyes and warmest smile I had ever seen. She was not only beautiful, Bernadette was the sweetest, the loveliest and the kindest person I had ever met. And when she said she loved me, I couldn't believe it, certainly not with the way I felt about myself most of the time.

She was of Italian descent and lived with her mother in a small, very pleasant one-family house in Richmond Hill, Queens that had been turned into a two-family residence. Bernadette had eleven sisters and one brother. I won't name them all except her only brother, Anthony. He was about ten years older than me, tall, handsome and with curly black hair. He was also a real card and a real nice guy.

I remember asking him one day what it was like growing up with eleven sisters. He grinned at me and said:

"I didn't learn until I was fourteen that I didn't have to sit down to pee."

Of course he was joshing. He was simply telling me in a funny and round-about way the problems a boy can have growing up with so many sisters in a house with only two small bathrooms.

Bernadette's mom, Mrs. Angelina Forcina, actually had sixteen children but four were lost at birth or shortly after. She wasn't quite five feet tall, had dark gray hair and a very warm and attractive face. I heard she had wanted to be a nun as a young girl but her mother wouldn't allow it. Instead she was told to marry at the age of fourteen.

Her husband, Alexander, a hard-working man who had been in the produce business most of his life, died of a sudden and massive heart attack at the young age of fifty-six. Bernadette was only eight at the time and very close to her father. She was devastated.

There was very little drinking in the Forcina clan including in-laws except for wine which was served on Sundays with a large, four-course Italian meal in the large dining room at Mama Forcina's house. That's why when I entered the picture, with little or no drinking in her family and all of her sisters marrying Italian men, I stood out like a sore thumb. Still, everyone accepted me and quickly dubbed me "dousie pots." That means "you're nuts" in Italian.

Everyone in my family also loved Bernadette when I brought her around to some gatherings while we were dating—everyone, that is, except my mother. She was cold and almost hostile the few times we were together. I think there were two main reasons.

First, my mother really liked my former fiancée Pat far more than I realized and was very disappointed when our engagement ended. Naturally, she blamed me. And I could feel all that rekindled the hurt and disappointment I caused her for leaving the seminary, something she never really got over.

The second reason was my mother didn't like Italians. I don't mean to put my mother down because I truly loved her for all she did to protect me as a child and instill in me the belief that I could achieve anything I dreamed. But like many folks back then, she had her prejudices and Italians were relatively high up on her list along with Jews and Blacks. That's why Bernadette felt the full brunt of her emotions.

But I have to add that my mother changed considerably for the better in the bias department over the years. This was especially true when my dad got sober and she began to meet so many recovered alcoholics of different colors and religious persuasions.

None of that, however, was why Bernadette and I eloped. She and I have discussed that many times over the years and I believe I've come up with the best explanation. I loved her so much I was afraid of losing her. So, when the opportunity arose to take her captive, I took advantage of it.

We were leaving Gallagher's Tavern after dancing most of the night. Bernadette and I loved dancing together. We still do. It was around eleven thirty. Even though she had just turned twenty, I knew Bernadette's mom liked her daughter home before midnight. That also gave me four more hours to drink with my bar-hugging buddies since the watering holes in New York stayed open until four in the morning.

Bernadette said she wasn't ready to go home. I asked what she would like to do.

"I want to stay with you," she replied very lovingly.

When she said that, it seemed like something burst inside of me. I was filled with an indescribable elation. The words I spoke next were even a shock to me.

"Then let's get married."

Her eyes filled with tears as she fell into my arms. We just sat there for several minutes in a warm, close embrace. The next thing I knew we were standing in front of a Justice of the Peace in Elkton, Maryland exchanging fourteen dollar gold-plated wedding rings we had just purchased from his wife and promising to love, honor, obey and care for each other until death did us part. I still remember the last words the Justice of the Peace said to us with his hand outstretched:

"I wish you lots of love, happiness and prosperity and that will be twenty dollars if you can afford it please."

How we got to Elkton and back after notifying our families by telegram is not as important as what happened next—coming home to face the music so to speak.

My mother glared at me and wouldn't say a word. Bernadette's mother was deeply hurt and kept repeating, "But why?" She had wanted to give her youngest child a beautiful wedding and now she was cheated out of that dream. She only requested that we live apart until we got married in the Catholic Church. It was eerily like what my sister Marilyn had gone through when she eloped with Eddie Dean.

Of course we agreed. Since there was no way I could stay at home with my mother's raging anger, I bunked at Marilyn's for the next two weeks. That's when Bernadette's brother, Anthony, walked her down the aisle at St. Benedict Joseph Catholic Church in Richmond Hill, Queens on March 27, 1955.

It happened to be Passion Sunday when, according to church rules, all the statues had to be covered with purple veils and no music was allowed at any church service. So Anthony sang "Here Comes the Bride" loud and clear for all to hear as he strolled toward the altar with his sister, my bride, on his arm.

My new mother-in-law held an informal but very nice wedding reception at her home. Marilyn shamed my mother into coming. My father, who liked Bernadette from the first time they met—and the feeling was mutual—got very drunk and very friendly with her sisters. My mother also got drunk and actually accused my dad of playing patty cake with Bernadette's oldest sister, Rose. She was a very pretty lady about his age. The next thing I knew, my mother was coming at my new bride with a knife. Anthony managed to take it away from her without creating a scene. I never could figure out why my mother loved knives so much.

Other than that, it was a lovely affair and an exciting way for us to start our new life together. On second thought, perhaps those remarks are a bit too glib because, looking back, Bernadette didn't deserve what she had just gotten herself into. She didn't know she was marrying into a family impacted by the disease of alcoholism. And she also didn't know she was marrying an alcoholic. But then, neither did I because I had no idea I was headed down that path.

We made love that night in our small, furnished apartment and then, much to her dismay, I had to run off to my job since I had been assigned to work as a nightside rewrite man. However, we did have a really enjoyable delayed honeymoon two months later at Arcadia National Park in Maine. It almost turned into a disaster when a huge antlered deer leaped out of the woods one day right in front of our car and I missed hitting him by inches.

A short time after we returned, Eddie Mahar, my City Editor, came over to me one morning as I was finishing a story for the first edition. He said he was promoting me to a By-line Feature Writer. I was literally speechless. At the age of twenty-one and with less than three years of experience behind me, I would now be covering and writing some of the most exciting, nationally-important stories most newsmen would sell their souls for.

Here I was a young man blessed by his Creator with the talent to possibly go far in a career I loved. Yet, little did I know that, like my father, that promotion would be one more great opportunity my growing craving to drink would take from me. But that was something I couldn't believe at the time since I had no idea how cunning, baffling and powerful alcoholism truly is.

Now that I was out of my parents' house, my younger sister Patty, who was about to turn eighteen, and my young brother Bobby who was nine, were left to face the continuing impact of my father's disease and my mother's anger. However, like Marilyn, Patty also soon found her way out by marrying a nice young fellow named Herb Gass, a pleasant-looking serious young man who worked as a carpenter.

To this day I can't say that she really loved Herbie, at least not the way I loved Bernadette or how I came to see that Marilyn loved Eddie. I only knew that my younger sister wanted to be out of that house so badly she was willing to accept the consequences of a somewhat troubled relationship in order to do it. And that trouble continued for many years.

With Patty gone, that left my kid brother to fend for himself.

One of the things Bobby remembers quite clearly concerning our parents was that at one point, rather than constantly trying to stop my father from drinking, my mother decided to join him. Perhaps she thought being with him at Monahan's Bar on weekends or at some other gin mill might change things somehow. Maybe she hoped my dad would become a more social drinker and come home with her when she was ready to leave. As he described it:

"That's what mom was, a social drinker. She knew when she had enough and could stop. But she could never understand why dad never had enough, and that was the problem. Fortunately or unfortunately, Monahan's was right down the block. Sometimes when mom was with him, she would call and wake me up so I could help her bring him home."

My brother, who was blessed by never having a serious drinking problem himself, remembers another one of my dad's favorite "watering holes" that, for a while at least, became a home away from home. The place was called appropriately enough Coo Coo's Bar & Grill and was located under the elevated train on Liberty Avenue in Ozone Park. I'll let him tell the story:

"Sometimes my mother would pick me up at school and we'd go to a saloon called Coo Coo's to meet my father. The bar served food so we'd often have dinner there. The place had a shuffle board table and dart board game in the back room where I'd entertain myself until they were ready to go home. That's when the trouble would start.

"Sometimes when my mother was ready to leave, my father would be so drunk he'd get violent because he didn't want to go. He would raise holy hell but I never saw him hit my mom. We would either leave without him or some men would help drag him to our car and throw him in the back seat where he'd fall asleep. Then, helping my mother get him out of the car and up those eighteen steps to our apartment was another story. Sometimes I don't know how we did it. Also, I don't know how he would get home when we left him at Coo Coo's because I was usually asleep by then."

My brother also recalled the many times my father would want to go out again after getting home. His excuse was always the same:

"I need to get some damn cigarettes!" he'd yell.

Bobby said my mother began keeping packs of cigarettes in a kitchen draw for such occasions. Apparently she still didn't realize he simply needed another drink. She refused to keep liquor in the house unless company was coming. According to my brother:

"The cigarette thing didn't always work very well. In fact, one night it turned into a near catastrophe. My father was very drunk and started to leave the house. My mother reached out and grabbed him by the back of his jacket. It turned into a push/pull contest across the kitchen table. Dad maneuvered to the doorway, dragging mom with him. They were both screaming at each other. My father managed to open the door to the outside hall and made one last lunge to pull away. I saw my mother's hands slip from his jacket, my dad lose his balance, and fall down all fifteen steps backwards.

"My biggest fear was that he would smash his head into the iron radiator at the bottom of the staircase. Thank God he didn't. Miraculously he wasn't hurt. He stood up, cussed at my mother and accused her of pushing him down the steps. He then opened the front door and headed for Monahan's Bar. I don't remember him coming back that night."

Bobby said things weren't always like that. With no one around anymore but him, he said there were some periods of calm. But what affected my kid brother was the same thing that used to concern me when I was his age and living there. You always knew there was another storm brewing. He told me once about one of those storms that almost turned into a hurricane.

"Sometimes when dad would come home very late and very drunk, instead of fighting with him, mom would wake me up and help me out of bed. She'd put my shoes on and a warm coat and take me for a long walk, hoping dad would be asleep or passed out by the time we got back home.

"But there was one particular night that stands out in my mind. I woke up to hear them yelling at each other in the kitchen. Suddenly mom came running into my bedroom like she was in a panic. Dad was chasing her with both of his fists raised. As she ran to the other side of my bed, I jumped up and stood between them. I had no idea what I was going to do. I simply stood there shaking.

"Dad stopped, looked at me, cursed at her and left the room. She could hardly breathe as she sat beside me on my bed crying. She continued crying until she heard the downstairs door slam shut. Once she thought it was safe, she tucked me back into bed. I'll never forget what she told me that night. She said dad was a good man but sometimes the drinking made him do some very bad things that he didn't really mean to do. She believed that someday he would change.

"In some strange way I understood what she was saying because when he wasn't drinking, dad would take me places like to the beach in the summer and sleigh riding in the winter. I always knew that he loved me."

I once felt the same way, especially when my father would do the same thing with me that he would do occasionally with my younger brother—take him deep sea fishing. Again I'll let Bobby tell the story.

"Whenever we would go deep sea fishing, it was always on one of those big fishing boats docked in Sheepshead Bay, Brooklyn. The boats were always crowded and the beer flowed like water. Mom would make us both some real nice sandwiches and tell my father to be sure he cleaned the fish at the dock before bringing them home. He would buy me sodas and then usually drink too much beer. But he always slept it off on the way back in because he cared about my safety and wanted to be sober driving home.

"Believe it or not, my father loved to cook the fish himself, either in a bunch of grease in the frying pan or baking it in butter in the oven. Of course my mother was left to clean up but she always seemed to enjoy those fish dinners. Those were the nights they seemed to get along best for some reason."

I remember telling my brother when we were together one day how I had promised myself I would never be anything like our father when I grew up. He understood what I meant. Little did I know I had already started down that road. I had no idea I would become as helpless as my father and unable to fulfill my good intentions, even though, like him, I had every reason to do so—a wonderful wife, an exciting career and great opportunities ahead.

Again, here I was in my early twenties and right in the heyday of journalism. And I was already a feature writer for the largest evening newspaper in the world, privileged to cover stories of worldwide significance as well as juicy events that made interesting front-page fodder aimed at building readership and circulation.

Since I still loved to dream, I began to see myself following in the footsteps of the great columnists we had at the Journal-American like Westbrook Pegler or Jimmy Cannon or Jack O'Brian or even Dorothy Kilgallen, the famous Broadway gossip columnist. I thought I might even hit the jackpot and become as famous as the nation's best known and most widely read columnist Walter Winchell who wrote for the New York Daily Mirror. He was syndicated in almost five hundred newspapers across the country. The more I drank, the bigger my dreams and with enough booze they would almost approach reality.

One of my first assignments as a feature writer was to do a series of articles about a tantalizing Café Society scandal in New York that involved the pint-sized heir to a huge oleomargarine fortune named Mickey Jelke. Apparently desiring to be an entrepreneur like his old man, the young, porno-loving playboy started a high-priced call girl service in Manhattan.

Soon everyone from judges to politicians and corporate executives to the rich and famous found themselves in bed with Jelke's delights. Pat Ward, the stunning brunette who headed the service for the oleomargarine heir, was finally caught accepting money for her "performance." She cut a deal with the prosecutor that blew the case wide open. Her prominent customers quickly scrambled for cover while she testified and sent poor Mickey away for three years in the Big House.

When I interviewed the sultry prostitute, she offered me a freebie if I would write nice things about her since she wanted to become an actress. I turned her down because I didn't think Bernadette would approve—of the freebie that is.

A news photographer caught me interviewing the call girl in front of the criminal courts building and shot a picture of us together. The photo wound up on the front page of the New York Daily News. My father bought a ton of copies to show his friends. My mother had something new to brag about to her neighbors.

While it was fun covering and writing stories like this juicy call girl scandal, nothing came close to an assignment I was given that October...one I've always considered the dream opportunity of my lifetime.

Being born in Brooklyn and raised a Brooklyn Dodger fan, I could hardly believe it when Eddie Mahar assigned me to write sideline feature stories involving the fabulous and historic 1955 Baseball World Series between the Brooklyn Dodgers and the New York Yankees.

The series was played at the original Yankee Stadium, "The House that Babe Ruth Built" which was located in the Bronx. The highly-ballyhooed event was christened The Subway Series because fans could take the train to watch their teams play.

The Dodgers had never won the World Series in seven attempts and in their last five they were defeated by the Yankees. But this time every single person in Brooklyn, whether they knew anything about baseball or not, swore that painful motto the sports media had coined, "wait 'til next year" would be blown away once and for all.

The tense and exciting series wound down to the seventh and final game. I had featured some of my biggest Dodger heroes in my first six stories, greats like gutsy third baseman Jackie Robinson, twenty-game winning pitcher Don Newcombe, home run hitting center fielder Duke Snyder, All-star shortstop Pee Wee Reese, Golden Glove first baseman Gil Hodges, and the glue that held the team together, catcher Roy Campanella.

Like every other Dodger fan, I wondered who would be the next hero to emerge and carry the team on to victory. Dodger manager Walter Alston opted to start the surprise hero of Game Three, the young right hander Johnny Podres. Many so-called knowledgeable sport writers said Podres had a tired arm and wouldn't last three innings. But the young pitcher's right arm must have gotten a good night's sleep because it managed to hold onto a two to nothing lead as the game neared its conclusion.

The Yankees had two men on base and only one out when their much-heralded catcher, Yogi Berra, came to the plate and sliced a long drive just inside the left field foul pole. The Dodgers' new and untested left fielder, Sandy Ameros, not only made a spectacular glove-hand catch but then fired a perfect throw to shortstop Pee Wee Reese. In turn, Reese fired a strike to Gil Hodges at first, catching Yankee base runner Gil McDougald halfway to second.

The crucial double-play gave Johnny Podres and The Brooklyn Bums a two to nothing victory and the first World Series championship in the team's history.

I remember calling the city desk from a phone booth in the stadium with the crowd still roaring in the background. I wanted to see if Mahar wanted me to play up any special angle for the feature story I'd be writing for the next morning's first edition. I'll never forget what he said:

"I want you to take the fucking pulse of every shit-kicker in Brooklyn. Find out how the hell they feel about finally winning a fucking World Series. I don't want any phony bullshit...just how the fuck they really feel in their gut."

Now, where would you think a feature writer who likes to drink might find a bunch of Brooklyn "shit-kickers?" You're absolutely right. I think I hit practically every bar from Bensonhurst to Canarsie and from Prospect Park to Coney Island.

Fortunately, I was riding in a Journal-American radio car with Mel Finkelstein, one of the truly great news photographers and a man who didn't drink. I mean, my dear friend Mel didn't drink any booze at all. But I remember how he chided me every time I would leave one saloon and stagger into another.

"If you keep it up," he said, "we'll never make it to the Dodger's celebration party. I thought that's what we were looking forward to—getting some good interviews and some good pictures."

"Just a few more shit-kickers, Mel," I promised. "Then we're off to interview the champs. Okay?"

When we finally did get to the Dodger celebration party at the old Montigue Hotel in the upscale neighborhood of Brooklyn Heights, I recall getting into a fight with Billy Lowes, a hot-headed Dodger relief pitcher. He accused me of making goo-goo eyes at his gorgeous, silver-haired girlfriend. I was simply asking her for directions to the Men's Room. The great center fielder, Duke Snyder, came over and broke up the fisticuffs before they went any further than a few serious misses. Lowes was pretty plastered too.

Then I remember trying to interview the hero of game seven, left fielder Sandy Ameros. But Sandy didn't speak English very well. Gil Hodges and Roy Campanella stood nearby laughing at me. I think one of them said I was so drunk that Ameros was speaking better English than I was.

The next thing I recall, I was sitting at a typewriter in the city room surrounded by the pile of notes I had taken that I could barely read. Thank God I also had a stack of clippings from sports writers on the morning newspapers who had covered the final game. It was almost six a.m. and my deadline was seven.

A copy boy kept bringing me black coffee and Art McClure kept hollering over asking when I'd have a few takes on my story. While my head was still circling somewhere over Brooklyn, my fingers started to pound the typewriter keys. I wasn't sure what words would be coming out on the paper.

When I finished my last take and handed it to the copy boy, I tried to sneak out before McClure had a chance to read it. I had a sense I was in real deep doo-doo, that my bacon was cooked and that my seat on the Titanic was slipping seaward or any other fearful phrase you might want to come up with. But before I could get five feet away from my typewriter, I heard the Night City Editor shout:

"Hey Borchert! Come over here!"

By the time I reached McClure's desk, my insides felt like they were ready to become my outsides. Beads of perspiration glistened on my forehead. But the words I heard from an editor I admired startled me and made me wonder if he was as drunk as I was.

"Listen," he said with the hint of a smile. "I just read some of your takes and I think it's pretty damn good stuff. From now on you should come in here the way you did this morning because you're a much better writer drunk than you ever were sober."

Then he laughed, patted me on the shoulder and went back to work. I was still in a daze when I hit the street, more so from McClure's comments than from my night of boozing. That my Night City Editor would give my drinking that much credit only fostered my belief that alcohol was my friend, not my enemy. Looking back now, I believe McClure, who loved to booze it up himself, might have been putting me on. Still, my interpretation of his words only made my slippery slope much more slippery and my one-way ticket to alcoholic hell closer to getting punched.

After all these years, there's one more thing I remember from that day when my team won its first World Series championship. That was the lead or opening paragraph of my By-line feature story:

"Like a giant comet roaring down from outer space, the realization that its Beloved Bums had finally won the World Series struck this borough last night with a mighty roar."

I'm sharing some of these exciting stories and deeply personal events in order to highlight how such a great opportunity afforded a young man could be so quickly and easily extinguished by a so-called "magic elixir." Yet it was to take me several more years to fully understand that the disease of alcoholism doesn't merely want to take away everything you have. It wants to kill you. Yet I continued to march blindly forward.

While I'm grateful for the talent God gave me, one of the greatest assets I had at the time was to be surrounded, supported and essentially mentored by some of the finest writers in the newspaper business, many of whom also drank to excess. There was Joe Faulkner for example who I still believe was a better writer than his famous cousin, novelist William Faulkner. Joe taught me to use one good adjective rather than three dull ones to help make a story crisp and clear. He bled to death from cirrhosis of the liver at three o'clock one morning sitting on the curb outside of Moochie's Bar.

Red Horan, who wrote historical novels at the rewrite battery in between running news stories and Bill McCulllum, a terrific feature writer himself, taught me how to think ahead. They said each paragraph should build to the next in order to hold the reader's interest. Like other writers I knew at the Journal-American and around town, they also suffered from what my Aunt Maggie used to call "the Irish virus."

So many truly great writers such as Ernest Hemmingway, Truman Capote, William Faulkner and Tennessee Williams, to name just a few died of alcoholism. While I'm certainly not putting myself into their category, neither did I learn anything from their sad departures. It was similar to my father not learning anything from the deaths of his alcoholic brothers.

But, as I've said, when you're young and healthy you tend to think you're immortal and can handle anything booze throws your way. That's why you don't see its effects creeping up on you. So I continued to enjoy my job and my marriage while the dark storm clouds gathered on the horizon.

Sober or not, I was privileged to witness and cover some very historic events during this period of time. For example, it was around the mid-1950's when the American Civil Rights Movement began to gain significant strength and newspapers like the Journal-American started paying attention.

Perhaps it was a form of white guilt, trying to make up for its recent past when it would quietly suggest that reporters and writers ignore many events involving the minority community. That's what I had experienced as a brand new police reporter who was trying to cover stories that were "the wrong color." That's why I was pleased when I was sent on a bus trip to Tuscaloosa, Alabama to interview the very first black girl ever admitted to the University of Alabama and then forced out three days later for manufactured reasons that were basically racial.

Her name was Autherine Juanita Lucy, a quiet, soft-spoken young woman who enrolled at the University on February 3, 1956 as a student in library science. As she headed for class on February 6, a hostile mob assembled to prevent her from entering the building. Some in the crowd began throwing things at her and threatening her with bodily harm. So the police were called, allegedly to secure her admission. However, that evening, University officials suspended the determined young woman on the grounds that it could not provide a safe environment.

Two days later I interviewed Autherine at her sister's home in Birmingham where she was awaiting further news about her suspension. The front page story I wrote that appeared under a banner headline the next day began with a courageous quote:

"They stoned me, they cursed me, they spit upon me, but they did not deter my efforts to receive a good education at the best university in the state of Alabama."

The story was picked up by the International News Service wire and sent to newspapers across America. I remember after the interview, Autherine's sister Bernice said to me:

"You better get out of town fast. One of these days some of you white folks are gonna get killed trying to help us." How right she was.

With the help of the NAACP, Autherine hired an attorney who filed suit against the school to have the suspension overturned. The lawsuit was not successful, however, and was used as a justification for the young woman's permanent expulsion. The school's president claimed that Autherine had slandered the University of Alabama and therefore was not worthy of being a student there.

Because of the unbelievable red tape in southern courts back then, it took twenty-four years for Autherine Lucy's case to wind its way up to the Supreme Court where her expulsion was finally overturned. Still determined to do so, she received her Master's degree in Elementary Education from the University of Alabama in 1992, twenty-six years after she had first enrolled.

To atone for the harsh and bigoted treatment of its first black student, some years later the university named an endowed scholarship in her honor and unveiled a portrait of her in the student union overlooking the most trafficked spot on campus. The inscription reads:

"Her initiative and courage won the right for students of all races to attend the University of Alabama."

I then went from covering and writing that very moving story which helped me overcome some of the prejudices I had grown up with to a very shocking event—one that made my wife Bernadette and me suddenly take greater security precautions with our own children.

On the morning of July 4, 1956, Mrs. Betty Weinberger who lived in the wealthy town of Westbury, Long Island, wrapped her month-old son Peter in a receiving blanket and placed him in his carriage on the patio of her lovely home. She then went inside for a few minutes while little Peter slept.

When Mrs. Weinberger came out to check on her son, all she found was an empty carriage and a ransom note from a kidnapper demanding two thousand dollars. He apologized for his actions saying he needed the money and that the baby would be returned "safe and happy" the next day if his request was met.

Despite the kidnapper's threat to kill the child at the "first wrong move," Mrs. Weinberger panicked. Hysterical, she called her husband Morris and then phoned the Nassau County Police Department and reported what had happened.

Morris Weinberger and the police requested that all newspapers hold off printing the story. They needed time to meet the kidnappers demand to drop off the ransom money at a designated spot near a busy parkway. Every newspaper in the city and on Long Island, including my own granted the request except the New York Daily News.

By the following day, more than two dozen news reporters swarmed Nassau County Police Headquarters in Mineola, Long Island and the ransom drop-off area where the kidnapper had never shown up. I was among them. For more than a month, I bounced back and forth from my home to a motel room in Mineola where I would stay for days interviewing detectives and other people and writing feature stories about the heart-breaking event. Because of its great human interest, the Weinberger baby kidnapping became a headline story in newspapers across the nation as well as on radio and TV.

It wasn't until the FBI entered the case that real progress was made. They began examining thousands of handwriting samples of individuals involved in all sorts of scams. They came up with a man named Angelo LaMarca, an addicted gambler, who lived in a nearby town and once had been arrested for bootlegging. The handwriting in his probation file matched the handwriting on the kidnapper's ransom note.

I'll never forget the day the FBI arrested the suspect. It was the morning of August 23, 1956. They stormed LaMarca's house, handcuffed him in front of his shaken wife and three small children and had him lead them to the remains of the Weinberger's baby son, Peter. What was left of his tiny body was hidden behind some bushes just off a busy Long Island parkway. Then they hauled LaMarca into Nassau County Police Headquarters.

Every news desk, radio station and TV outlet in the New York metropolitan area had been alerted to the arrest. By the time the now much-hated kidnapper arrived surrounded by FBI agents and Nassau County detectives, there had to be at least fifty to sixty reporters and news photographers jammed into the police station in Mineola, Long Island along with radio and TV outlets.

I found a spot on the platform of a staircase leading up to the detectives' squad room. I could view all that was happening and I sure as hell didn't like what I witnessed. In fact, it shocked me.

Yes, I knew these reporters were human like myself and were emotionally worked up by the gruesome crime of kidnapping and killing an innocent baby. But to actually see them spitting at and throwing soda cans and garbage at LaMarca as he was being led to the booking desk was something I thought shamed my profession. I feel the same way to this very day. I always believed that reporters and news writers were supposed to be observers of bad human behavior, not participants in it.

I left rather upset that afternoon, wrote my feature story at the Mineola motel, called it in to a rewrite man in the city room and then got very drunk. I didn't get home until the early hours. I kissed my wife, crawled into bed and slept all day.

Since I knew the Angelo LaMarca story inside and out by now, my City Editor had me write occasional feature stories about him, his family, his trial and his conviction all the way through to his execution. That took place in Sing Sing's electric chair on August 7, 1958, less than two short years after his arrest. To be honest, you don't want to witness a man die such a horrific death no matter what he did. And while I felt very sorry for the Weinberger family, I also felt sorry for the LaMarca family. They were marked as social misfits for the rest of their lives.

While things seemed to be going great on the job front, there were signs on the home front that signaled possible trouble ahead. I paid them no heed. Neither did Bernadette, mainly because she had absolutely no experience in the world of alcoholism.

We had only been in our furnished apartment a short time when we were able to buy our first home in the fall of 1955, thanks to the ingenuity and generosity of Bernadette's mom. She had a close friend who loaned us some money to make a down-payment on a two-family house in Floral Park, Long Island. It was a quiet residential community filled with many young families and small children. Believe it or not, a two-family house then only cost $16,000.

Our mortgage payment was seventy dollars a month and we were getting seventy-five dollars in monthly rental from the upstairs tenant, another young couple. Still, from almost the very beginning, I had difficulty meeting my mortgage commitment.

Then we had our first little girl. She was born on February 14, 1956, Valentine's Day, which I felt was a good omen. We christened her Judith Ann after Saint Jude who is known as the patron of hopeless cases.

Boy did that turn out to be appropriate.

CHAPTER TEN

Becoming My Father

Even in the heyday of journalism, young newsmen like me didn't make all that much money. It didn't matter how hard you worked, how creative you were, how many hours you put in or how many exclusive stories you broke. Salaries and pay increases were usually based on a contract negotiated between each newspaper and The Newspaper Guild which was a union affiliated with The International Federation of Journalists.

As I said, no matter how good you were or how bad you were didn't make much of a difference. Salaries were set by the union wage scale and increases were based on longevity.

My dad belonged to a union as did most of my uncles and many of my older cousins like Albert. They were called trade unions and generally covered workers in manufacturing and construction and other types of industrial and commercial occupations where there had once been serious worker abuse. But I could never understand why a creative business like the one I was in had to be unionized.

Perhaps that's why I began to feel cheated sometimes when I'd cover a major event or come up with an exclusive interview or have a banner front page By-Line story. I was making a lot less than some gray-haired beat reporter nearing retirement who slept on his desk half the night and turned in maybe one or two stories a week. It didn't seem fair. I learned later on they called the kind of thought pattern I was developing self-pity.

That thought pattern first began to weave its way into my immature subconscious brain when I was given the opportunity some months earlier to work with one of the Journal-America's most popular columnists, Dorothy Kilgallen, better known to most people then as The Voice of Broadway.

She had gone to Cleveland, Ohio to create some gossip stories about the famous murder trial of Dr. Sam Sheppard. He was the handsome young orthopedic surgeon accused of brutally murdering his attractive wife, Marilyn. She was four months pregnant when found in a pool of blood on the staircase of their stately home in Bay Village, Ohio overlooking Lake Erie. I was assigned to take Dorothy's notes every afternoon and write a feature story under her By-Line for the next day's paper.

I had never met the respected columnist who later starred on the TV show, *WHAT'S MY LINE,* but we became very friendly on the phone. Not only that, she was always very generous with her compliments about me to Eddie Mahar and others at the paper concerning the feature pieces I wrote for her.

As it turned out, the jury refused to believe the young doctor's alibi that his wife was killed by a bushy-haired, one-arm intruder who had knocked him unconscious as they fought on the stairway in his home. He was convicted of second degree murder in January of 1955 and sentenced to life in prison.

Dr. Sheppard's family hired a well-known attorney, F. Lee Bailey, to appeal the case all the way to the Supreme Court. The judges found five violations of the convicted doctor's constitutional rights during his trial which they termed "a mockery of justice." He was finally set free. The surgeon's story became the subject of several books, several movies and a major television series.

But as I was writing those features about the trial under the By-Line of Dorothy Kilgallen, the thought did occur to me that she was making millions while I was making a mere pittance doing so much of her work.

So the seed of self-pity was planted early but it took a while to germinate and grow.

In truth, I should have been shouting gratefully from the roof tops about the position I was in and the breaks I was getting at my age. And I was starting to make a fairly decent living had I not been squandering much of it on drinking and betting a few ponies at Aqueduct and Belmont race tracks.

To be really honest, as the days, weeks and months passed by, I was also becoming so consumed with my own ego and ambition that I wasn't paying enough attention to the growing responsibilities I had as a husband and a father.

As a result, I soon found myself establishing relationships with a rather sordid list of usurious finance companies and loan sharks that my father had been patronizing for years. They included street money lenders like Richie Baldino, a muscled, olive-skinned man in his fifties who walked with the aid of a very heavy wooden cane which he used to threaten deadbeats.

At the same time, Richie happened to be one of the friendliest and most approachable loan sharks to frequent Moochie's Bar. He knew my father well. He was always eager to lend you what you needed right on the spot.

I think my money problems started to become apparent to me one Friday afternoon in the fall of 1957. I had taken one too many advances on my paycheck so I didn't have enough cash to bring home. I happened to pass by a storefront window with glittering gold lettering on it reading Beneficial Finance Company.

The name seemed to echo in my brain. I didn't remember at the time but later it came to me that this lending organization, like Richie the loan shark, was another one of my father's sources of borrowed income. I stopped and glanced in. The bald-headed man behind the counter sort of waved and smiled. So I walked in.

Fifteen minutes later I walked out with fifty dollars in my pocket. It was enough to buy groceries for Bernadette and me, baby food for Judy and to pay a few bills. It was a simple solution that was to turn into an extraordinary problem. It was also something I managed to keep from my wife until the roof started caving in.

Our second daughter, Charlotte, came along on July 22 of that year and the weight of my financial responsibilities grew a little heavier. That's when, I'm ashamed to say, I began giving myself an unofficial pay increase. Since the newspaper reimbursed me for all the expenses I chalked up covering stories, including the costs for driving and servicing my car, I started adding a few bucks here and there.

When I would stop for gas or have the oil changed, I'd have Louie who owned the service station give me a blank receipt so I could fill in a fictitious amount. He was only too happy to oblige his friend, the big shot writer. If I interviewed someone over lunch, it would often be at a place where I knew the manager or the head waiter so I could put my thumb on the scale when it came to the bill.

In other words, I found devious ways to steal from my employer and cynical ways to excuse it. I did find ways to make amends some years later, however, but in the meantime I walked around filled with fear that I'd be found out and everything would come to a crashing halt. Still, I kept on doing it because I felt I had to. I needed the extra cash. I was slowly getting deeper and deeper into debt and saw no way out.

One of the ways I justified my malfeasance was always being available for any assignment and doing the best possible job I could. In fact, there were many times I went overboard to get a scoop just to salve my conscience.

A good example of that was the evening of February 1, 1957 when I got a call at home from the city desk about a Northeast Airlines plane carrying ninety-five passengers and a crew of six that had just crashed on Rikers Island.

That was New York City's main jail complex, a four hundred and thirteen acre island with ten separate prison buildings that sat in the middle of the East River between the borough of Queens and the tail end of the Bronx. It was only a short distance away from the runways of LaGuardia Airport, and back in 1957, was only reachable by ferry boats.

It was almost six-thirty and we were just finishing dinner. I threw on a heavy coat and hat, kissed Bernadette and my little girls goodbye and jumped into my car. Despite the fact that it was snowing rather heavily, I made it from Floral Park to the Manhattan side of the Triboro Bridge in less than half an hour. I then had to weave my way down to a pier on the East River where special ferry boats were shuffling fire, police, physicians, nurses, Northeast Airlines officials and other emergency personnel back and forth to the island.

Through the blowing snow I could see the blaze from the plane crash in the distance. I reached the pier and hooked up with a crowd of reporters and photographers still waiting for a ride to the scene. They were all hollering at a police lieutenant and his two sergeants who were hollering back that the officials had to go first.

Rikers Island, as I discovered when doing research for my story, was always a rather unique place aside from being a prison community. It was named after a Dutch settler, Abraham Rycker, who somehow acquired the land in 1638 from the officials of New Amsterdam. His descendants owned it until 1884 when they sold it to New York City for $180,000.

The Rycker family allowed the island to be used as a military training base during the Civil War. Since there were barracks and other structures built to accommodate the union troops, New York City correction officials turned them into jail cells when they purchased the island some years later. The night of the plane crash, there were more than nine thousand prisoners on Rikers Island and more than one thousand prison guards and other support staff.

Fortunately, while we members of the press corps continued to harangue the police for not allowing us on a ferry, a public relations rep for Northeast showed up to assure us he'd get us on the next one. He didn't know anything about the death toll or possible survivors but he did fill us in on the accident itself. In other words, we had a mini-press conference in a snowstorm. He only told us the bare facts. The rest came out in an investigation.

Northeast Flight 823, a two-year old DC-6A four-engine propeller aircraft, was originally scheduled to depart from LaGuardia for Miami International Airport at 2:45 p.m. However, due to the heavy snowfall, a sky filled with traffic and the time required to clean the snow and ice off the plane's wings, the departure was pushed back to 6:01 p.m.

Although the pilot reported to the tower that the nose wheel was skidding slightly on the snow-covered runway, the plane was cleared for takeoff at the northeast end of the field. Upon establishing a positive rate of climb, the landing gear and wing flaps were retracted and the engine power reduced.

Flying on instruments without any outside visibility, the plane slowly gained altitude as it passed over Flushing Bay. But instead of proceeding northeast, the pilot began making a gradual turn to the left.

As Flight 823 approached Rikers Island, its altitude was insufficient to clear the high trees covering a hilltop at the far end of the complex. The DC-6A hit the trees, spun out of control and crash landed. It finally came to rest within fifteen hundred feet of the point of first impact. All four engines exploded into flames.

Before the Northeast public relations rep could answer any of the questions he was being pummeled with, another ferry boat pulled up to the pier. The police shouted for everyone in the press contingent to climb aboard. By now my hands and fingers were almost numb from trying to take notes in the snow and brisk wind. But they had thawed out by the time we pulled up to the dock at the prison island.

All the way across the East River I plotted what I intended to do upon arrival at the crash scene. To get any kind of a scoop, I first had to prevent the morning newspapers, mainly the Daily News and the Daily Mirror, from carrying anything significant about the tragedy, such as first-hand accounts from survivors or the heroics of Rikers' prison inmates helping in the rescue.

It was now after nine p.m. and I knew the deadlines for the morning papers were around midnight. Therefore I had to keep their reporters from calling in stories for the next three hours. There was only one way to do that which was the way Hank Eberling, my drinking buddy at the World Telegram and Sun had shown me about a year before -sabotage all the telephones anywhere near the scene of the story. There were no cell phones back in those days.

While all the other reporters and photographers headed for the crash site the moment we docked, I looked around for the nearest security guard. I found one almost freezing to death at a nearby gate.

"I'm a newspaper reporter for The New York Journal-American," I said identifying myself. "Can you tell me where I can find a telephone?"

"In the Administration Building at the top of the hill," he replied through chattering teeth. "All the offices are locked but there's five pay phones in the lobby. The warden kept the building open for you fellows."

"Thanks," I said. Then I remembered to ask one more really important question. "By the way, do you know when this ferry will be headed back?"

"Probably won't be before midnight," he replied. "The boat captains are all busy handling the emergency units."

I thanked him and quickly scampered up the hill and into the large, dimly-lit Administration Building. I first made sure all the offices were locked so there would be no other phones available. Then I went into each of the five phone booths and unscrewed the covers on the speaker end of the telephones, removed the electronic speaker devices and screwed the speaker covers back on. This would prevent anyone on the other end of the line from hearing what was being said.

I put the electronic devices in my coat pocket and hustled back down to the scene where the plane wreckage was still on fire. I felt confident I had just screwed my morning paper pals out of their stories and myself into a very large scoop.

At the site of the crash I learned twenty passengers had been killed and seventy-eight injured, many critically. The six crew members had also survived, some with serious injuries including the flight captain who was badly burned on his face and arms. They were all being treated at the prison hospital which had been extended into the prison mess hall to handle the large number of patients.

Since I now had time, I interviewed a number of the prison inmates still at the site, short timers who had been allowed out of their cells to help prison guards drag survivors from the wreckage. I later learned that thirty of the fifty-seven inmates who assisted with the rescue effort were released from jail the following week and the other twenty-seven had six months taken off their sentences.

My next stop was the prison hospital where most of the reporters were finishing up their interviews with those survivors who weren't that seriously hurt. I started following suit until I had a stroke of good fortune. I happened to ask a nurse who was passing by where I could find the plane's flight captain. She told me he was in a private room and couldn't be disturbed.

The place was in chaos, mainly from the influx of doctors and nurses from Manhattan who had volunteered to help. As they scrambled around treating patients, no one seemed to notice me peeking into various hospital rooms. That's when I spotted a blond-haired man in his early fifties lying in bed with tubes in every orifice. His reddened face seemed to be inside of a big, clear bubble. It was actually his facial skin that was badly swollen and filled with liquid due to the severe burns from the crash. My instincts paid off one more time. He turned out to be the flight captain.

Being in severe pain, I wondered at first if he would even talk with me. But he did, just for a few minutes, because he wanted to explain how the crash wasn't "pilot error." I believe he wanted it on the record in case he didn't make it.

I recall generally what he said, all of which I put in my exclusive story:

"Things turned bad as soon as we lifted off. The driving snow and wind gusts prevented us from climbing as fast as we needed to. We were over Flushing Bay and flying on instruments so we couldn't see a thing.

"When we banked to the west as planned, I tried to gain more altitude, but the wind gusts must have shifted preventing us from doing so. Suddenly the plane shuddered. I knew we hit some obstacle—those huge trees on the edge of Rikers. I knew we were going in.

"There was no time to lower the landing gear. From experience I knew we had to be at the open end of the island. So I came in belly-up on the grassy field hoping to salvage the aircraft and as many passengers as possible. I hear most of them were saved thank God."

His pain seemed to be getting worse. He started to grimace. That's when I left. I already had what I came for—another great scoop.

It was almost midnight by the time I returned to the Riker's Island dock to catch the ferry back across the river. I think I was the last one to arrive. The wind and snow were still whipping loudly across the surrounding fences but weren't making nearly as much noise as the crowd of reporters who were bitching about the sabotaged telephones and the ferry delay.

"Hey Borchert!" Mac Levy of The Daily News shouted as I climbed aboard. "Where the hell have you been—fucking with telephones by any chance?"

"Fucking with what?" I replied innocently enough.

"The pay phones in the Administration Building," Bud Stahl of The Daily Mirror cut in very angrily.

"Hell no!" I answered emphatically. "I don't need a phone. My deadline's not until seven o'clock."

Then Mac Levy gave me a very accusatory look. "We already missed ours because some bastard sabotaged all the phones. Any idea who it might be?"

I simply shook my head and shrugged my shoulders, then found myself a seat. Everyone knew it had to be someone from an afternoon newspaper or maybe a wire service reporter. But they all denied it including me.

It was close to another hour before the ferry's captain arrived and we finally took off. By that time everyone on the boat was arguing with everyone else. Bud Stahl was even threatening to have The Newspaper Guild investigate the matter, but nothing ever came of it. But I must admit I did lose a few friends who always believed it was my handiwork.

Before checking into the city room, I checked into Mooche's Bar to warm up. It may sound like an excuse but I was really freezing right down to my tail bone. It was now past midnight and I was glad I didn't see my father in there, although it wouldn't have been that big a surprise. I downed a few double shots to ignite my pilot light and a few more to get the gas burner going. I was feeling pretty good when I arrived in the city room a short time later.

Art McClure couldn't believe I had scooped the morning papers and would even beat the first editions of the afternoon papers with my exclusive interview with the airline's captain. The Night City Editor played my feature story of the heroic captain under a banner headline on the front page and my story about the inmates helping to rescue survivors in a three-column spread on page three.

I believe it was after five when I finished and headed for an all-night joint in the Fulton Fish Market just south of Wall Street for a nightcap. I didn't get home until very late that that morning.

It was probably around that period of time when I started to occasionally call in sick because of a real bad hangover or pains in my stomach from drinking too much. Of course I didn't use those excuses. Actually, it was Bernadette who would do the calling and she would get very angry with herself and with me for having to lie. I remember her saying to me one morning:

"I'm sick and tired of lying for you! I'm not calling anymore. If you can't make it to work then call yourself."

"Then let them fire me," I said, trying to frighten her. "I don't give a damn. I'm too sick to call."

I think she continued to make those calls more out of fear of survival than any real concern for me. And as I continued my slow downward slide, Bernadette began to feel trapped. She knew it would only be a short time before I'd be back in the same trouble again.

One day when she was pressing a pair of my pants, she found a check in a pocket that read: $ 000.00. It was one where I had taken all my salary out in advances and forgot to throw the check stub away. My wife told me some years later that the thought of having no money, no way to buy food for the children or to pay the bills frightened her so much she began to think she made a serious mistake marrying me.

But we had two children now and another on the way. She felt it was too late to do anything about it. So she kept her feelings to herself and went on as best she could, constantly praying to God for help.

Love can get lost for a while amid such fear and confusion. Sometimes it can even die. Bernadette was already beginning to see that our relationship and our family life were slowly becoming dysfunctional which was a word she always hated. But how else would you describe it. And seeing that blank check only helped confirm it.

It's terrible what alcoholics do to the ones they love the most, mainly their wives and their families. We may say we don't mean to do it, yet we do it just the same and for the same reason—another drink. That's how powerless we become over alcohol and that's how I became like my father, a man I never wanted to resemble in any way, shape or form.

To make matters worse, I started getting a hunch that Art McClure and maybe even Eddie Mahar were becoming suspicious of my excuses for taking days off now and then. In fact, Art, who was old enough to be my father, talked with me one night about his concern that my life was getting out of control.

"You've got to slow down on your drinking, son," he advised in a rather father-like fashion. "I think all of this success has gone to your head and you don't know how to handle it.

"I know a guy who drinks as much as I do shouldn't be giving advice to other people. But I don't want to see you screwing things up. You've come too far and you're still a very young man.

"If Mahar starts to think you're drinking too much, believe me he'll come down real hard on you. Booze almost ruined his career. He was about to get fired, his wife was leaving him and even Cardinal Spellman who Eddie worships stopped talking to him. He's been white-knuckling it ever since. Maybe that's why he curses so much.

"Take it from me, you can really go far or you can wind up in the toilet. That's your decision."

I know Art was looking out for me so I followed his advice, at least to some degree. I slowed down on my drinking, paid more attention to my wife and family and worked even harder to show everyone I was okay. But I never stopped drinking completely. After all, booze was my friend, right?

With the pressure on, I was fortunate to be handed another a great opportunity to get the heat off and show my abilities were still intact. I happened to be at my desk in the city room the day of October 4, 1957 when the world's first satellite was launched into outer space. It was a Russian satellite called Sputnik One and, perhaps because the other rewritemen were so busy at the time, I was assigned to write the lead story.

The Soviet Union claimed Sputnik was sent into orbit to celebrate the International Geophysical Year and study the earth and the solar system. However, after gathering public opinion on my own and through other sources, I wrote in my story that many Americans feared the Soviets had planned more sinister uses for their new rocket and satellite technology.

In fact, I even began getting concerned myself after I called up leaders in the U.S. scientific community asking for their comments. I was told by those who insisted upon remaining anonymous that our government officials, military officers and scientific experts were all caught off guard by the Soviet's technological achievement. They said the Soviet goal was to launch the first Russian Cosmonaut into space within a very few years.

My front page story concluded with the very chilling fact that Sputnik One was some ten times the size of the first planned U.S. Satellite which was not scheduled to be launched until the following year. That meant America had a long way to go just to catch up with the Soviets in what was now being termed "The Space Race."

I wrote several follow-up pieces, basically interviews with American rocket scientists and military strategists. But I learned as the world turned that few had any direction in mind until President John F. Kennedy came along.

Embarrassed by the fact that on April 12, 1961, only four years after Sputnik, Russian Cosmonaut Yuri Gagarin became the first human in space, President Kennedy issued his historic challenge—that America would have a man walking on the moon before the end of the 1960's. That challenge was met.

At the same time, I was still continuing to have challenges of my own, both at work and at home. The bills were piling up, I had fewer financial sources to borrow from and I was trying to keep it all a secret from Bernadette so she wouldn't get upset. I've learned since then that secrets are like cases of dynamite. Any spark (related or not) can cause a monumental explosion taking everyone out.

In searching for ideas that might solve my financial woes, the thought occurred that we could probably sell our two-family house for more than we paid for it. That small amount of equity would still be enough to pay off all the bills Bernadette knew we had and some other bills she didn't know about. Hopefully, there would also be enough for a down payment on a small one-family house further out on Long Island.

We were driving home from a party one rainy night. I didn't think I was really that drunk but had just enough to give me the courage to discuss my idea with my wife. She seemed agreeable at first to sell the house, but only if we bought a place closer to her mother. She not only loved her mother a great deal but also still felt guilty about hurting her by eloping. I honestly don't know why I opposed her suggestion. Perhaps I thought homes near her mother would be too expensive. I had heard houses were much cheaper in places like Deer Park, Long Island which, I must admit, was a considerable distance away.

We started to argue. I think I was afraid that if we didn't follow my plan exactly, there wouldn't be enough money to solve my financial problems which I didn't care to discuss in any detail at that moment.

The argument got heated. It was either going to be my way or the highway. I remember she started bringing up things that night that I didn't want to hear—things that I would drink over so I wouldn't have to think about them.

"You make a good salary but we never have any money," she began. "You get angry every time I ask about it.

"You never spend much time with the children. You promise to take them to the park or the merry-go-round but you never do.

"When I want to visit my mother or one of my sisters you always have something else to do

"You're never around when I need you.

"You never take me in your arms anymore and tell me how much you love me."

My big ego couldn't handle hearing the truth about myself. No, I was the hot shot newspaper writer she should bow down to. I was the one who worked my ass off and was never shown enough appreciation. I was the one who was going to accomplish such great things that she'd regret every bad thing she ever said about me. It got so heated I wound up doing something I'll always regret whenever I think about it. I realize there's still amends to be made after all these years.

I managed to angrily zig-zag my way through traffic and get into the right hand lane. Then I screeched to the curb, jammed on my brakes, reached over, pushed her door open and shoved her out of the car into the pouring rain. Bernadette was carrying our first son at the time. I was totally blinded by fear and rage fueled by all that I drank at the party. I knew how outrageously wrong I was as soon as I took off and headed for the nearest bar. I had left her stranded alone in the pouring rain.

When I stopped at some noisy joint and downed more shots and beers, I kept thinking about Bernadette getting soaking wet, catching a cold, getting pneumonia and how it might affect the baby. I should go back. But would she still be there? It was probably too late. I learned later that she was able to call a cab and get home safely, but thoroughly drenched. Fortunately she didn't even come down with a sniffle.

I got so drunk that night I went into a blackout. I woke up the next morning in my car parked behind a saloon some miles away from Floral Park. Neither my wife nor I can remember how we patched things up. But we did. I went on the wagon, at least for another while. And I put the discussion about moving temporarily on the shelf.

Our first son, William, Jr. was born on September 24, 1958. He was a sickly baby. He had rashes all over his body, was colicky and needed a special baby formula to drink. I've wondered at times if that could have been related to that terrible incident with Bernadette. Thank God he grew up to be a strapping and healthy young man.

In addition to having more incidents at home, I was also having a growing number of troublesome incidents at work. A few were related to some stories I was assigned to cover which, in my attempts to turn them in something bigger than they were, drew more of my City Editor's growing ire toward me.

One was a juicy show biz tale I still brag about to my friends. It involved the most notorious playboy and gigolo of that era, an intriguing character by the name of Porfirio "Rubi" Rubirosa and his relationship with the once titillating Zsa Zsa Gabor.

The story unfolded on one of those slow news days earlier that year when a brief article came across the Associated Press wire from Las Vegas. It said Rubirosa had an argument with the blond showgirl and punched her in the eye. The AP also sent a photo showing the beautiful blond Zsa Zsa wearing a black patch over her right eye. Of course the playboy, who was married to the Woolworth millionairess Barbara Hutton at the time, denied the whole thing claiming Gabor was simply looking for publicity to boost her career.

It so happened that Zsa Zsa was flying into New York City later that afternoon since she had landed a role in a new Broadway musical.

While Mahar didn't like obvious publicity stunts, he knew readers always jumped at the chance to lap up some hot show business dirt, particularly if it involved the country's famous, headline-grabbing gigolo and a rising star like Zsa Zsa. So he sent me out to Idlewild International Airport which was later re-named John F. Kennedy Airport to interview the ambitious showgirl.

Before heading out, I stopped by the newspaper's morgue or research library to check into Rubirosa's background. I found myself quite impressed. Many who knew him well said the handsome playboy, now in his early fifties, had once been a political assassin who in between assignments supplemented his income by servicing rich and famous women and making love to radiant young movie stars.

Ian Fleming once said he based his James Bond character on Rubirosa because, according to the famous fiction writer, "he was a true renaissance man"—an adventurer, tennis player, soldier, diplomat, chef and world-class polo player. He also raced his Ferrari on the Le Mans circuit in Europe.

Rubi, as he was known to most of the vulnerable young ladies he chased, had been romantically involved with beauties like Rita Hayworth, Jane Mansfield, Veronica Lake, Eartha Kitt, Delores del Rio and of course Zsa Zsa Gabor. His greatest coup, however, was marrying Doris Duke, the richest woman in the world who had a net worth of over eight billion dollars from good old Texas oil.

That marriage lasted almost two years before she ditched him for cheating on her. Rubirosa, however, was awarded several million dollars in the settlement. He then went on to wed the second richest woman in the world, Barbara Hutton, to whom he was still married when his relationship with Gabor hit the headlines. By the time I reached the airport, I had already decided to try and find the famous gigolo to get his side of the story.

I was a little surprised to see the airport press room packed with reporters and photographers. But then, as I said, it was a slow news day. Zsa Zsa was escorted in by her press agent, a paunchy guy with a big cigar. The showgirl sat on the edge of a desk, inching her skirt higher and higher until the popping of the photographers' flash bulbs almost drowned out questions from a slobbering press corps.

Finally the gorgeous blond straightened herself out and we all got down to business. Yes, she said, the story was true. And yes she said, she was still in love with Rubi. But no, he hadn't promised to leave his filthy rich wife for her. As I stared at this sexy creature giving silly answers to stupid questions, I began to ask myself a question—what was wrong with this picture? Then it hit me. She wasn't wearing the black eye patch she had on in the Associated Press photo from Las Vegas. So I shouted out:

"Hey, Zsa Zsa! Where's the black patch?"

She gave me the coyest smile.

"Here darling," she said. "Take a good look."

Then she lifted her skirt all the way up. She wasn't wearing any panties. And she wasn't a real blond.

The place went crazy. The reporters just stood there goofy-eyed. The photographers started climbing all over each other to take the picture of the year or at least the picture of their lifetime. Before most of them could pop more flashbulbs into their cameras, the paunchy press agent had his tease of a showgirl out the door and on the way to a waiting limo. But I already had the answer to my question. I also realized that even a sharp, intelligent and experienced playboy like Rubi can be set up by someone who wasn't even a real blond.

It was already past five, much too late to catch the paper's last edition. Besides, despite the shock effect of a naughty showgirl, I really didn't have much of a story. So I decided to stick by my intention to get the other side from the alleged pugilist.

My next stop was at the ritzy Park Avenue apartment building where Barbara Hutton owned a lavish penthouse for her frequent stays in Manhattan. I just had a hunch that Porfirio might be there trying to smooth things over. I was right. But it was also where I ran into some unexpected trouble.

When I showed my press card and a ten dollar bill to the young gatekeeper behind a large mahogany desk, he said Mr. Rubirosa was there but had ordered his driver to pick him up at eight p.m. Since I had more than an hour to kill, I walked three blocks down to the Regency Hotel and killed most of it at the bar.

I was waiting when the playboy walked out of the apartment building and headed for his town car. I remember stepping in front of him and asking if we could talk for a moment.

"Excuse me, Mr. Rubirosa. I'm a writer with the New York Journal-American and I'd like to get your side of the story concerning you and Zsa Zsa Gabor."

He pushed right past me toward his limo. Then I did something very stupid. I grabbed his arm.

"She says you punched her in the eye but I know you didn't do it," I blurted out. "What really happened and is your wife upset?"

He stopped and gave me the most threatening look I had ever seen in my entire life. Then he said:

"Get the hell out of here or I'll have you fired!"

As his chauffeur opened the limo door and I watched the playboy climb in, I did another stupid thing. Being half loaded, I shouted out:

"Why don't you just go 'F' yourself like you do with all your 'F...ing' broads.

Suddenly remembering the background information I read that this guy had once been a political assassin, I turned and high-tailed it out of there as quickly as my slightly drunken legs could carry me. The whole thing exploded early the next morning when I showed up to write my story for the first edition. Mahar was fuming.

The City Editor was red-faced when he told me Rubirosa had called the publisher of the Journal-American who he knew personally telling him all that had happened and demanded that I be fired. That was, in fact, what I expected. Instead, Mahar actually defended me, saying I was only doing my job and that everyone uses profanity when they get upset. He promised to straighten me out and that he'd keep me on a tight leash and away from Mr. Rubirosa and anyone associated with him.

In spite of his defense, Mahar was really pissed with me. I remember him saying something along the lines of:

"I don't like being called on the fucking carpet by the publisher of this fucking paper because one of my reporters steps over the line! You get it? Maybe you're just a little too young to be handling a scumbag like

Rubirosa even though you had the balls to do it. I must give you credit for that."

Then he softened just a bit. "You're not getting fired. I'll take the heat. But why don't you take your head to the fucking cleaners and get all the shit washed out. Then maybe you can think straighter the next time around!"

I never did get to the cleaners and my continued drinking only filled my head with more shit…or perhaps I should say with stinking thinking. For my two biggest screw-ups were right around the corner.

The once-famous Tommy Manville, an off-beat Manhattan socialite who was heir to the multi-million-dollar asbestos fortune, was getting married for the thirteenth time. He loved publicity so he announced it to the whole world. Art McClure thought it would be a fun story so he assigned me to cover the wedding ceremony which was held at the Waldorf Astoria Hotel. Mel Finkelstein came along to take some pictures.

Tommy Manville was considered something of a clown, even by people in his own set. But he was also sneakily admired for his number of conquests of beautiful young women and his extravagant bank account. He took equal pride in his ability to attract gorgeous blondes and the shock of overgrown white hair that adorned his wrinkled head. At the time of his death at the age of seventy-five, it was estimated that he spent more than two million dollars on marriage settlements.

While he reveled in all the publicity surrounding each of his trips to the altar, Manville sought privacy in his large waterfront estate on Premium Point in New Rochelle, New York, not far from his Manhattan abode.

He equipped it with burglar alarms, peephole doors, armed guards, a public-address system, a radio in every room and twenty telephones. He called the estate his Fortress and often wore two heavy pistols in his belt which he said were to protect the guests he would occasionally entertain.

Manville's long list of conquests included show girls, actresses, chorus girls, secretaries and stenographers. His thirteenth marriage, which by the way won him an entry into the Guinness Book of World Records, was to a lovely twenty-year-old model from Texas by the name of Christina Erdlin.

The wedding ceremony was swift but the party afterwards went on for hours. The booze literally flowed like the wine at Cana. I got very, very drunk, went into another blackout and woke up in my car at ten o'clock the next morning. I was still in the Waldorf-Astoria parking garage. I had missed my deadline for the story I was supposed to write for the first edition.

When I called the city desk, Bobby Spellman told me that McClure had already left but that Mahar wanted to talk with me. Boy, did I get a reaming this time. To him, missing a deadline was like shooting the Pope. It was unforgiveable. He said all the other papers carried their own feature stories on Manville's thirteenth marriage, some on the front page with pictures. The Journal-American had to run "a piece of a shit story from the Associated Press" on an inside page. He was sure the publisher knew Manville and would be on him again for such poor coverage.

A City Editor who once thought I was worth grooming as a feature writer was now ready to fire my ass for sure. He kept saying it was the last straw. I kept apologizing and blaming it on forgetting to set my alarm clock. He knew it was a bald-faced lie.

"I'm too busy right now for all this shit," is what I think he said. "If you didn't have a wife and kids, I'd fire your fucking ass right now. But you're back on the police beat. No more By-line features. Starting Monday you're peddling your papers at Manhattan Police Headquarters. Maybe that'll help keep your ass out of all those fucking bars."

Before I could say another word, he slammed down the phone. I just sat there trying to figure out what to do next.

Over the course of my drinking career I gradually came to believe that I could usually think more clearly with a few good belts, especially when I was uptight or felt cornered. That belief was still with me. But why did I decide at that moment to drive all the way back downtown to Moochie's Bar to have a few? I could have gone right inside the hotel and had all I wanted. But before I could give it a second thought, I was on the East River Drive heading for the lower east side.

When I look back, I realize that the impact of Mahar's anger and resulting punishment must have affected my alcoholic brain in some strange way. I began to ask myself dumb questions like was all this really my fault? Maybe I got married too young? Maybe I had kids too soon? Maybe I wasn't as good a writer as I thought.

What can you do when the pressure gets so great you really need a few drinks just to relax? You have to do what comes naturally. But why did it almost always lead to trouble? And every time I would ask God for some help, why would He always turn me down while taking good care of everyone else? What can you do when the whole world seems to be stacked against you?

Then another strange thought occurred to me. Perhaps I was going to Moochie's intending to see my father. This way I could thank him for being such a great role model when I was growing up. I would kiss him on the cheek and express my gratitude for showing me how to wreck a loving family and a promising career. Maybe I would pat him on the back for always being there when I needed to talk over a problem or get some direction.

As I drove down to my favorite watering hole, I found myself blaming everyone but myself for the situation I was in. I had a wife whom I felt didn't love me anymore, a City Editor who refused to understand my problems, a father who was an uncaring drunk and a God who wanted no part of me. My self-pity was growing exponentially, my blame-game was in high gear and my resentments were popping out my eyeballs. Yes, it was everybody else's fault, especially my father's.

Sure enough when I pulled to the curb on South Street and walked into the smoky saloon, he was standing there bellied up to the bar as usual. He was on his break after the first edition had gone to press, the edition that should have carried my story about Tommy Manville and his stupid, meaningless, almost laughable thirteenth marriage.

The moment my dad saw me, he knew there was something terribly wrong. My clothes were wrinkled, my eyes were red and I needed a shave. Even before he said hello, he looked at me with a frown and asked:

"What's wrong? You look like hell."

I nodded to Frank Moochie, the owner who was tending bar. He knew my drinking habits as well as he knew my father's. He poured me a double shot of rye and a beer chaser. As I picked up the shot, my father grabbed my arm and said:

"I asked you what's wrong."

"I screwed up," I responded rather sharply. "I missed an assignment and Mahar wanted to fire me. He demoted me instead." Then I downed the shot and beer.

"Maybe he's just trying to teach you a lesson. From what I hear things aren't going that well on the home front either. If I were you I'd get back in my car and head for home. Drinking's not going to solve anything. Believe me, I know."

Maybe I took his remarks the wrong way because it was like someone threw a bucket of hot water in my face. I saw red. That's when I remember suddenly losing control.

"Who the hell are you to be giving me advice!" I said loud enough to attract attention. "I should go home? What about you? You think you're some kind of great role model?"

"That's enough," was my father's angry reply.

"Why? Aren't you proud of the way I've followed in your footsteps? I'm a drunk just like you and doing what drunks do—fuck up!"

"I said that's enough!" he insisted.

"Enough?" I responded. "Who says it's enough. Come on, let's have another drink. It's never enough, is it?

I thought I saw my father's eyes water up as he turned and walked quickly out of the noisy saloon. I took a deep breath and tried to calm down. I could feel a lot of eyes staring at me. I signaled Frank for another shot and beer. After I downed them, I realized the one thing my father was right about was the home front.

I knew I should head for home and, as they say, face the music rather than have it play on. But I knew I didn't have the guts at that moment or wasn't quite ready to get involved in another argument with my wife. I knew my emotions were still raw and out of control and I might only cause more damage trying to explain the unexplainable.

So instead I asked Frank Moochie, who was a real good friend, if I could rest for awhile in one of the back rooms that customers often used for their shindigs. No problem he said. I didn't realize how exhausted I was, both physically and emotionally. I dozed right off on a cushioned bench and slept until well after four o'clock that afternoon. I remember, because when the final edition of the newspaper was put to bed, Moochie's bar would get packed. The noise level woke me up.

I washed in the Men's Room and straightened up as best I could. My father was nowhere in sight when I came back out to the bar. Frank said he left and never returned. Then he poured me a double shot of rye with a beer chaser on the house.

Why didn't I just go right home then? No one can answer that question except another alcoholic. I knew I shouldn't have had that shot and beer. It's the first drink that gets you drunk, not the thousands that follow after. It's like when you get struck by a train, it's not the caboose that kills you, it's the locomotive. Once that first shot went down, it was like my ass suddenly got cemented to the barstool with Crazy Glue. I was once again powerless over alcohol.

Jimmy Healion, another drinking buddy who worked in the Journal-American's circulation department, showed up shortly after six. His wife was a nurse and was working the late shift at Bellevue Hospital. We continued drinking together and sharing our woes until around nine. That's when Jimmy got the itch to go over to Greenwich Village and listen to some jazz.

"The Village," as most locals called it, was considered the Bohemian conclave of New York City and a haven for budding artists. It also attracted all kinds of musicians, particularly those who loved to play jazz and folk music.

The Mamas & the Papas made their start there as did Peter, Paul and Mary, Simon & Garfunkel, The Lovin' Spoonful, and singers like Bob Dylan, Barbara Streisand, Bette Midler, James Taylor and Carly Simon.

Many great writers also penned their early works in The Village's small, homey, walk-up flats such as Truman Capote, Jack Kerouac, James Baldwin, Maya Angelou and Dylan Thomas. But all Jimmy was looking for that night was some nice, cool jazz. So I decided to go along even though I always knew my pal had a nutty side to him.

He told me I was too drunk to drive my car. Since he didn't have a car himself, and since he thought taxis were too expensive, he did something awfully stupid, something again only real alcoholics would think was perfectly sane. He borrowed one of the Journal-American's newspaper delivery trucks, one that had keys in it because it was scheduled to go out on a route.

I really don't remember much of what happened the rest of that night. I was in and out of blackouts. I think I recall listening to some black jazz musicians in some over-crowded saloon. I think I also recall Jimmy having trouble maneuvering the delivery truck through some old and narrow Village streets. I think he also side-swiped a car but didn't bother to stop.

What I remember most vividly was coming to with a start on Jimmy's parlor couch around nine that morning. He and his wife, Jeanie, lived in a small apartment complex only four short blocks from the Journal-American building. His wife was screaming at him to "get that drunken friend of yours off my good couch!" So I got up, washed my face, found my car and drove home.

Neither Bernadette nor I can remember what happened when I finally did show up looking almost like that proverbial Bowery bum. Whether we argued about my lies or she found it senseless to do so at that moment we can't say. What I did suspect, however, was that she was rapidly reaching the point of hopelessness when it came to having a simple, loving marriage and the feeling of security that came with it.

I was awakened early the next morning by a phone call from Bobby Spellman. He said the truck drivers union was raising holy hell about two wacky drunks who worked for the paper stealing one of their trucks. When it was finally returned in the wee hours of the morning, one of the drivers on the loading platform recognized the culprits. He said one of them was a writer by the name of Bill Borchert.

Bobby said the entire city room was still trying to peel Mahar off the ceiling. He was so angry he didn't even want to waste his best curse words on me. He only wanted Bobby to deliver me a message.

You're fired!

CHAPTER ELEVEN

How Far Is Down?

Just for the heck of it, and because I've broken so many of them, I looked up how Webster's Collegiate Dictionary defines the word "Promise." It says:

"A declaration that one will do or refrain from doing something specified or, a declaration that gives the person to whom it is made a right to expect or to claim the performance or forbearance of a specified act."

When promises are made, they should immediately be encased in steel or cement because they can be so fragile, so easily broken. In fact, I lost count of how many promises I broke to Bernadette, especially during those years of uncontrollable drinking. Yet, I still had the audacity to make another one after losing my job.

First I offered my heartfelt apology for bringing so much hurt and shame into her life and into the lives of our innocent children. Even though none of them were old enough to recognize or understand what was going on, they suffered too from the fallout.

Then I made another one of those typically phony, hypocritical promises to never drink whisky again. I included a caveat of course that I might have an occasional beer because beer doesn't get you drunk. I'm sure you've heard that bogus statement before. I said I would only have a few and never go overboard. And I meant every word of it. Wouldn't you if you had such a loving and forgiving wife, three wonderful children, a big mortgage, a lot of other debts and no income?

My wife's brain was probably numb at the time from hearing the same slobbering pledges over and over again. But perhaps somewhere deep inside she held on to the hope that one day one of my promises might come true. So she forgave me again and agreed to start over one more time. It didn't occur to me until much later on that she and I were doing the same dance my mother and father did for so many years.

During those first few days after receiving Mahar's final decree, I focused on three things: first, making phone calls to contacts I had in the media hoping to find another job; second, spending more time with Bernadette, and third, taking the kids to the park and the merry-go-round or just playing with them around the house. I guess I wanted them to know they really had a father who loved them. I enjoyed it so much I was beginning to believe my own promise.

I think it was around the middle of that week when I got a call back from a fellow named Jack Roach who was the Assistant Bureau Chief for United Press International in the city. I had met him at several press functions and he said he liked my work. He also said he was leaving UPI to help start a weekly news magazine for McGraw-Hill Publications and might need a good feature writer. He told me if I were interested, he would be back in touch in a few weeks once they had outlined their staff requirements.

That Friday night I got an unexpected call from Art McClure. He said they had finally scraped the City Editor off the ceiling and he had a quiet, intelligent talk with him about me and my escapades. They both agreed they might be throwing the baby out with the bath water. Art didn't put it quite that way.

"I was speaking with Eddie about you the other day," he said. "We both agreed we all had to sow our wild oats. I said maybe you were over that now, including hitting the bars."

"I think I've learned my lesson the hard way, Art," I replied.

"Good. Glad to hear it because you know Mahar always liked you. You were one of his favorites. In fact he said you might still be redeemable. What do you think?"

"I sure hope so."

"He's thinking about bringing you back to write obituaries...that it might give you some humility and maturity."

"Obituaries? But...isn't that usually a job for a much older guy?" I asked without the least bit of humility.

"If you mean Fred Granger, he's retiring as the Obituary Editor. That's why the job's come open. I'm thinking if you kept your nose clean, it could be a way of working yourself back up the ladder and have a paycheck for your wife and kids in the meantime. But if you're not interested..."

"No. No," I answered very quickly. "I really appreciate this, Art. I really do. And I'll work my ass off. Tell Mahar thanks for me."

After I hung up I realized I was now facing one of those "a bird in the hand or two in the bush" situations. Should I wait for Jack Roach to call me back with a possible offer to work on a brand new magazine, or should I follow McClure's advice and accept a ghoulish job at the paper in hopes of doing again what I really loved at some point in the future.

I chose the bird in the hand. Even though I had mixed emotions about writing obituaries, I swallowed my pride and tried to express my gratitude to Art for running interference for me. While writing obits was something I considered rather demeaning, I was happy to be back on the payroll.

My wife also had mixed emotions about the new position I was being offered, but for other reasons. Yes, she was very happy and relieved that I would be bringing home a paycheck again, hopefully without too many advances taken out. But she was unhappy about the hours I would be working—from one to nine in the morning. It would not only upset her routine with the children and the house but such crazy hours would also add undue confusion to the new start we had promised to make together

I told her it would only be for a very short time. I said I would do everything I could to get my old job back. But that was not to be the case.

Right from the outset I hated what I had to do, phone up funeral homes around the city to find out what well-known people had dropped dead that night. If it was someone fairly significant, I'd have them messenger me a photo so we could run it on the obituary page. It wasn't anything like covering the wake of band leader Tommy Dorsey at Campbell's Funeral Home, meeting famous people and then writing a feature story about the event.

What I learned was the publisher wanted to spruce up the obituary page and have the death notices written like they were brief news stories, especially if they were about prominent people. I guess Mahar figured I could do what the publisher wanted while atoning for my bad behavior at the same time.

At first I was surprised that undertakers worked such weird hours. But then, people die around the clock and have to be embalmed, dressed up and made up to look at least as good as figures in a wax museum. That takes time. So I learned that these death mask artists actually enjoyed my calling them at one or two o'clock in the morning because it gave them a break from their otherwise gloomy activities.

My desk was in an alcove off the city room, some distance from the city desk and the rewrite battery. Whenever I'd get itchy or bored, which was frequently, I'd stroll over to bother McClure or to chat with some of the night rewrite guys. They started kidding me, calling me names like Jack the Ripper or the ghoul from the graveyard or Edgar Alan Poe's right hand man.

I'd try to kid back but it was difficult. I sorely missed being where they were, writing real stories about real live people. I started getting so depressed it became noticeable. One guy in fact told me I had my head so far up my rear end I needed a porthole in my stomach to look out. I found that rather descriptive.

For the first few weeks, the obituary page began to sparkle if I may say so myself. The obits were crisp and highlighted by photos of the more prominent deceased. But then I found myself struggling to stay on the straight and narrow and not sneak across the street to Moochie's Bar for a few quick ones before closing time. But it was a losing battle.

As much as I wanted to keep my promise to my wife, as much as I wanted my old job back, as much as I wanted to be the kind of man everyone could be proud of, the maniac in my brain wouldn't let me. I had a mental obsession for alcohol which always turned into a physical compulsion once I picked up that first drink.

When I'd arrive at my desk around one in the morning, I would first call a whole bunch of undertakers to get a head start on things. Then I'd hop over to Moochie's, down four or five shots and beers and come back to write those obituaries. If I didn't have enough to fill the page, I'd clip a few out of other competing newspapers and send them into the composing room together with my own stuff.

I'd then head back to Moochie's just before closing time. Charlie Moochie, Frank's younger brother who had one crossed-eye, spoke with a lisp and had a huge beer belly, would always pull down the shades and let good paying customers like me stay an extra half hour or so. Then I'd shuffle my way back to the city room with a container of rye and soda stuffed in a brown paper bag.

I didn't realize that our lazy janitor was leaving old editions of other newspapers lying around for days. Since I gradually began using more of their obits than writing new ones myself, we were now printing stories of people who died more than a day or two ago. I started getting notes from Mahar in my city room mailbox saying he wanted what he called "fresh obits"—people who passed away within the last twenty-four hours.

I remember one night at Moochie's having this crazy conversation with Charlie about "fresh obits."

"How do you like writing about dead people?" was the way Charlie started off. "It would give me the creeps."

"Sometimes I feel like I'm standing in the middle of a graveyard reading a bunch of tombstones," I laughed.

"Would you write one about me if I dropped dead right now?" asked one of the other four drunks still in the place.

"He only writes about famous people, not nobodies like you," Charlie responded as if he needed to defend me for some reason.

"I haven't been writing about anybody lately," I admitted. "I've been using the obits from other newspapers and my City Editor's getting pissed. He said he wants fresh obits."

"What the hell's a fresh obit?" Charlie said as his crossed-eye almost went straight. "When you're dead, you're dead. You're not fresh anymore."

"I agree," said the other drunk.

"Makes sense to me too," I nodded. "But you try telling him that." Then I added, "Hit me again, Charlie, and buy my friend here another drink before he drops dead."

By the time I left Moochie's around four that morning, the maniac in my brain was telling me Mahar should go to hell and leave me alone or write the damn obits himself. How important were they anyway. Dead people don't care one way or the other. Besides, I didn't have time to be calling all those damn strange undertakers every night, not when I had to keep Charlie Moochie company.

Even when I did get around to calling some funeral homes, I'd often doze off before I had written enough obits to fill the page. Then I'd have to scramble around tearing them out of those other papers in order to meet my deadline. I must have found a pretty old newspaper one morning because we printed the obituary of a prominent man who had died three days before. I knew both Mahar and McClure would probably be after my scalp one last time. So I called Jack Roach before he called me.

Fortunately, Jack was ready to staff up the new McGraw-Hill magazine. He offered me a job writing features at a salary considerably higher than the one I was making along with a more generous expense account.

When I came into the city room early the next morning, I thanked a rather pissed off Art McClure for all his help, left my written resignation in Mahar's mailbox and bought everyone a going-away drink at Moochies. But my heart was heavy as I walked away from a career I really loved. I vaguely remember Art saying to me as I was leaving:

"You know the expression...jumping from the frying pan into the fire? That's what you're doing. I'm sorry to say it but I think you're going to keep screwing up until you get your life under control. But I wish you luck anyway."

I don't remember whether we shook hands or not. I only recall that I had a feeling he was absolutely right and there was nothing I could do about it.

The insanity that comes with the disease of alcoholism sometimes makes you think you're back in control of your life when actually your life is totally unmanageable. Now that I had this great new job and was no longer being threatened by people I felt didn't understand or appreciate me, I was king of the hill—or so my screwed up brain was telling me.

I thought Bernadette would be delighted I was getting a bigger paycheck and would be working regular daytime hours. But she had mixed emotions. First of all, she was justifiably upset that I had never talked to her about the possibility of changing jobs before I accepted Jack Roach's offer. She wasn't aware of the circumstances behind my decision to quit the paper. That's why she couldn't understand why I would leave a career as a newspaper writer when I had always told her it meant more to me than anything else in life, except her and the children of course.

Actually, all she really wanted was to be part of such important decisions. She was sick and tired of always being left in the dark. She would often tell me quite emotionally that husbands and wives were supposed to share their thoughts, their dreams, their aspirations and their problems, including financial ones.

On that subject, she wanted to know why we were suddenly getting phone calls and letters again about late payments from the electric company, the gas company and the bank that held our mortgage. I first replied it was because my pay was cut when I was fired and re-hired. That wasn't true. Then I said until I started making more money, we should consider selling the house as I had once suggested. We could then pay everybody off and start fresh in a larger but less-expensive house on Long Island.

This time Bernadette didn't start an argument right away. She conceded that with our two girls in one small bedroom we certainly did need more space. So she gave in and we began to look around.

It was Christmas of 1958, when Santa Claus brought us an unexpected present. We learned we were expecting our third child, our first boy. He was born the following September and we named him William after me. Since it was now absolutely clear that our two-family home could no longer accommodate all five of us, Bernadette reluctantly agreed to buy a larger but less expensive house we had seen in Deer Park, Long Island.

I'm sure the lack of space wasn't the only reason she agreed to move. I tend to think that Bernadette was so bewildered by my behavior, the constant lack of money, having a fourth child at her young age and a sickly one still in diapers that she just decided to turn it all over to God.

Bernadette was raised a staunch Roman Catholic and remained so all her life while I continued to have my ups and downs regarding the church. Like everyone else, I'm sure my wife had her moments of desperation and wondered why a loving God was allowing so many bad things to happen. Without her deep faith, however, I don't know if we would have ever made it together.

Deep inside I knew she really didn't want to move so far away from her mother and her family. So to salve her feelings, I made another one of those stupid, hypocritical promises. I told her that once we got back on our feet financially, if she didn't like being so far out on Long Island we would buy a place closer to her mother. I didn't realize it then but, in a way, I was actually being prophetic.

It was either in March or April of 1959 when we moved all our belongings into a cute Cape Cod-style house on Hass Avenue in the small town of Deer Park. To this day, Bernadette is convinced I wanted that house because it had a great big bar in the finished basement. That could be true. It doesn't change the fact that I had just foisted another heavy burden on a young woman who already had enough to bear.

First of all, we only had one car which I needed most of the time for work. That left my wife trapped way out in the sticks. She had to take buses or cabs or ask the neighbors for help whenever any of our children would get sick and would need to see a doctor. As I said, she was many, many miles away from her family she always enjoyed visiting. And on top of all that, she didn't particularly care for the pastor of the nearby Catholic Church.

It was also a very long drive into the McGraw Hill headquarters building in Manhattan where my new office was located. I did ride the Long Island Railroad at times which took more than an hour and a half each way. Sometimes I had to work late into the night or I was unable to get off a bar stool at some new haunt I had found. Between staying overnight at a hotel from time to time and travelling around the country to cover stories, I was away from home more and more.

As for my job, I wanted to make a real success of this new opportunity. I was determined to get off to a good start. I felt certain that Jack Roach, now my boss and editor of the start-up publication, had checked around before hiring me. There was a good possibility he had heard some stories about my drinking and my screw-ups but decided to give me a chance anyway. At least that's the way I was reading it. But he never let on one way or the other. Instead he was very complimentary and encouraging.

"I think you're just what this magazine needs," Jack told me at lunch one day shortly after I started. "Even though our focus is on business, economics and politics which can be pretty dull stuff, there are plenty of interesting characters behind the scenes—chief executives, entrepreneurs, congressmen and the movers and shakers on Wall Street. That's where you come in."

"Tell me exactly what you want me to do," I replied.

"Just what you did at the Journal-American. You're a great interviewer. Find out what makes these people tick...why they're so successful and powerful. Get inside their heads."

"No holds barred?" I asked.

"Well, we're not talking about Zsa Zsa Gabor or that playboy, Rubi Rubirosa," he laughed. "We have to be a little more discreet. But if you write some great feature stories about some real interesting people in the world of business or politics, I think that can really help perk up the magazine and build our circulation."

For the first five or six months I managed to do a bang-up job. I was practicing what the so-called know-it-alls in the alcoholism rehab business call control drinking. The problem was they really did know it all because pretty soon the wheels started to come off and that downward spiral fueled by lack of control began to pick up steam.

Since the new weekly magazine was designed to cater to the business and investment community, Jack suggested I get warmed up by doing a series of features on the hottest investment bankers on Wall Street. To be on the safe side, I interviewed those wealthy, fast-talking egomaniacs in their ornate offices rather than over a liquid lunch which several of them suggested. One guy pressured me so much to continue the interview at his favorite pub that I cut it short. Since it takes one to know one, I believe he was a heavy drinker too and I just didn't want to take any chances.

I also interviewed and wrote stories about a well-known entrepreneur who was working on artificial voice communications and the chief executive of the Illinois Central Railroad who had just introduced the first buy/lease program for freight cars. The first was a big deal for the technology industry and the second for major shippers and tax loophole experts.

Then along came the Allie Reynolds fiasco which put the first nail into my coffin.

Jack, who by now was very happy with the job I was doing, decided to develop an overview story on the oil and gas industry in the United States. He wanted us to cover all interesting facets of the business. For example, he had discovered that the retired, once-great New York Yankee baseball pitcher, Allie Reynolds, owned a large oil-based mud company in Tulsa, Oklahoma. Figuring that was certainly an interesting facet of the business, he asked me to fly out and do a feature on him and his company.

I really don't recall if Jack was a Yankee fan or had any interest at all in baseball. Even though I was still a rabid Dodger fan, I was really looking forward to meeting this incredible major league baseball legend.

Albert Pierce Reynolds was a Creek Indian from Bethany, Oklahoma. He was arguably the best relief pitcher in the history of The New York Yankees. Appropriately enough, he began his career as a starter for The Cleveland Indians but joined the Yankees in 1947 where he became known as Super Chief.

Together with two other outstanding major league pitchers, Vic Raschi and Eddie Lopat, he helped the Yankees record five consecutive American League pennants and World Series titles from 1949 to 1953. Well-known Yankee Manager Casey Stengel once said of his Super Chief:

"Reynolds was two ways great, which is starting and relieving, which no one else can do like him. He has guts and his courage is simply tremendous."

In 1951, Allie pitched two no-hitters in one season, a feat only a handful of major leaguers ever accomplished. And in 1952, his combined record as a starter and a reliever was 20-8. But his legend was built primarily on his post-season performances.

In six World Series relief appearances, the Super Chief recorded either a victory or a save each time, including the clinching games in the 1950, 1952 and 1953 championships. When he retired from baseball in 1954 and returned to his home state, the phenom started a mud company in Tulsa rather than speculate on drilling for oil himself and possibly losing all he had saved.

As a native of oil-rich Oklahoma, Reynolds knew from studying the industry how important oil-based mud is in reducing the cost of tapping proven reserves or bringing in wildcat wells. While my feature story was to be partly about the famous Yankee reliever's baseball career, it would also focus on his success in business. So I did a little research before my trip to brush up on the use of mud in the oil and gas industry so I could ask intelligent questions.

I learned that when applied to the well site, oil-based mud which is an emulsifier produces a high drilling rate, lowers drill pipe torque, and drag and reduces differential sticking. While expensive, oil-based mud greatly reduces the problems of drilling through shale and in high temperature holes.

So, now being an overnight expert, I headed for Tulsa. It was October 8, 1958 when I landed and checked into the Mayo Hotel, the finest place in town. It seemed like everyone there was going crazy. That very afternoon, believe it or not, the Oklahoma Legislature had passed a bill allowing for the first time the entire state to go "wet." That meant you could now buy liquor by the drink openly at a public bar. Before that, you could only buy it by the bottle or the barrel from an illegal bootlegger.

Naturally I joined the celebration. I woke up the next afternoon in a smelly room at a second rate hotel across town with wrinkled clothes, not knowing how I got there and with vomit all over the floor. Somehow I managed to crawl into the bathroom and threw some cold water on my face. Then I called Allie Reynolds. I apologized profusely for missing my morning appointment, told him I had gotten sick and asked if I could come right out to his company.

He was more than slightly annoyed. He said his afternoon was completely booked but that he could possibly meet with me the next morning. But I was on a deadline. I had to be back in New York the following day to write my story in time for publication. So I pleaded my case. He gave me fifteen minutes to interview him on the phone, something I could have done from my desk at the magazine had I not celebrated his state's big drinking event the night before.

It was a terrible interview. I told Jack the baseball great had some last minute business come up and could only talk to me a short while. I know Jack didn't believe me. I also knew he wasn't going to call Reynolds to check and embarrass himself for having an undependable writer on his staff. So he let it go and published the story anyway.

The last nail in my coffin came when I was sent to Las Vegas, Nevada to cover an important two-day business convention at the Riviera Hotel and Casino focused on the waning economy and government policy to support it. The gathering, which boasted some high-powered speakers, began on a Monday morning. I arrived that Sunday afternoon to be on hand for the opening talks.

Casino hotels are very seductive places. They offer so much free booze it would be committing a crime to turn it down. The only thing I remember about that Sunday night was seeing almost all of Victor Borge's performance in the main showroom of the hotel and sending Bernadette a post card with his picture on it. She still has that post card and takes it out once in a while to remind me of the fun I was having while she was struggling way out in the sticks of Long Island.

Victor Borge had always been one of my favorite, laugh-a-minute performers. The internationally popular Danish comedian, conductor and pianist was often referred to as The Great Dane and The Clown Prince of Denmark. He performed with philharmonic orchestras around the world and shared the stage with such stars as Frank Sinatra, Judy Garland and Barbara Streisand. I had the privilege of getting to know Victor personally some years later when I lived in a town called Rye, New York and he lived in nearby Greenwich, Connecticut.

Victor Borge also had the longest running one-man show on Broadway called Comedy In Music which finally closed after more than eight hundred and fifty performances. I've often wished I had seen his whole show that night at the Riviera but I drank so much I was in and out of blackouts. It continued that way over the next two days.

The convention ended on Wednesday morning. I was scheduled to be on a plane back to New York late that same afternoon so I could write my story Thursday morning in time for publication. When I came to early that Wednesday morning, I was so hung over I couldn't remember how much of the event I had covered or how many people I had interviewed, if any. Like my coverage of the Brooklyn Dodgers World Series event some years before, I had notes scattered all over, most of them illegible.

Fortunately I had a press kit of the event that contained outlines of the speeches that had been given. But I knew my boss wanted personal comments from the more important people in attendance and I didn't have them, or at least couldn't read them. I couldn't think straight, so I went down to the Riviera bar for an eye-opener to help me think straighter.

I struck up a conversation with a rather well-dressed, red-cheeked guy at the bar who said he had been at the convention. He said he knew those important people Jack had wanted me to interview and what they thought about certain matters when it came to the economy and the government.

So I interviewed that guy over a few more drinks, quite a few more in fact. I think his name was Teddy or Eddie or Freddie, something like that. I'm not sure. But it didn't make any difference. From what he claimed he knew, I now had a lot of good quotes I could put into the mouths of those important people I never got around to interviewing personally. While it seemed a bit like cheating, I decided to take the chance, hoping it would get me out of a potential jam.

I was dead wrong. It got me into an even worse jam. Jack liked the story, but when it appeared, a few of those important people I didn't really interview called the magazine threatening to sue. They said they had been misquoted and their words taken out of context by some writer they had never even met. Before I was fired, I resigned.

By this time, my father was well aware of my downhill slide. Why not? He was still on one himself. But despite his own problems and his continuing battles with my mother, he was now contacting Bernadette from time to time. While she would create alibis for me, mostly out of shame at this point, he could read between the lines. During my absences, he would often drive out to check on her and the kids. Despite the fact that he had little money himself, he would always leave her something, saying it was for the children.

As I've said, my wife loved my father, not because he would give her money, but because he cared so much for her welfare and that of his grandchildren. Without my realizing it, he was deeply concerned about what was happening to them and to me. Even though she knew my dad also drank too much, Bernadette believed he was someone she could still count on if ever things got too bad.

My mother-in-law was also aware of my heavy drinking at this point and the problems it was causing her daughter and her grandchildren. It wasn't anything Bernadette had told her, again because she was ashamed of what was going on and didn't want anyone to know. It was her mother's intuition and some family gossip that made her realize things weren't going right with us

Bernadette also tried to keep our problems secret for another strange and unexplainable reason. She felt that she was causing some of the problems herself because she wasn't attractive anymore, that she wasn't a good enough wife or a good enough cook or a good enough housekeeper. That she wasn't smart enough or much fun to be around anymore.

That's how sick alcoholics can make their spouses. In truth, my wife was still more attractive and better at everything than anyone else I ever knew. She just couldn't figure out why I didn't seem to appreciate her anymore. That was because I didn't appreciate anyone or anything anymore.

I remember so clearly the first time my mother-in-law came all the way out to Deer Park to see us. It was on a Saturday in late November. She was disturbed from the moment she walked into the living room and saw our children playing on a bare wooden floor. As I've said, mama was a quiet, soft-spoken woman who rarely raised her voice. That particular Saturday she spoke out quite clearly.

She told me in no uncertain terms that my children could get pneumonia playing on such cold floors. She said if I didn't have enough money to buy a warm rug, she would pay for it herself. In less than four hours, I had thick brown wall-to-wall carpeting covering the entire living room floor and hallways.

I was surprised with my poor credit I could still buy the carpeting on time payments. I knew that what was left of my financial resources would soon be coming to an end. And now with the loss of another job, desperation was beginning to set in.

Suddenly, from out of the blue, I received a call from my old drinking buddy, Hank Eberling, the fellow who had been with the World Telegram and Sun when he showed me how to sabotage telephones. Hank was now at WOR radio in Manhattan working at the news desk with the long-time voice of the station and its news director, John Scott. He said they were looking for someone to write features along with the news and to come up with ideas for radio interview shows. He mentioned my name to Scott and told him about my news experience and the many headline stories I had covered and written.

Two weeks later I was working for WOR at a pretty handsome salary. Even though I still didn't think God was in my corner, the opportunities were still coming for some reason. I'm the one who kept screwing them up.

I quickly learned that Scott was quite the prima donna and a stickler for deadlines. He carefully explained to me as though I were some kind of a nitwit that radio was a whole lot different than newspapers and magazines. I remember him saying:

"We report the news every hour on the hour. That means the copy needs to be ready at least fifteen to twenty minutes before broadcast time. It can't be one minute late. And it has to be completely accurate. We can't run apologies on page thirty like you guys did in your newspapers. By accurate I mean no typos or misspellings and everything double-spaced so it's easily readable.

"Between the news and weather and all the interview shows going on, things are happening around here all the time. That's why there are no breaks except lunch and most of us have it brought in. Now, do you think you can handle all that?"

"I think so, John," I said very politely even though I wanted to punch him right in the mouth. I began to sense he also knew a little too much about my past and wanted to watch my every move. I realized there wasn't any room for my bad habits.

Desperation can keep you afloat for just so long. Once again I tried not drinking until after work but soon started bringing in little nips to get by during the day. I'd down them in the bathroom and then gargle with Listerine and chew breath mints. I knew I needed this job because it was quite evident I was running out of options. If I didn't make it at WOR, where could I go from here? I constantly felt doomsday was right around the corner. Still I drank.

One day Hank told me he had bumped into an old friend of ours, a fellow named Ed Pitman who had been a press photographer at both the Journal-American and the World-Telegram before getting fired for being drunk too often on the job. He was down on his luck and shooting pictures of tourists for ten bucks a pop at a place called "Sammy's Bowery Follies." He asked us to stop by for old time's sake. So I went with Hank one night against my better judgment.

First of all, few people know that The Bowery is the oldest thoroughfare on Manhattan Island going back to the Dutch settlements there in the late 1600's. It was originally a path called Bouwerij Road that connected farmlands to estates in the heart of New Amsterdam which became New York City. Peter Stuyvesant, the last Dutch governor of New Amsterdam, had his own farm along what is now called The Bowery.

By the early 1800's, as the population grew, farming in the area gave way to the well-heeled who built fine residences there. The Bowery became a broad boulevard and the neighborhood gained in respectability and elegance.

Before long it began to rival Fifth Avenue as an address. Famous New Yorkers like the very wealthy John Jacob Astor and the respected philanthropist Peter Cooper had residences there. People were proud to say they lived on The Bowery.

Around the time of the Civil War, however, the area began to decline rather rapidly for some reason. The mansions and shops gave way to low-brow concert halls, high-priced brothels, German beer gardens and then pawn shops and flophouses. By the 1890's, The Bowery was a center for prostitution and bars catering to gay men and lesbians.

What helped further darken the climate and the streets of this once elegant area of New York City was the Third Avenue El train that ran above the Bowery from 1878 to 1955. During that period it became populated largely by drunken men who were called Bowery Bums and the area became known as "Skid Row."

One particular bar on The Bowery between Houston and Stanton Streets became a very popular "Alcoholic Haven" as Life Magazine was to describe it some years later. Its owner, Sammy Fuchs, began to notice that uptown swells would have their limo drivers slow down as they passed his place or sometimes they would actually stop in just to gape at what they referred to as the dregs of humanity that filled the place.

So Sammy decided to capitalize on the attraction. He hired five ex-vaudeville show girls who weighed about four hundred pounds each to sing and dance for the crowds and mix with the bums on sawdust-sprinkled floors. He changed the bar's name to "Sammy's Bowery Follies" and before long it was filled with tourists, politicians, bankers, actors and others out slumming for the night.

Besides operating the kind of bar that no longer exists in Manhattan, Sammy Fuchs performed a lot of good deeds in the neighborhood. He helped feed, clothe and sober up some of his most downtrodden customers and established a dental clinic for poor children. That's why he became known as The Mayor of The Bowery.

My friend Ed Pitman made out well shooting pictures of tourists and uptown swells posing with real live drunks or one of the overly plump showgirls. But, being a terrible alcoholic himself, he never saved a dime. After Hank and I chatted with Ed that night, I would drop by on occasion to have a few drinks with him. We'd grow melancholy swapping stories about "the old days" in the newspaper business. I would sit there and wonder why so many people were so fascinated by Bowery Bums.

When I was getting drunk with Ed one night, I asked him that same question. He gave me a most intriguing answer.

"It's the same reason why people like to watch high-speed car races or dare devil trapeze artists or bloody boxing matches," he said. "They're hoping to see a serious accident or people die right before their eyes. In a place like this, they're really seeing the walking dead."

Then Ed turned to me with a very serious look on his face and said something that I've never forgotten.

"You better slow down kid or one of these nights these swells will be coming in here just to look at you."

The know-it-alls in recovery groups call alcoholism "the disease of denial." They say that's what kills people, denial. Boy, did I have it in spades. While I never forgot my drunken friend's remark, I paid little heed to his warning that night. I simply laughed and ordered another drink. After all, there was no way I could ever become a Bowery Bum.

Yet, without realizing it, I was dragging the Bowery into my own home every time I showed up. Bernadette was grateful that I rarely drank in the house but she would often get very angry, and rightfully so, when I would come home so drunk that I'd spend most of the next day sleeping it off.

I made one last serious attempt to stop drinking forever. That was when our second son was born on September 8, 1959. We named him Lawrence Jude Borchert. You will notice that Bernadette wasn't giving up on Saint Jude the patron of hopeless cases. I'm sure that saint tried very hard to help, but I was a real tough case.

When I lost my job at WOR radio for missing too many deadlines, we also lost the house in Deer Park. But I never told my wife the truth about what had actually happened. I did a few years later and she forgave me once again. Don't ask me why.

Since I had fallen behind on my mortgage payments, I called the mortgage loan officer at the bank and gave him a real hard luck story. In turn, he offered me ninety days to catch up before starting foreclosure proceedings. That gave me time to sell a different story to Bernadette.

I'm not proud of any of this, but lying was now a big part of my agenda as it is with most alcoholics. I told my wife that with four young children, she could definitely use a little more help than I was providing. I suggested we sell our house, put the equity into a savings account and move into her mother's finished basement until we could find our own place near her.

Bernadette could always smell a rat from five thousand miles away. I'm sure she suspected there was a lot more behind my latest scheme than I was exposing. But she had it with all the anxieties and frustrations. She had it with the isolation and lack of money. She had it with Deer Park and all its difficulties and disappointments. And she especially had it with me.

My wife told me once that the prospect of being with her mother meant safety and security not only for herself but mostly for the children. She would no longer be fearful of living out on a limb while watching me rapidly saw it off.

So we moved into mama's basement. The children slept in cribs and on day beds around the walls while Bernadette and I slept on two cots behind the oil burner. And as for looking for a place of our own, my mother-in-law suspected it was all a sham from the start. But for a little while she allowed me to keep up the charade until I got sicker and sicker. It became obvious after awhile that looking for a house was a complete waste of time and only led to more resentment and despair for Bernadette.

At one point my wife finally had enough of me. She could no longer handle not only my drinking, but all the pain, anxiety and misery that went with it. Despite having four children, she was still a young, attractive woman who had a desire for a better life. So she told her mother she wanted to leave me.

I had never taken the time to get to know my mother-in-law very well. I knew she went to church every morning and always appeared to be kind, loving and God fearing. But I had no idea she had such great spiritual insight, the kind that was to keep Bernadette and me together until I was ready to get well.

Mama simply told her daughter that she couldn't leave me at that point because I was a very sick man who needed her help. She believed that I truly loved her daughter and our children and that I wouldn't be doing the things I was doing unless I was very sick.

My wife loved her mother deeply and had so much faith in her that she stayed with me and continued to put up with my terrible disease. She shared all this with me some time later. I was glad because I never could understand why she stayed. I probably wouldn't have under the circumstances. Most men don't.

Through the recommendation of another old newspaper buddy, I managed to hook on with a small public relations company in Manhattan called A.A. Schecter & Associates. The owner, Abe Schecter, had been the first news director of NBC-TV and was one of the warmest, most decent human beings I had ever met.

Having been around the block a few times, I think Abe knew from the start that a man of twenty-six who was red-faced, slightly bloated and sweats a lot probably had a drinking problem. But he gave me every chance. He said I wrote the best press releases in the firm and was pleased every time I managed to get a story about one of his clients into a newspaper or magazine or as a guest on radio or television. But my liquid lunches were now starting before noon and lasting until three.

When Abe finally had to fire me, I think I remember his exact words:

"You're a terrific writer and you do a great job for me and my clients when you're around. The problem is, you're not around often enough for the money I pay you. So I have to let you go.

"I could give you a long speech about what I think you should do, Bill, but it would probably be a waste of time. I just wish you the best."

That's when my period of being unemployed and unemployable began. It also started my periods of what you might call professional panhandling and bad check writing.

I would call up whatever friends I had left in the media and invite them to lunch. Then I'd pour out my tale of hard luck, borrow whatever I could "until next Friday when I get paid" and let them pick up the tab. It was one sure way of running out of friends very quickly.

As for bad checks, my game was to frequent a particular bar for a week or so, long enough to become quite friendly with the bartender, manager or owner. Then, usually late on a Friday afternoon, I'd announce with a great deal of drama that I had forgotten to cash a check at the bank before it closed. And I had to have some money for the weekend.

Since I was now such a good customer, they would usually ask how big a check I needed to cash. Then I would write out a check for as much as I could get and they would never see me again. However, I felt that sooner or later some bar owner would track me down and turn me in so I was always running scared.

I began to hate living in my mother-in-law's basement, mainly because it was a constant reminder that my whole life was going down the toilet. But there was also another reason.

To approach the basement stairs you had to pass by the dining room where my mother-in-law would generally be sitting. It didn't seem to matter whether I came in at four in the afternoon or four in the morning, mama would always be there at the dining room table praying. She would have the Old Testament of the Bible and the New Testament, a book on the lives of the saints, a stack of prayer cards, a prayer book and two sets of rosary beads. That's what I call praying.

The trouble was, I knew she was praying for me and I didn't like it one bit. I felt she was putting me down, interfering in my life and shoving God in my face. It made me feel like a helpless, useless bum which I still refused to admit. Since I was usually drunk at the time, I would often yell at her, demanding that she mind her own business and stay out of my life—that I didn't need her damn prayers. She wouldn't say a word. She would just keep on praying.

By this time I was an even sicker, more selfish and very self-centered man who gave no thought to the fact that here was a woman who was feeding his wife and kids while I was paying her no rent at all. Mama was seeing how I was hurting her lovely daughter and innocent grandchildren and never said a word to me. She knew it wouldn't do any good and might provoke an argument. In fact, she would never even turn and look at me. She would just keep on praying.

The God my mother-in-law was praying to I no longer had in my life. I had asked Him one too many times for His help but He never came through. He never gave me what I thought I needed, a lot of money and another good job. I would wake up in some doorway or in a fleabag hotel and scream out one of those foxhole prayers:

"God, I know I've said it a million times before but this time I really mean it. If you help me out with a job so I can borrow some money to take care of things, I swear I'll change. I'll go back to church and be the kind of person You want me to be. Just help me out this one time and I'll never ask You again. Please."

Then things would get worse because I couldn't stop drinking and I'd always blame it on God. Despite my years in the seminary studying to be a priest, prayers had now become like ashes on my tongue. So I stopped praying and just walked away from my Creator. I am deeply grateful that He never walked away from me.

Whenever I would leave that basement, allegedly to find work, I rarely told Bernadette where I was going or where I might be should she ever need me which was now seldom the case. I just had to get out of the place and get a drink. For some reason I just happened to mention one day that someone I knew was starting a communications business and might need my help as a paid consultant. The story was true except for the paid consultant part. I said we'd be meeting at the Yale Club in the city.

That happened to be the very same day our oldest daughter Judy, who was now five, came down with a high fever from a urinary tract infection. It was so bad, the doctor told Bernadette to drive her to the hospital right away. After checking her in, she was able to reach me and asked if I would meet her there.

When I nearly fell out of a cab drunk in front of the hospital, my wife was so ashamed and embarrassed she began to cry hysterically. I now weighed over three hundred pounds and didn't shower often enough. I had become a fat, sloppy, stinking drunk who was almost completely out of control. Bernadette begged me not to see our daughter in such a condition. I knew she was right so I abided by her wishes. That's when she calmed down.

She hadn't eaten anything since breakfast and it was now late in the afternoon. Even though I knew she didn't want to be anywhere close to me in my condition, we wound up going a Chinese restaurant near her mother's house. Much of this I don't recall because once again I was in and out of a blackout. But Bernadette did fill me in at a later time.

Since I had borrowed some money from my sympathetic friend at the Yale Club, I had some drinking funds in my pocket. My wife recalls I ordered eight dry Rob Roys that day. It wasn't easy for me to shock her anymore but this time I did. I'll never forget the tears in her eyes and the near hopeless sound in her voice when she looked at me and asked:

"Why? Tell me why. Look at you. Why are you doing this to yourself? Will it ever stop?"

Now I was shocked. I didn't mind much anymore when she would scream and holler at me for coming home drunk and causing chaos because I deserved her anger. But asking me a question I couldn't answer, why I drank…it was a question I had been asking myself for years. And it was a question I just couldn't handle. That's when something inside of me snapped. I suddenly felt like I was coming apart. I was like a little boy lost in the woods and afraid he would never find his way out. That's when I realized I desperately needed help. So I reached out to my wife.

"There's something wrong with me, Bernadette," I said with tears now flowing down my face, "I feel like I'm crazy or going crazy. I really need help but I don't know where to go. What am I going to do? You have to help me."

I was very fortunate to be married to a very strong woman. For some unexplainable reason she still had some love left for me because she knew what love was. It's not just a warm, fuzzy feeling. It's a decision and a commitment to be there for someone when it's not easy to do. But on this day I saw the girl, the lady, the woman I once knew I couldn't live without. And she was about to save my life.

When we arrived home, she phoned Dr. Altruda who, since we moved back to Queens, was once again our family physician. When she explained my situation, he gave her the name of a psychiatrist whose office wasn't that far away. Two days later, on a chilly Saturday morning, I found myself sitting in front of Dr. John Bronchoto, a thin, pleasant-looking man with a small bald spot on top of his head. He was in his fifties and wore half glasses and a pencil mustache.

For some reason I was very nervous about seeing a shrink. I now know it was just an excuse to stop at Fred Funks saloon on my way for a few doubles to calm my jitters. I think the good doctor smelled them on my breath the moment I sat down and laid my fat belly on his desk.

I remember looking around for some kind of a couch to lie down on.

I thought that's what you did in a psychiatrist's office. At least that's what you see in the movies. You lie down on a couch and tell the shrink all your troubles. For a moment I wondered whether or not he was a real psychiatrist. Then he interrupted my drifting thoughts.

"I'm sorry, but what did you say your name was again?" he asked looking over the top of his pince-nez.

"Bill," I replied rather nervously.

"How old are you, Bill?"

"Twenty-seven."

"Twenty-seven? What are you doing in a psychiatrist's office at the age of twenty seven?"

"Because I think I'm crazy…or at least going crazy."

"Tell me why you think you're crazy."

I didn't know where to begin, so I started by telling him I was doing a lot of things I didn't want to do…making promises I wasn't keeping …hurting my wife and family…losing jobs…living in a basement …getting into bar fights. That's when he stopped me. He leaned across his desk and asked:

"Tell me Bill, how much do you drink?" I was now sure he smelled my visit to Fred Funks.

Still, his question surprised me. Believe it or not, I was still having difficulty looking at my drinking as my real problem. Sure I knew I drank too much at times but that was to relieve the pressure and put up with all the problems in my life, like not having enough money; the pressure of getting married too young and having too many kids; having a drunk for a father; God being against me; my lack of good luck and the IRS threatening to come after me for not having filed my income taxes in six years. Those were the things causing me great stress and anxiety and those were the things I wanted to talk about.

But this psychiatrist kept asking what I drank, how much I drank, how often I drank and why I drank. For some reason or other I found myself telling him my entire drinking story. It took him less than ten minutes to come up with a diagnosis. He slipped off his glasses, gave me a very knowing look and said:

"Bill, I think you're an alcoholic."

I couldn't believe what this skinny little shrink just said to me. I reacted very angrily. I pulled my fat belly off his desk, sat up straight and replied:

"Are you calling me a Bowery bum because that's what alcoholics are!"

"No, only when they're in the final stages of their disease. You're on your way but you're not there yet," he said in a much more caring tone. "But if you keep on drinking the way you have been drinking, the Bowery is right around the corner. Believe me. I know what I'm talking about."

It took a moment for his diagnosis to sink in. Even though I wasn't quite buying it I asked:

"What should I do? Keep coming back to see you?" Then I heard the worst of the news.

"No. Psychiatry really can't help most alcoholics. You'd only be wasting your time and your money seeing me. And if you decide to keep on drinking, you'll need the money. But if you decide to stop, there's a twelve step program I know that can help you. I'll give you a phone number to call."

The man was so honest he pissed me off. On my way home the thought occurred to me that I'd rather be diagnosed as crazy then alcoholic. Crazy people can drink. Alcoholics should stop. But I had gone to see this doctor for help and felt I really didn't get it, at least not the kind I had expected. What do I do now?

Since I was sure he'd be reporting his diagnosis to Bernadette, I was more open than usual with her about my visit and what the psychiatrist had said. She pleaded with me to follow his advice. I was in no position at this juncture to disagree. So I called the number he gave me.

It was a few days later, near the end of March of 1961, when I managed to find my way into a twelve step meeting in a Protestant church basement. I found a bunch of old guys there telling war stories about their drinking escapades. At the age of twenty-seven, I'd bet I was the youngest in the room by more than twenty-five years.

The first thing that turned me off was when one of them told me the same thing that shrink said, that I had a disease called alcoholism that couldn't be cured but could be arrested. A disease I thought? What a slick way of getting myself off the hook after all the crap I pulled. I'd rather they had told me the truth, that I was nothing but a selfish, stinking, lousy, filthy, low-down piece of garbage. Then I would have believed they were on the level.

I went to those twelve step meetings for almost two months with the firm intention of giving their program a real shot. But being an alcoholic still in denial, I had cut back on my drinking but never completely stopped. That's why the maniac who was still living in my brain was able to convince me this thing didn't really work or that I had at least another twenty-five years before I needed it.

I remember the night I was sitting across from Bernadette on one of our basement cots next to the oil burner and telling her I didn't think I had to go to those meetings anymore.

"Why not?" she asked with a concerned look on her face.

"Because I already learned what was the most important thing to know," I said, trying to sound convincing. "I found out that if I continued to drink the way I was drinking, someday I could have a whole lot of trouble. So I'm going to take it real easy from now on."

It was like that scene from the movie, "The Exorcist." My wife's head seemed to spin completely around. I recall her glancing toward the oil burner next to her, up at the low-hung basement ceiling, over at our children sleeping on day beds and one in a broken crib, then looking back at me and shaking her head. I could almost read her lips repeating what I said: "Someday I could have a whole lot of trouble." I think she finally realized how sick I was. Then she rose slowly from her cot and went upstairs. She was so lost and bewildered she had nothing left to say.

So I started again, slowly at first, but then my drinking gradually picked up. That summer was dreadful. I remember two guys from Smitty's Bar & Grill down the street helping me put my car up on blocks in the driveway. Every time I had seventy-five dollars to get it registered, I got drunk instead. That's why whenever I'd make a few bucks, I wasn't able to drive the children to the beach or take Bernadette shopping. Yet she still hung in there.

Sometimes when I was drinking late in the city and the smelly, low-class bar I was in either closed or threw me out, I'd manage to talk a cabbie into driving me home. I would give him the wrong address and then pretend I had to go into the house to get some cash. I'd stagger to a side door, then sneak quietly through several backyards and find some bushes to hide under. I'd lay there sucking on the rest of a pint for an hour or so until I felt the cabbie had gone. It was a very shabby and shameful thing to do. One night I dozed off under a bush and woke up with ants crawling all over my face.

That Christmas I had been on a drunk and in blackouts for several days. I never bought a tree for my family. I think it was either Christmas Eve or the night before when I was staggering home and spotted this beautifully decorated, well-lit Christmas tree in the foyer of an apartment building that had no doorman. So I staggered in, unplugged the tree and dragged it out with me. What terrible things we drunks do.

I'm not sure why I never managed to get that tree all the way home. Something tells me I might have seen a police car passing by and threw it over a fence so I wouldn't get myself into trouble. Fortunately my mother-in-law had bought a very nice tree for her house which Bernadette and the children helped her decorate.

It was the first week of April, 1962. I awoke with a start in another two dollar a night fleabag hotel room that stunk of urine and stale beer. My clothes were terribly wrinkled and smelled almost as bad as the room. My growth of beard seemed to be stuck to the mattress from having slobbered in my sleep. I remember staggering into the filthy bathroom and looking into a small mirror. What I saw staring back disgusted me.

I came out and sat on the edge of the bed. My mind wouldn't stop. It kept reeling off every single calamity in my life and all the reasons I shouldn't even be around anymore. My wife and family were still living in a basement. No one would hire me. My bad checks were bouncing all over New York. I was sixty-seven thousand dollars in debt to banks, finance companies and loan sharks. I was convinced the FBI would be arresting me at any moment for not having filed my income taxes for more than seven years now. I hated myself and was in complete despair over every bad thing I had ever done and all the people I had harmed.

At the age of twenty-eight, my life was over. There was absolutely no reason for going on. I was also absolutely certain that God hated me too and had a special place reserved for me in Hell.

As tears of self-pity once again flowed down my face, I stood up and walked to the window. I opened it and crawled out on the window ledge. I think I was on the eighth floor facing an air shaft. There were cables and telephone lines crisscrossing all the way down to the bottom. I sat there and waited for the courage to jump.

CHAPTER TWELVE

A Man Named Benny

Suicide, as they say, is more often than not a permanent solution to a temporary problem. Depression, however, can rob you of the ability to judge whether problems are temporary or permanent. And I was in a deep depression.

All I saw as I sat on that window ledge was blackness. That maniac in my brain that I often speak of was working overtime. He refused to let any light shine through, any hope that things could possibly work out, especially my relationship with my wife and family. He convinced me it had gone way past the point of forgiveness.

I felt like I was facing a huge mountain of difficulties and there was no way over it, around it or through it. But the longer I sat there, the more frightening my final solution began to appear. The courage I thought I was waiting for seemed to be drifting farther and farther away. Deep down I began to sense that I didn't really want to die. I just didn't know how to live.

As I continued to stare down into the darkness of the air shaft, my fear increased. I could almost see Hell staring me in the face. I felt completely abandoned. I tried to pray. That's when I had a sense that God, Whoever or wherever He was, didn't want me to jump.

But addiction is a tough beast to tame. It's not easily defeated. It wants to kill you. Maybe it was the cowardice in me that changed my mind or perhaps it was some spiritual force. I wasn't sure at the time. But I slowly swung my legs in from the ledge and took a deep breath. After a moment I decided what I should do. Self-pity was to be my guide and self-will was to light my path. That's because my plan called for doing things my way one more time.

I felt certain that Bernadette would be much better off without me. So would my children. I knew that because I grew up with an alcoholic father. I would go back to that dingy basement, pack a suitcase and leave. As a single mother, my wife could get on welfare or find a job. I knew her family would come to her aid. And whatever money I was able to make, I'd be sure to send it to her. Maybe she could even find a nice guy with a few bucks and get married again. I wouldn't like that. But then, no matter what, she'd be a whole lot better off without a stinking drunk like me hanging around.

I would simply disappear, maybe even change my name so the authorities couldn't find me. For some strange reason, I thought about all those guys I saw at Sammy's Bowery Follies and others pan-handling along the filthy streets to get another pint of Old Irish Rose, a wine that never saw a grape. They had disappeared in plain sight. But that was one place I swore I would never wind up. Then I looked around at my surroundings and saw I was already there.

After washing as best I could, I still felt wobbly when I reached the lobby. It was filled with torn carpeting and broken chairs and a few drunks sleeping it off because they couldn't afford even the cheapest room. I had close to twenty bucks in my pocket so I bought two bottles of cold beer from the old black man behind the check-in desk. I drank them both and then headed for the subway.

My wife was ironing clothes when I walked down into the basement. The kids were upstairs with my mother-in-law. I couldn't look Bernadette in the face because I didn't want to see how she would look back at me. I was sure she hated me and would be happy when I was gone. I believe I mumbled something like:

"I came home to pack a suitcase and leave. I'm getting out of your life for good. I've decided you'd be a whole lot better off without me."

She just kept ironing. Then I think I said something like:

"You could go on welfare and make more money than I'm bringing home. Most of all you'd have some peace for a change, not putting up with all the crap I've been giving you for so long. I'm really sorry."

What I expected to happen didn't. There was no assent or dissent. There was neither surprise nor relief. There was no immediate reaction at all. I just stood there and watched her continue to iron. After a moment, she put the iron down, turned and looked at me. There was no anger on her face, only sadness and confusion. Then I remember her saying:

"Before you leave, do you think you owe me one last favor?"

I lowered my head and murmured:

"Yes. I guess so."

What came next I wouldn't have expected in a million years. I thought I was talking with a woman who couldn't stand the sight of me, had more respect for a rusty nail, someone who despised me for everything I had done to her and the children. But instead of the venom I anticipated, the words coming from her lips were more an expression of compassion and caring.

"For God's sake, Bill," she said, "why don't you give that twelve step program another chance?"

How would you respond to a judge who gave you parole instead of a death sentence? How would you react to a doctor telling you your cancer was cured? Bernadette's words had that same effect. I didn't know what to say or what to do I was so blown away.

I know it sounds rather corny, but I felt I didn't deserve the forgiveness I thought I saw on her face as she spoke. It was like those old guys in that Protestant church basement telling me I had a disease that could be arrested instead of saying I was just a plain old piece of garbage. As I stood there staring at my wife, that's what I felt like—just a plain old piece of garbage.

Instead of trying to hug her or thank her for her concern, I bolted. That's right, I bolted. I ran back up the basement steps and down three blocks to a bar on Liberty Avenue. I ordered two double shots of rye so I could think straight. I got one down, then glanced into the mirror behind the bar. The problem with mirrors is they're all like that psychiatrist I went to see. They're just too damn honest. A mirror will always tell you the truth.

That night the bar mirror told me I was at the end of the line, that I couldn't go on any further. I was either going back to the window ledge in that fleabag hotel or signing myself into some booby hatch or joining those fellows with the war stories so they could teach me how to stay sober.

I pushed the second double shot away and went back to my mother-in-law's basement. Without fully realizing it, I was ready now to receive God's grace and follow whatever His will was for me. I had finally hit my bottom.

The first thing I did was take a shower in mama's bathroom. When I came out nice and clean for a change and wearing a fresh pair of pajamas, the phone was ringing. It was for me. Being a saver, Bernadette had kept some phone numbers I had given her of men I had met at meetings the previous year. She had called a guy named Joe and he was calling me back.

"I hear you're having a lot of problems again with the booze," he said very kindly. "Would you like to give our program another try?"

God answered for me. "Yes, Joe," I said. "Yes, I would."

It was around seven-thirty on the evening of April 8, 1962 when a big old 1954 dark blue Packard pulled up in front of my mother-in law's house. It was driven by a short, stout man with thick eyeglasses, thinning black hair and a broad smile named Benny Michaelson, a jeweler by trade.

The car was filled with five other sober men including the fellow Joe I had spoken with the night before. Despite my girth, they managed to squeeze me into the back seat. I had no idea at that moment how my whole life was about to change. As we pulled away, I saw Bernadette and her mom standing on the front stoop. I don't know whether they were smiling or crying.

As I sat there between two other sober alcoholics, I suddenly realized I had been drunk for so long I had no idea how the world around me had changed. I didn't know, for example, that THE WEST SIDE STORY, a musical with that sad song "Maria" I played on every jukebox in every bar I drank in had just won an Oscar for the Best Picture of 1962. Neither did I recall that my old baseball team, the Brooklyn Dodgers, were starting the season off in California as The Los Angeles Dodgers. Perhaps it was better I didn't remember. I might have been tempted to have a drink.

Then there was Scott Carpenter, a Project Mercury astronaut, orbiting the earth three times in the Aurora 7 space capsule. I had long since lost track of The Space Race I once wrote about. And Johnny Carson taking over as the host of NBC's The Tonight Show, a post he held for thirty years. I used to laugh through my sad, drunken tears at Moochie's Bar watching him host the best show on TV.

But the year I finally hit bottom, 1962, was also the harbinger of some very troubling events. First, there was the Cuban Missile Crisis which brought the United States and the Soviet Union to the brink of nuclear war. Not as serious but personally disturbing to me was the 1962 newspaper strike in the city. It lasted more than four months, spelled the eventual death of a number of newspapers including the New York Journal-American in 1966 that cost a lot of jobs for some guys I knew and spelled the end to the real heyday of newspaper journalism in New York City. It also brought back a lot of haunting memories.

I remember I was awakened from my reverie by the guy sitting next to me, a gray haired man in his early sixties who had a slightly bulbous nose.

"I'm Ralph," he said, shaking my hand. "I think I met you last year when you were sniffing us out," he added with a smile that showed two missing upper teeth. "Sometimes it takes awhile to pick up the scent. I hope you get it soon."

"I hope so too," I replied.

"Just keep your ears open and your mouth shut," he advised, "at least for awhile. That's the best way to learn when you're brand new. And if you have any questions, don't be afraid to ask. Okay?"

"Sure. Thanks Ralph," I said.

When we arrived at the same meeting I went to a year before in that Protestant church basement in Woodhaven, Queens, at least half a dozen sober men shook my hand and welcomed me back to what they called

"The Woodhaven Group." I felt flattered that some of them like Ralph remembered my name. One of them handed me a hot cup of coffee in a chipped white mug. Benny, who drove the Packard, pulled me aside. I had really enjoyed listening to him speak as we rode together with the other alcoholics. I especially loved his laughter since I hadn't laughed in a long, long time. He looked me right in the eye and said something like:

"I'm glad to see you back. My name is Benny...Benny Michaelson. I don't know if you remember me or not but I'm the fellow who told you the last time around you were full of shit. I knew you weren't ready. Are you ready now?"

"Yes, I think so," I replied.

"I think so doesn't cut it," he said very seriously. "You look like you've been through the mill and back so maybe you are ready now. Remember this. Halfway measures avail us nothing. You've got to give this program one hundred percent or it won't work. Do you think you can do that?"

It seemed like that window ledge in the fleabag hotel flashed before my eyes along with that double shot of rye I left on that bar on Liberty Avenue.

"Whatever I have to do, I'll do," I said with as much sincerity as I could muster. "I can't go back to the way it was. I don't want to go back to the way it was."

"Good. Then I advise you to get yourself a good sponsor who can lead you through the twelve steps of this program and do whatever he suggests." Benny started to walk away when I grabbed him by the arm.

"What about you," I asked. "I don't really know anybody else here and what you said makes a lot of sense. Would you be my sponsor?"

He gave me a warm smile and replied: "Let's talk after the meeting. And by the way, I suggest you sit right up front. You can hear better that way."

Three men from another area of Queens spoke that night, telling their drunk stories and how they found sobriety. One was in his late thirties which made me feel like I wasn't the only relatively young guy who screwed up his life. He made me feel even better when I heard him say:

"It doesn't make any difference how old you are or how young you are, whether you're a man or woman, black or white. And it doesn't make any difference what you drink, how much you drink or how often you drink. It's how the drinking affects your life—what it does to you is what really counts."

After the meeting, Benny led me into the small church kitchen where members were already bringing in their coffee mugs, dirty ashtrays (you could smoke in church basements back then), cake plates, knives, forks and spoons and putting them on the counter. The man I had asked to be my sponsor filled up the sink with hot soapy water, then turned to me and said: "You wash. I'll dry."

As I rolled up my sleeves and loaded everything into the sink and began washing, the strangest kind of feeling came over me. It was a good feeling. I recall it so well. I felt like I was now part of this club or group or whatever you wanted to call it. Something told me it was going to work whatever it was—that if I did what was suggested, it would keep me sober.

Benny told me later I had this good feeling because by washing those dishes I was doing something for someone else instead of just for myself which was my usual modus operandi. He told me I was performing a service for others—that being selfish and self-centered was the way most alcoholics had lived their lives. He said I would have to change that if I wanted to stay sober.

Benny dropped everyone else off first before taking me home. The first out was Jimmy Beggin, a man in his late fifties who had deep scars across the palms of both hands as a result of leaping from a subway platform and grasping onto the third rail. He was in a deep alcoholic depression at the time. He had tried to make it look like an accident so his distressed wife and family could collect his insurance.

Like me and the window ledge, something saved us both and I was beginning to think it might have been God. Jimmy was sure of it. He told me that after he had bounced off the electrified rail, people pulled him back onto the platform just before a train rolled into the station.

Next to hop out were Johnny Grimes and Joe Smith, both in their fifties who had lost very good jobs from drinking and were having difficulty finding new ones. Then Ray Wallace whose wife divorced him for drinking, Eddie Moylin whose wife threatened him with divorce and Sal Cavuto who had a bad liver the doctor said would kill him if he didn't stop drinking.

You can learn a lot from guys struggling to stay sober while riding in a car with them. It's like having a meeting going to the meeting, having a meeting at the meeting and having another meeting on the ride home. When Benny pulled to the curb in front of my mother-in-law's house, he stuck out his hand and said:

"Okay. I'll be your sponsor if you still want me to be. I just wanted to see how committed you really were to getting sober. Washing all that stuff tonight convinced me."

Then he added: "I've learned from being sober more than nineteen years now that we alcoholics don't like to be told what to do. So I'm only going to offer you suggestions, I mean about the things that keep me sober. But, if you don't follow my suggestions, you might just as well get yourself another sponsor. Okay?"

"I'll do whatever you say, Benny," I remember replying. "Like I said, I really want to stay sober and change my whole life for the better. I want to stop hurting people."

He picked me up every night at eight o'clock for meetings that were held at nine throughout the borough. He knew so many people in the program and they all seemed to love the guy. He introduced me to many of them but I just couldn't remember most of their names. One night I told him I was concerned about my memory, that maybe my drinking killed too many brain cells. He offered me two suggestions:

"You don't need a very good memory if you tell the truth. And try walking around with a pencil and piece of paper in your pocket so you can jot down things that you want to remember."

Then he looked at me and laughed, "Stop worrying. The longer you stay sober, the better things will get—whether you want them too or not."

As the days, weeks and months passed by, Benny continued to drop everyone else off first so we could spend some time together talking. He knew I had a lot on my mind. He told me one night I was a walking garbage can with the lid about to blow off. That's why I needed to get stuff out by sharing it with him.

This one particular night as I started to climb out of his car, he grabbed my arm and pulled me back in.

"I can tell something's been bugging you the last few days. I've been waiting for you to open up. If you don't get it out, that's how we wind up drunk."

After a long, painful pause, I said as I looked out the window:

"Every time I go into that house, I feel like I don't deserve to be there after all I've done to my family. And when I see Bernadette and the kids, I feel even worse, dragging them down into a basement. I've got so much guilt piled up inside of me, Benny, I feel like just running away. And the longer I stay sober, the more I come to realize how much I've really hurt them. I just can't forgive myself and I don't know what to do about it."

He reached over and turned off the ignition. Then in the silence of his big old Packard, he looked at me and said something that changed my life and helped me find a better understanding of and relationship with my Creator.

"You still believe in God, don't you Bill?"

"We haven't been on very good terms in a long time. But yes, I believe there's a God," I replied.

"Do you believe God has forgiven you for all that crap that's still driving you nuts and could lead you back to a drink?"

I envied Benny. He was Jewish and by now I knew he had a loving God in his life, a God he called his very best friend. Every morning he would get down on his knees and ask his Best Friend to help him stay sober and every night on his knees he would thank Him.

On the other hand, as I've said before, I sometimes still had this childish image of God being this old guy on a throne watching me like a hawk. Every time I'd do something wrong, zingo—my name would go into his big book in capitol letters. And the way I was raised as a child in the Catholic Church, I thought everything I did was wrong.

But in the seminary, I really got to know a lot more about God through His Son, Jesus Christ. I came to believe that Jesus died a horrible death on a cross in order for all my sins to be forgiven. So, while I was sometimes caught between the fear of justice and the joy of forgiveness, deep inside I believed that God truly loved me because He sent His only son to die for me. And "What greater love can one man have for another than to lay down his life for him." This was what I had once believed until booze almost completely eradicated it from my soul. At that moment, I would have loved to believe it again.

As all of this was rushing through my mind, my sponsor hit me with that big one:

"Do you believe that God as you understand Him has forgiven you?"

"Yes," I answered. "At least that's what I want to believe, Benny."

"Are you bigger than God?"

"Of course not."

"Then if you want to believe that God has forgiven you, why can't you forgive yourself?" he concluded.

The wall came tumbling down. Being sober now for almost two months, my mind was clear enough to understand what Benny was trying to tell me. I was letting my guilt beat me up so that the disease of alcoholism could kill me. But God as I wanted to understand Him had already forgiven me. I also knew now that He had also taken me off that window ledge so that I could learn how to forgive myself and lead a happy and sober life, His way, not mine.

Before leaving the car, my sponsor said it was time we began working the twelve steps of our program together before the lid on my garbage can finally blew off and spilled everything all over the place. I took the first step with him that night:

"We admitted we were powerless over alcohol—that our lives had become unmanageable."

The next eleven that were to come read:

"Came to believe that a Power greater than ourselves could restore us to sanity.

"Made a decision to turn our will and our lives over to the care of God as we understood Him.

"Made a searching and fearless moral inventory of ourselves.

"Admitted to God, to ourselves, and to another human being the exact nature of our wrongs.

"Were entirely ready to have God remove all these defects of character.

"Humbly asked Him to remove our shortcomings.

"Made a list of all persons we had harmed, and became willing to make amends to them all.

"Made direct amends to such people wherever possible, except when to do so would injure them or others.

"Continued to take personal inventory and when we were wrong promptly admitted it.

"Sought through prayer and meditation to improve our conscious contact with God as we understood Him, praying only for knowledge of His will for us and the power to carry that out.

"Having had a spiritual awakening as the result of these steps, we tried to carry this message to alcoholics and to practice these principles in all our affairs."

Benny was buying me lunch one day when he asked:

"What do you think it is that really attracts you and me to this program, Bill?"

Being a smart ass I said, "The free coffee and cake."

"No, seriously," he smiled. "Ever hear of something called 'unconditional love?' We don't judge each other. We put others first. We anticipate their needs and try to help them out of tough spots. We'll go to any length to help another alcoholic. Isn't that the big attraction?"

"It sure is," I replied, apologizing for being such a smart aleck. "It's like you and all the other guys being concerned about someone like me."

"I have another suggestion for you" he said as he looked directly into my eyes. "Take it home, this unconditional love. Take it home and practice it like you do at meetings with your family. You'll see how much it will change everything for the better."

It did. Of course, nothing happens overnight. It took me awhile to get as sick as I did so I knew it would take a while to get well. But Bernadette began to gradually notice my new concern for her. And I started helping more with the children, trying to change Larry's diaper without regurgitating, taking the older ones for walks or to the park and especially going to Sunday Mass with the family.

My wife and I began to talk again. It wasn't easy at first. We both seemed to be walking on egg shells. But it did get better except for one thing. I still didn't have a job. While Bernadette wasn't pushing me, Benny sure was. He kept reminding me I had responsibilities, a wife and four children. But I was afraid to leave the house by myself. I thought I might be tempted to drop into a bar before getting on the train for Manhattan.

I think I had also been afraid of bumping into my old loan shark, Richie Baldino. He had been looking for me everywhere since I still owed him almost seventeen thousand dollars. I hadn't borrowed that much, but the high vigorish or interest on the money he lent me never stopped adding up. But then something happened that both shocked and confused me. Richie dropped dead from a sudden heart attack. Not knowing what to do about the money I owed him, I told Benny all about it.

My sponsor asked if Richie worked for the mob and would anyone else be coming after me. I had never heard that my favorite loan shark was mobbed up, only that he worked with his older brother Jules who was also dead. That's when Benny simply said, "Then just pray for him." I still do on occasion and hope he's happy doing business in "loan shark heaven."

Now relieved of that huge financial pressure, I finally followed my sponsor's suggestion. I got down on my knees one morning and asked God to keep me sober and help me find some work. I spent that day in the city calling on guys I considered old media buddies. But I had so many blackouts from drinking I didn't remember how badly I had treated many of them during my professional pan-handling days.

Most were polite but it was obvious they wanted no part of me. So I came home very discouraged. Here I thought I was in such a good spiritual place after my talks with Benny. But I was about to learn you can't take such things for granted. You have to work at it one day at a time.

Bernadette was in the kitchen with her mother feeding the children. She asked how my day went. I didn't want to talk about it. She knew there was something wrong so when I went downstairs she followed me. With the news that my loan shark was off my back, I shouldn't have been so sullen and ill-tempered. But I was. And I had no reason for starting an argument except that I used to salve such bad feelings with a few drinks. Now I felt naked and unprotected.

My wife wanted to discuss what was going on. I didn't. She said things and I said things and before you knew it the old self-pity was back.

"What the hell's the sense of staying sober anyway!" I shouted. "Nothing's going right. I can't find a job! No one wants to hire me. And you expect things to change right away."

"I never said that!" she shouted back. "I know it's going to take time."

"And I can tell you're never going to forget all those things I did when I was drinking. You'll always keep bringing them up."

"You don't make it easy to forget. Listen to you right now. I didn't start this!"

I suddenly remembered that one of my brothers-in-law who enjoyed a beer now and then had been over visiting recently. I knew he had left some cans in my mother-in-law's refrigerator. I moved past my wife, and ran up the stairs. She was right behind me.

I grabbed a beer, went into the dining room and popped it open. Bernadette started to cry. She stared at me with that hopeless look back on her face and said:

"I don't understand what's going on. But if you drink that, don't blame me."

Just then the telephone rang on a nearby table. It was for me. Eddie Moylin, a member of the Woodhaven Group group, was calling to see if I could go with him on "a twelve step call." That's what the program calls it when you pick up a sick alcoholic who wants help and take him or her to a meeting or to a dry-out place if they need it.

I couldn't believe what had just happened. I get a call for help from a fellow alcoholic just when I'm about to take a drink myself. The can of beer dropped from my hand. I stood there stunned as tears filled my eyes. I knew that this was no mere coincidence, not after having gotten down on my knees that morning and asked my Higher Power for help to stay sober. That was the last serious urge I ever had to pick up another drink.

A few days after my near slip, I received a surprise phone call from Abe Schecter, the public relations executive I had worked for rather briefly the year before. He said he had heard through the proverbial grapevine that I was sober and looking for a job. He asked if I could meet with him in his office the following Monday.

As I mentioned earlier, Abe was one of the nicest and most decent men I had ever known and he proved it to me again when I sat across the desk from him. I remember what he said to me that morning just like it was five minutes ago.

"I told you when I had to let you go that you always did a terrific job for me when you were here. I'd like to offer you that account executive position back on two conditions. First, that we do it the same way your friends in that twelve step program I hear you're in do it—one day at a time. I'll pay you forty dollars a day for every day you show up and put in a full day's work. That will come to two hundred dollars a week.

"Second, if you don't show up two days in a row, the deal is off. I hope that doesn't sound too harsh, Bill, but I've had drinkers on my staff before. If I see I can count on you, the job is yours for as long as you want it. Okay?"

I thanked him, shook his hand and was back working for Abe the very next day. That evening I brought Bernadette home two crisp twenty dollar bills in a plain white envelope. We both had tears in our eyes as we hugged for a very long time. It wasn't the money. It was the feeling that our hopes were beginning to turn into reality. We both knew now that it would take time, but we also knew we were on our way.

At the end of every day, I would walk out of A.A. Schecter & Associates with forty dollars in my pocket and a pat on the back for a job well done. Before the end of the month, I was a permanent staff member making ten thousand dollars a year which was a thousand dollars more than I made the year before. And Abe and I became much more than worker and boss. We became very close friends.

I don't believe it was any kind of a coincidence that when Abe passed away some years later, his wife called and asked if I would deliver the eulogy at his funeral. While I was stunned, she said Abe always felt good about giving me a hand up when I needed it. He was very proud of how I took advantage of the opportunity. I was barely able to read my eulogy notes through misty eyes, I loved that guy so much.

While my life was continuing to improve, my father's life was continuing to go in the other direction. Then something occurred that opened the door to his decent much wider. His middle brother Herb, the one he was closest to, passed away.

The doctor said my Uncle Herb had died of cardiac arrest brought on by extreme alcoholic drinking. My dad was totally devastated by his brother's passing. I think it finally hit him that three of his four brothers died from the same disease. Yet, my father was still unwilling to admit the same malady was killing him too.

Science tells us today that alcoholism generally runs in families. If one parent is an alcoholic, the children have a fifty percent chance of becoming alcoholics. If both parents are addicted, there's a ninety percent chance that at least one or more of the children will become alcoholics. My father and I were both born standing right in front of the bull's-eye of alcoholism watching as the poisoned arrow made a direct hit on both of us.

My dad went on a two week bender after my uncle's funeral. He almost lost his job. My mother knew by now that I was sober and was in a program that was helping me stay that way. We had talked about it a few times. Even though she couldn't accept the fact that I was a real alcoholic, she was happy my life was back on a positive track. Also, with her and Bernadette being on better terms, she was coming by to see her grandchildren more often.

However, things had gotten so bad at my parents' place that my mother called me at work one day pleading with me to talk to my father. Benny suggested I not go but I guess I still felt I had all the answers even though I didn't understand most of the questions. I always had to learn the hard way. My sponsor said it's virtually impossible to speak intelligently with a drunk when he's drunk, especially your own father. Something told me I still had to give it a try.

I pretended I was just dropping by for a visit that Saturday afternoon. My mother spent the day with Aunt Helen to make sure my dad and I would be alone. He was sitting at the kitchen table eating a sandwich and drinking a beer when I walked in. He needed a shave and had a slight buzz on but wasn't really drunk.

"I thought you died and went to Heaven," was how he greeted me. "We haven't seen or heard from you or your wife since your Uncle Herbie's funeral. Everything alright?"

"Couldn't be better," I smiled, then quickly added, "Well, that's not exactly true. Things could be a whole lot better but we're getting there."

Then he looked me straight in the face and said: "I can see you're still not drinking."

"I can see you still are," I replied, sounding just a little too flip. He noticed it. I could see it in his face and hear it in his voice when he responded the same way.

"Did your mother ask you to come over and talk to me?"

"You know how rough it got for me, dad," I said, trying to sound a bit more caring. "Hell, I even tried to out myself, things got so bad. I don't know if you knew that or not. I just couldn't see any other way. Now…well, this program I'm in seems to be working for me. It's keeping me sober. Even guys a lot older. Just the other night at a meeting…"

He cut me off. I could tell he was getting pissed off.

"Look, it may be great for you. I can see that. But you've got your whole life ahead of you. Mine's practically over. So don't be coming over here trying to sell me a bunch of snake oil. Besides, it's too late trying to teach old dogs new tricks. So let's just forget it."

"That's a bunch of crap and you know it," I replied, now getting pissed off myself. "Don't you think you can at least…"

He stood up and cut me off again. "I'm still your father. Don't think you're so damn self-righteous that you know what's good for me!"

Then he pushed past me saying very angrily: "Excuse me. I have to go to the bathroom."

I waited a few minutes and then realized I was fighting a lost cause. So I left.

The thought struck me as I was heading home that I just left the man I swore I would never be like, the man who was still so blinded by his alcoholism that he wouldn't even consider the possibility of changing and finding a better life. This was also the man I became.

Then another thought struck me. While I never wanted to be like my father, now I wanted him to be like me. How big can one's ego get. So I laughed at myself and decided to do what I had been doing with almost everything else in my life lately. I turned my father over to God.

My mother was naturally disappointed when she called to find out how things went. She told me they had been invited to a wedding reception the following Saturday and she didn't want to go. But my father insisted. It was the daughter of one of his closest friends whom he worked with for many years in the pressroom.

It just so happened I had been invited to speak at a twelve step meeting that same Saturday night and my car was still sitting on cement blocks in my mother-in-law's driveway because I didn't have enough money to get it fixed. The engine needed work. So instead of asking Benny or someone else to take me, I suggested that if my folks were going to the wedding, I'd come over and drive them. Then I could take their car to my meeting, pick them up on my way back and take them home. I had no idea what I was in for.

My father got so drunk at that wedding reception he started taking bottles of booze off the tables of other guests. He kept saying that a damn cheapskate must be running the affair. He told his friend and fellow pressman that the food was lousy, the band stunk and that his daughter was the ugliest looking bride he ever saw. They were ready to engage in fisticuffs until a few sober guests pulled them apart.

My mom was so embarrassed she was ready to leave without him. That's when I arrived. She begged me to get my father into the car before things at the reception got even worse.

Taking my parents home that night brought back painful memories of my childhood. My father wanted to jump out and go into every bar we passed to get cigarettes. My mother kept screaming and hitting him for embarrassing her in front of so many friends and others she had just met.

To be honest, I couldn't wait until I finally managed to get my father into bed, kissed my mother goodbye and left. Despite those bad memories and the smell of all the booze my father had sopped up, never once did I think about having a drink myself. Instead, I prayed all the way home that my father would some day find what I had found.

It was around noon the next day when our phone rang. I had just returned from Sunday Mass with Bernadette and the children. It was my father. He sounded really hung over. I was more than stunned when he asked if I was going to "one of those meetings of yours" that day. When I said I was going at three o'clock, he asked if he could come with me. I was really taken aback. He claimed the silence at his place was killing him. My mother wouldn't believe he didn't remember anything about what happened at the wedding reception and refused to talk to him.

He drove over and picked me up at my mother-in-law's house but wouldn't come in. I didn't know what to say to him on the way to the meeting and he didn't know what to say to me. So it was a short, quiet ride. Benny was there with his good friend Charlie Alexunis who was about my father's age, fifty-five.

Charlie had boxed in the Golden Gloves, a once famous national pugilistic contest. He claimed he came in third as a middle weight. He had long eyebrows, one cauliflower ear and a square jaw. He also had a loud, gravelly voice but you could hear the kindness and understanding in it every time he spoke with a newcomer to the program. That's the voice my father heard that day.

We were early so we grabbed a cup of coffee and a doughnut and sat across from Benny and Charlie at a long metal folding table. As we began to talk, I'll never forget how Charlie reacted when my father tried to use his same old worn out bromide that you can't teach old dogs new tricks.

"You don't mind if I'm honest with you, do you Bill?" he smiled.

"No. Go right ahead," my dad replied not knowing what to expect.

"What you just said is a bunch of crap and you know it down deep. I'm probably your age or a little older and I've learned a lot of new tricks in this program that have kept me sober for more than fourteen years. I even consider the twelve steps we practice great new tricks."

"I only meant..." my father started to say. Charlie finished his sentence.

"That you don't know a damn thing about getting sober and staying sober. Neither did I at first. But isn't that why you came here with your son today... because he's found something that might work for you too?"

"Maybe. I guess so," my dad replied with a slight touch of reluctance.

"Then why don't you give it a try," his new friend said, his gravelly voice filled with encouragement. "We simply don't take one drink one day at a time. And we don't do it alone. We do it together, with each other. That's why we come to these meetings for support...and to learn more new tricks."

They both smiled.

"It's never too late, Bill," Charlie continued. "Hell, I hear you still have your wife and family. My wife threw me out fifteen years ago. I'm ashamed to admit it but I was a real nasty drunk. I used to push her around a lot. I've tried to make amends but she won't forget. Even after I got sober it took a few years before my kids would speak to me again."

"My wife should have thrown me out a long time ago too, Charlie," my father confessed. "Why she's put up with me I'll never know. How do you make up for all that stuff?"

"By staying sober and working the steps of our program," Benny answered. "That's how we become the kind of guys we've always wanted to be."

I could see my father was suddenly embarrassed by the tears welling up in his eyes. Charlie noticed and struck out his hand.

"Give us a try, Bill," he smiled again. "You won't be sorry. You've got nothing to lose and everything to gain."

My father shook Charlie's hand. Before the conversation could continue, the meeting started. I could see my dad listening to every word the speakers were sharing.

I couldn't get over how they really hit it off, my dad and Charlie Alexunis. For the next two weeks they were inseparable at meetings. My father had the shakes for days as he struggled to dry out but it was great watching him as he tried his best to latch onto the program.

I really can't explain how I felt seeing my father finally get sober after so many years and knowing what it would mean to my mother and our whole family. But then the joyful hopes that were building inside of everyone around him were suddenly dashed by this cunning, baffling and powerful disease.

From what I learned, my father kept trying to apologize to his pressman friend for the way he had acted at his daughter's wedding. But his friend refused to accept his apology. Then one day at work, the father of the bride really told my dad off in front of their whole crew saying he was nothing but a mean and stupid old drunk who everybody had been covering up for and supporting for years. My father couldn't handle the shame and ridicule.

My mother called to say he went on another bender, that he hadn't been to work for several days and was spending most of his time in his old haunt, Coo Coo's bar. I called Benny to ask what I should do. He told me to do nothing and then asked where my father was hanging out.

The next thing I knew, Benny and Charlie showed up at Coo Coo's and talked my dad into going into a dry-out place in Hoboken, New Jersey which was run by a sober Jesuit priest. He spent seven days there detoxing, came out, went back to meetings with Charlie who became his sponsor and never had another drink.

My mother finally found the husband she had always been praying for and I found the father I had always wanted. But just as my father and I were starting a brand new relationship in sobriety, my life took a completely unexpected turn. And since I was now learning how to accept life on life's terms, I didn't need a drink to think it over.

It was just after Labor Day in September of 1962 when a very successful public relations executive I had known named Dick Cheney called with an exciting and most unexpected proposition.

I remember the day because we were now living in the upstairs apartment in mama's house since the tenants had moved out. It consisted of a living room, small kitchen, one bedroom, a bathroom and a large finished attic room where the children slept. It was crowded but it was paradise compared to the basement. By the way, I forgot to mention we had five children by now. Our son, John, had been born on February 27, 1961, nine months after another one of our "let's start all over again" periods.

Also, I had recently gotten my old black Buick off the cement blocks in the driveway and had it refurbished, to some degree at least. Money was still very tight since I still had other old debts to pay off.

Dick Cheney was the Executive Vice President of Hill & Knowlton, the largest public relations organization in the country. I had gotten to know him when I worked for McGraw-Hill Publications and WOR radio. He was one of the few contacts I hadn't tried to professionally pan-handle so our relationship had always been cordial.

He had heard through some mutual friends that I was back in the public relations field working for Abe Schecter who he also knew and respected.

Dick had a very important client in Dallas, Texas called the Murchison Brothers who were very heavily invested in oil wells and related industries. They were now buying stock life insurance companies all around the country. Their largest was a firm in Nashville, Tennessee called Life & Casualty Insurance Company.

The problem was a growing number of stockholders of those companies were accusing the Murchisons of using the insurance investment portfolios to prop up some of their riskier ventures. As a result of those charges which began to appear in the financial media, the white hats of these proud Texans were beginning to turn black. Dick needed to hire a good public relations guy to get them cleaned up. Thinking I could be his man, he called to see if I had any interest in undertaking such a challenge.

When he told me the job would start at a salary of twenty-five thousand dollars a year with generous benefits, I sure did have a lot of interest. In fact, I almost dropped the phone. It was more than twice what I was presently making. The hitch was, however, that I would have to move to Nashville and work out of an office at The Life & Casualty Insurance Company which was the heart of their growing insurance enterprise.

The city of Nashville, Tennessee was famous at that time for two things that were linked at the hip—country music and The Grand Ole Opry. While today the city's metropolitan area boasts a population of more than one and a half million people, it was less than three hundred thousand back in the fall of 1962.

It was originally a small settlement on the banks of the Cumberland River called Fort Nashborough until the railroad came through. With access to both river and rail transportation, the area became an ideal shipping port and grew very rapidly. It became a city known as Nashville in 1806 and was named the permanent capital of the state of Tennessee in 1843.

While the Civil War set the prosperous southern metropolis back on its heels economically for a short period of time, its solid manufacturing base and financial stability quickly re-fueled its upward momentum. When it became the home of country music and a major music recording center, that added significantly to Nashville's attraction and growth.

I knew none of these things when Dick Cheney first called. In fact, I don't remember if I had ever heard of Nashville, Tennessee before and if I did, it was probably from my history or geography studies. Bernadette didn't know anything about it either when I filled her in on Cheney's proposal.

She just stood there with a frightened look on her face. Why not? It should have been no surprise since I was still so self-centered I wanted everything to go my way. Look at me, my ego said. I'm on my way back. Already everybody wants a piece of me. It takes time to get rid of character defects like that. Sometimes they can only be whittled down a little bit at a time. But I was working on it.

That's why I knew there was no reason to expect my wife to be the least bit excited about leaving the safety of her mother's house. Why should she put her trust and that of our children into the hands of a drunk who had been sober less than seven months?

As much as I wanted a quick fix to our financial situation, there was no way I would force my wife to move that far from her family and friends ever again. I did it once before when we made that disastrous move to Deer Park, Long Island. And that was only a few hours drive, not nine hundred and thirty miles away. I was sober now and wanted to keep our improving marriage and relationship together.

Without my knowing it, however, Bernadette sat down and discussed it with her mother. As I said before, I had come to admire my mother-in-law for her great insight and spiritual perception. I believe it came from her absolute faith in God and her trust that He would always protect those who asked for His protection. And by now I had come to appreciate all the prayers she had said for me. My wife told me what her mother had said when they spoke:

"A wife's responsibility is to help and support her husband and be by his side wherever he has to go. Your husband is well now so if he has to take a job out of town to do better for his family, then you should go with him. You must trust that God will take care of both of you and the children."

Still, it took a strong woman to face her fears and walk through them.

My sponsor Benny told me when I came back to the program that I shouldn't make any major decisions during the first year of my sobriety. This sure was a major decision and I wasn't sober a year yet. After I explained the Nashville situation to him, he said:

"You've come a long way in a short time. Maybe your Higher Power thinks you're ready to go even further. Since the company wants to fly you down to meet with all the top executives, here's what I suggest.

"Take Bernadette with you and stay over a day or two. Tell them you want to look around and see what Nashville's like. They'll understand. Then see what kind of twelve step program they have there. If it's a good one, then I'd consider taking the job."

So Bernadette and I went to Nashville together. I discovered that no one at Life & Casualty or in the Murchison organization had checked my background. They took Dick Cheney's word that I was the best man for the job and rubber-stamped my hiring. To this day I wonder what would have happened if they knew they were hiring a recovered alcoholic who had screwed up every opportunity he had been given in the past.

The company's president, Guilford Dudley, Jr., didn't find out until I had already started turning the Murchison Brothers' black hats back into white ones. However, out of growing concern that someone at the company might see me going into a twelve step meeting, I decided to tell him myself. He said he knew some very successful people who had recovered from the disease of alcoholism and simply wished me the very best. The matter never became a big deal and we became very good friends.

The day after my company interviews were over, Bernadette and I found a large open twelve step meeting in downtown Nashville. We were warmly greeted by a group of sober men and women and their spouses. We loved everyone we met there and everything we saw during our whirlwind trip. We were so high emotionally by the time we headed for home that we didn't need an airplane to fly us back.

Abe Schecter was the last one I spoke to about my decision. He said he regretted I had to leave, but there was no way he could match what I was offered. We both understood. We also understood that this was not the end of a wonderful relationship, that if either of us could help the other, we'd be there to do it. And that did happen on several occasions.

Since the Murchison Brothers were under growing stockholder pressure, I agreed to start my new job in Nashville the first week of October. I stayed at a quaint, five-story hotel called The Noel in a large, clean room only a block and a half from the Life & Casualty building on Union Street and Fourth Avenue in downtown Nashville.

My plan was to return home a week or so before Christmas, celebrate the holidays with our families and then pack up and drive to Tennessee with Bernadette and the kids. She suggested we rent a small house there until we could afford to buy one. She was still concerned about my tendency to spend money we didn't have and get into more debt.

However, when I mentioned the idea of a small rental house to Alfred G. Brown, a prominent Nashville real estate executive who was suggested to me by the president of my company, he smiled politely and said:

"That's out of the questions. As Vice President of Public Relations, you have a very important position at Life & Casualty. You must have a very nice home in one of our upscale communities since you'll probably be entertaining the who's who in Nashville as well as special friends and business associates."

So Mr. Brown, who was a handsome, exquisitely-dressed man in his early forties with a pleasant southern accent, started showing me some very fashionable homes in some very fashionable areas. But the more he showed me, the more I began to feel like a fraud and imposter. Also, by now I had renewed, at least to some degree, my faith and trust in the basic integrity of people. That's why I decided to take this fine gentleman into my confidence.

"Pull over, Al," I said one afternoon as we were headed for still more fashionable homes for sale. "We need to talk.

"Please keep this between you and me but I can't afford to buy any of these wonderful homes you're showing me. I've had some serious setbacks, so you might say my new job here is like my starting over. That's why I don't want to waste your time."

Either Alfred G. Brown appreciated my honesty or he liked a good challenge for after a brief moment he looked at me and smiled again.

"You still can't settle for a small rental house in some so-so neighborhood. Let's not be too hasty because I think we can work this out."

I soon discovered why this real estate mogul was so successful. He could put together ingenious financial deals and pull a rabbit out of a hat at the same time. He managed to get me a second mortgage to put down as a deposit on a first mortgage and arranged with Life & Casualty to cough up more than a few bucks for moving expenses and incidentals.

Bernadette and I wound up moving into a lovely, brand new, four-bedroom red brick ranch house sitting on top of a pastoral hill in the attractive, upscale community of West Meade, twenty minutes from my office. My wife was both shocked and frightened when she first saw the place until I explained why and how we could comfortably afford it. After all, back then twenty-five thousand dollars a year went a long way even when you were paying off past debts.

So two days after Christmas, we all crammed into my old Buick and headed south. The car's hood wouldn't close so I tied it down with a piece of rope. Our few possessions together with some furniture my mom and dad and Bernadette's mother chipped in had been sent on ahead in a small rented truck. Bernadette had forgotten a pole lamp so she stuck that in the back of the car between two of our children.

This really was starting over again and it was wonderful and exciting. Bernadette loved our neighbors in West Meade and our new pastor, Father Joe of St. Henry's Catholic Church which was only ten minutes from the house. I went to twelve step meetings almost every night and before long had good friends all over town. And I enjoyed my job immensely. It was a real challenge but filled with professional satisfaction since I was now part of the solution instead of being part of the problem.

However, shortly after arriving in Nashville, I began to worry about the matter of not filing an income tax report for eight years. Out of both fear and shame, this was something I had managed to keep secret from my wife and also from Benny, my sponsor. But now, since I was trying to get my life straightened out, this was something I knew I had to face before the Feds came down on me. Still I let it drag on until I began having trouble sleeping.

Bernadette already had her hands full getting us all settled so I decided not to tell her until I could figure out how to handle the situation. I was embarrassed to call Benny but I did. After reminding me about facing the truth in all my affairs, he suggested I first turn the matter over to my Higher Power and then find a good accountant or someone who knew something about taxes. I followed his advice.

I had met a businessman named George Goodall in my twelve step group. George, who became a very close friend over the years, was a bachelor in his late fifties. He was thin, medium height, always wore a bowtie and had thick white hair that made him look like a prominent U.S. Senator. He owned an auto insurance agency so I figured he would know something about taxes.

Over a cup of coffee I told George the whole story.

"So what else is new," he smiled. "It took me more than five years to pay off all my debts after I got sober, including the IRS. They're a bunch of scoundrels."

"Do you have any suggestions for me, George?" I asked, almost pleading.

"I sure do so stop worrying," he replied, calming most of my fears. "I have a friend in the program who I think can solve all your problems."

He was absolutely right. George's friend was a man named John Whitney who just happened to be the head of The Internal Revenue Service office in Nashville. You can't make those things up and nobody can tell me this was simply another mere coincidence. It got even better.

A few weeks after I had given him what little tax information I had, he called me into his office to discuss the results of his investigation into my case. With a big grin on his face, John explained that while I hadn't filed my tax reports, the IRS had been deducting taxes from every pay check I had ever received.

"After penalties and interest for not filing your tax reports," the Nashville IRS chief said, "the Federal Government owes you sixteen hundred and eighty dollars.

"Sometimes it pays off to face the truth," John added.

Bernadette was delighted to hear the news but made me promise once again to stop hiding things from her no matter what they were or how bad. Then, believe it or not, we had another baby a few months later, our sixth child and our fourth son, Robert. He was born on September 25,

1963. It put an even greater burden on my wife. That's when we reached out to her mother to come down and spend a little time with us. Mama loved caring for little babies. After all, she raised twelve of them. She was overjoyed and said yes immediately.

By this time, my mother-in-law had become an important spiritual source in my life. She literally practiced what she preached. Here was a woman I once despised because I considered her praying for me to be an embarrassment. Now this same woman had become someone I truly admired and loved. And I knew she had come to care for me a great deal too.

I flew to New York to accompany her back to Nashville. It was her first flight. I'll never forget sitting next to her as the plane taxied down the runway getting ready to take off. She was a bit nervous and was praying her rosary. I remember leaning over to her and saying:

"I hope you're praying for me, mom, because if this plane goes down, you're going up. I'm probably going the other way."

She squeezed my hand and smiled: "Not anymore."

Seeing the happiness on my wife's face when her mother walked in meant more to me than anything I could possibly have imagined. It was another step on the road to making amends for the past. It was another unearned blessing from a loving God.

I was sitting in our den one night doing some writing. Mama had just tucked everyone into bed including Bernadette and the baby. She now had her hands filled with The New Testament, her holy books, her prayer cards and her Rosaries and was heading for the dining room to do some praying just as she always did at home. She noticed me in the den, came in and sat beside me on the couch.

I believe I mentioned that mama was a rather small woman, not quite five feet tall with pretty gray hair and sparkling dark eyes. She made sure she wasn't interrupting me, then slowly opened her New Testament and rubbed her hand across the page. Her words will never leave me.

"All my life I've been reading this New Testament which is about all the miracles that Jesus performed. Then I read this book, about the lives of the Saints, and hear again about all the miracles that they performed in the name of Jesus.

"After reading all this, I've often wondered what it would be like to see a real miracle."

Then mama reached up, put her hand on my shoulder, looked into my face and said almost in a whisper:

"And now I have."

CHAPTER THIRTEEN

Hope and Love Spring Eternal

Everyone in America knew exactly where they were at 12:30 p.m. on November 22, 1963 when President John F. Kennedy was shot by Lee Harvey Oswald while riding in a motorcade in Dallas, Texas. It was that big of a shock.

I was at old Idlewild International Airport in New York City, now JFK. I was ready to board a plane for Nashville after holding a series of meetings with stockholders of the insurance company I was now representing. I had also managed to spend some time during my trip with my mom and dad and my mother-in-law.

Shortly after we took off and broke through a thick layer of white clouds, the pilot came on the intercom to announce that President Kennedy had passed away. I could see and hear many people around me crying.

Despite the sadness of his death, people continued to celebrate the joy of his life and what he gave to us all. Most of us will never forget those immortal words he spoke on the day of his inauguration on January 20, 1961:

"Ask not what your country can do for you. Ask what you can do for your country."

Perhaps the reason I identified so strongly with those remarks was because I was now trying to live by a similar philosophy in my twelve step program. It essentially said:

"Ask not what you can do for yourself. Ask instead what you can do for others."

I applied this principle first to my family. Living a stable and sober life for the very first time as an adult gave me the opportunity to be a real husband and a real father. That meant coming home for dinner every night; bringing home flowers and candy out of love instead of manipulation; helping our older children with their homework, reading bedtime stories to the younger ones and taking them all to interesting places and on fun vacations.

As the years passed it meant teaching my boys how to play baseball, football and basketball and cheering them on at their wrestling matches; managing their Little League teams; attending father-daughter dinners at school; driving my girls to their volley ball games and debate competitions and even coaching my wife's softball team.

I kept two appointment books—one for business appointments and the other for family commitments which I rarely missed. While there was no way all of this could make up to Bernadette and the children for all the hurt I caused, my attempt at trying to make amends strangely enough brought a great deal of joy into my own life..

My father had also adopted the same mindset and was showing it in almost everything he did, particularly in his relationships with his family as well as with his fellow alcoholics.

Since he was working steadily now and not blowing his salary on booze, he and mom were very generous with us and their grandchildren whenever they would come down to Tennessee for a visit. And we kept giving them ample reasons to visit—three more grandchildren during the five and a half years we lived in Nashville, Robert, Walter and Daniel. That made eight in all.

Dad enjoyed coming to meetings with me and getting to know those southern alcoholics I hung around with. He would remark that they spoke funny but said the right things. Each visit brought us closer. And my mom would frequently take me aside to tell me how much my father had changed and how well they were getting along together despite his going to meetings almost every night.

Bernadette and my mother also developed a much better relationship during those years in Tennessee which went by much too fast. And their improved relationship carried over when I was given my next great business opportunity in Shaker Heights, Ohio. It was the next place I was given another chance to advance my career. And while this opportunity had a very prosperous upside, it also had a very emotional downside.

Neither Bernadette nor I wanted to leave Nashville since we had developed such a fondness for the community and the wonderful way of life we were enjoying. But as I looked at it, we now had eight children that had to be fed, clothed and educated. The financial package I was being offered in Ohio would assure a comfortable future for all of us. Between salary, bonuses and stock options, I would be making more than eighty thousand dollars a year. In 1966, that was a whole lot of money. It still is.

My wife was much more reluctant to leave than I was. She kept saying that money wasn't everything and I knew she was right. Peace and happiness meant so much more. But then I asked, why couldn't we also find that in Shaker Heights, Ohio.

So once again my wife talked things over with her mother and basically received the same answer. Mama said wives go with their husbands wherever they have to go. While I didn't have to go, I really thought it was best.

I think between her mother's advice and the fact that Shaker Heights would be closer to New York City and her mother's home helped ease the decision and make it just a little less difficult for Bernadette to make the move. Also my wife did love the large, six-bedroom house with its rolling green lawns we were able to buy in that upscale Cleveland suburb.

I also discussed my new offer with both Benny and my dad. They suggested I pray about it. So I asked my Higher Power to remove greed, pride and ego from my decision and let me know what His will was for me. I hate to sound like a Holy Roller, but when I was doing things my way, it cost me jobs and two dollar rooms at flea bag hotels.

It was the fall of 1966 when I joined a relatively small, one hundred and twenty million dollar public company called ATO as its Communications Director. ATO was in the commercial fire sprinkler and fire protection business and was headed by a chief executive who had very ambitious plans. Twenty-four months later we had purchased eighteen other companies for stock and had become the fastest growing conglomerate in the country, approaching a billion dollars in sales.

My primary responsibility was to plan and coordinate all public relations, advertising and shareholder activities each time we bought another business. I was traveling so much, I rarely got my rear end out of one our private jets

With the company growing at such a rapid pace, my task would have been near impossible were it not for a terrific public relations guy I brought on board named John Donnelly. He became more than my right arm. John took over for me when I left ATO but jumped ship himself a few years later to take on a spokesman role for the NASA. We remained close friends until the day he passed away.

Fortunately during my travels I was able to make twelve step meetings in various cities around the country which proved to be quite interesting as well as extremely helpful to my sanity. I still maintain contact with a number of the sober people I met during those jaunts.

But Bernadette hated Ohio. She missed the polite southern hospitality she had gotten used to along with the slow pace of things. She said St. Dominic's Catholic Church and school in nearby Cleveland Heights couldn't compare to Father Joe and St. Henry's in Nashville.

Since I was away so often, the biggest thing that bothered Bernadette was not having a husband coming home every night for dinner or a father spending time with the children. It brought back too many bad memories. The job began to unravel our family life. One of the few highlights that year was my dad playing Santa Claus for the kids when he and my mother came to visit that Christmas.

After two years, the stress and tension of the job and the boorish, egotistical behavior of the company's chief executive started me looking elsewhere. An executive recruiter asked if I'd be interested in the position of Vice President of Public Relations for Dow Chemical Company. It would be another "white hat-black hat" situation since Dow was making all the napalm for the fire bombs being dropped over North Vietnam and being excoriated for it in the media as well as in marches on the nation's capital by anti-Vietnam War groups.

One of the executives on my company's management team whom I was close to suspected I was planning to leave. He was a great guy named Jim Gilligan who, believe it or not, was ATO's chief financial officer. He didn't have any love for our chief executive either. I remember he said to me over lunch one day:

"Why the hell would you think about going to Dow Chemical. They have all kinds of problems. And who says they don't have a narcissistic president there too.

"With all your experience you should be thinking about starting your own public relations firm. If you need any capital, hell I'll back you. I'm sure our pals Dale Coenen and Jack Doerge will too. And I bet George Herzog over at Cleveland Trust will also throw in with us. He sure likes the job you've done with our company stock."

So I followed Jim's advice and put together a business plan. He and the three investors he spoke to put up a total of three hundred thousand dollars which enabled me to launch my own communications enterprise in New York City.

Bernadette nearly hugged me to death when I discussed it with her. Now she could really be close to her mother and share all of our good fortune with her. But she never had the chance. Four months before we were ready to make the move to New York, mama passed away. She was 76. Bernadette cried for days.

My mother-in-law had been ill for some time but seemed to be regaining strength whenever we would visit her. She had been staying with her oldest daughter, Georgianna, who had been taking care of her. We visited mama with all the children that Christmas. She passed away on our flight back to Cleveland.

Being there at her crowded wake trying to consol her heart-broken daughter filled me with both warm and painful memories. But the one thing I couldn't get out of my mind was that night in Nashville when we sat together in the den and how she had looked at me and called me one of God's miracles.

I knew by then what mama meant. She had witnessed first hand a drunken, irrational man who had abused her daughter and grandchildren by his words and his actions until he finally found a spiritual program that had arrested his disease—a twelve step program that turned him into someone who was trying to practice unconditional love. To her, I had been resurrected and was seeking to live the kind of life she had always lived herself.

As I've said, my mother-in-law was able to see what had happened long before I could. Perhaps that's why it occurred to me as I watched my father progress in his recovery, that if I were a 'miracle' according to mama, he certainly was also.

According to Webster's Collegiate Dictionary, the word Miracle means:

"An extraordinary event manifesting a supernatural work of God and an extremely outstanding or unusual event, thing or accomplishment."

My father certainly met that definition. His whole life was changing right before my eyes. Not only was my mother enjoying the fruits of his sobriety, so were my sisters and my brother, Bobby.

My younger brother was going on seventeen and planning to follow the same path I took at a slightly younger age. He had decided to become a priest which naturally delighted my mother. But this time I think my father was very joyful too. However, when it came to my mother, I had a sense she was a little less exuberant because of her past experience with me.

Bobby said it was during his junior year of Catholic high school when the Montfort Missionary Order gave a retreat on vocations. It stirred his spiritual feelings and made him decide to join their Order. He was told to pray every day for the next year to find assurance that he was making the right decision. He was also told to pray for his family members that they may overcome any problems they might have.

My kid brother believed it was during his senior year of high school that his prayers and those of some Montfort Missionaries he knew helped my father finally find sobriety in a twelve step program. He couldn't believe the drastic change that took place. And he couldn't stop telling me all about it. He wasn't aware that I had seen it all from the front lines.

"Dad went to meetings every night," my brother told me. "In the beginning mom complained because he was still leaving home right after dinner, but at least he was coming back sober. It took her awhile to try and understand it and get used to it. Now that she's finally accepted it, their life together is the best it's ever been.

"I would see dad get down on his knees at his bedside every morning and every night to pray. One day I asked him what he prayed for. He said he prayed for his family and also that God would keep him sober one more day. He also told me he thanked God every morning for the gift of life and what he did with his life during each day was his gift back to God.

"And he was always helping people, driving them to meetings, to hospitals, even to the unemployment office to help them find a job.

"One day when we were alone in the living room he told me how sorry he was for not being a good father when we were all growing up. He prayed constantly that one day he could earn back the love of his family and be the father he always meant to be.

"It's amazing what a spiritual person he's become and I really admire him for it. I will never forget the day he and mom drove me to the seminary out in Bay Shore, Long Island. After we dropped off my belongings at the dormitory, we walked around the seminary grounds and made a visit to the chapel. When we said goodbye with hugs and kisses, it was the first time I had ever seen dad cry. I think it was also the first time he ever hugged me and kissed me like that."

Bobby remembered a real funny story that happened around that time which, though an innocent slip of the tongue, did embarrass my mother for a while.

To support his decision to become a priest, my parents joined an organization called The Montfort Auxiliary which helped raise money for both the missions and the seminary. Being new members at their first meeting, the head of the group asked my mom and dad to introduce themselves. As background, I must mention that at closed twelve step meetings, each member introduces himself or herself as "My name is blank and I am an alcoholic." It became almost second nature to do so.

After my mother politely introduced herself as Mrs. Ruth Borchert, the mother of new seminarian Robert Borchert, my dad stood up and said loudly and clearly, "My name is Bill Borchert and I am an alcoholic." His slip of the tongue naturally engendered some laughter. My mom was mortified. But no real damage was done. In fact, my parents were asked to serve as President and Vice President of the auxiliary the following year and remained on the board for the next six years.

In the meantime, the public relations company I started in the summer of 1968 grew quite rapidly. My four financial backers had strong connections with a number of large public companies. With those connections and a good public relations pitch, many of them became my clients.

Since my right arm at ATO, John Donnelly, wasn't available, I brought in another close friend Walter Barrett who I met years before in the seminary to help me run the firm. He had been doing public relations work and raising money for the Catholic Charities organization and I knew he was a stickler for details. Since I was usually busy writing press releases, brochures and annual reports or out consulting with new clients, I needed someone inside I could rely on to hold things together. Walter was as solid as they come.

Bernadette soon found us a lovely tri-level home on a nice piece of property in a town called Rye, New York in Westchester County. It was a quiet, rather wealthy community located about thirty miles north of the city, easily accessible to Manhattan by train. Despite its whisky-related name, you rarely saw a Rye drinker staggering down its streets. But that didn't mean there weren't a number of recovered drunks meeting regularly in church basements around town.

There was also a small social club that hosted a twelve step meeting twice a week. It was considered the most fashionable group in the area. Some of the members were so wealthy they seemed to be completely out touch with the principles of humility and service. They actually hired someone to serve coffee at the meetings, bake cakes and cookies and then clean up.

I remember how strange I felt the first few times I attended their discussion meetings. It wasn't just the fact that I was being served rather than serving that bothered me, it was also the topics they chose to discuss. They were mostly on feelings, pharmaceuticals and what kind of social events to avoid.

At the first group business session I attended, several members politely suggested I leave if I didn't like the way they conducted their meetings. Eventually a number of middle class drunks like me began showing up. That led to the hired help being eased out and the principle of service being reinstated. I remained a member there for almost twenty-five years.

In my business, I dealt with a lot of investment banking firms on Wall Street trying to get their financial analysts to say nice things about the public companies we represented. One day in the spring of 1970, I received a call from a gentleman named Larry Fox who headed a very active medium-size investment firm. We had become friends in a rather strange way. One of my client companies was bought out by a conglomerate he had helped finance. He told me he owed me one.

Over lunch Larry said he was putting together an exciting new enterprise that I might find of some interest.

"It's an independent motion picture production company that will not only make movies but manage and promote talent as well," he explained. "We're calling it Artists Entertainment Complex. We figure having stars under management contracts would give the company leverage to attract production financing."

"Sure makes sense to me, Larry," I said. "I'm a real movie buff. What would you like me to do, promote the company for you?"

"No," he smiled, toasting me with his dry martini. "I want you to be part of it. I've already brought in three other partners who have a lot of good connections and a lot of experience in managing and promoting talent as well as making movies.

"But we need someone who cannot only promote talent but also read film treatments and spec scripts and turn good story ideas into real great stories for the big screen. My guys have looked into your checkered past and found you used to be great doing that for newspapers, magazines and even radio. I'm sure you could do it for movies too."

His sweet talk was working. I was getting really interested in his proposal. I once dreamed about making movies and now I couldn't believe the opportunity was actually being offered to me.

"If you're interested," Larry continued, "your public relations firm could be merged into the new company for stock. Of course before you decide anything you'll want to meet with the other partners to see if the chemistry is right and all that stuff. But what do you think so far?"

I toasted him back with my coca cola. "I'm interested," I replied.

A few days later I met and decided to join forces with Marty Bregman, an insurance agent who wrote policies on stars like Elliott Gould, Barbara Streisand, Bette Midler and Al Pacino. That led him to giving them financial and career advice as any good talent manager would do.

Norman Weiss was a great talent agent who, among others, represented a hot new group from England called The Beetles during their first U.S concert tour. At their first American performance in St. Louis, Missouri, Norman told the press, "The Beetles drew more people in one day than Jesus Christ drew in three years of preaching." That statement made headlines but got Norman into a little hot water with a lot of Christians.

And then there was Roy Gerber, the biggest booking agent in Las Vegas whose main claim to fame was marrying the same woman three different times. Well, that's not exactly true. Roy also did know just about every big star who headlined in the casino showrooms throughout the popular gambling mecca.

We set up shop in midtown New York and produced our first movie in 1971. It was called *KANSAS CITY BOMBER* and starred the still lovely Raquel Welch as a Roller Derby queen. To be honest, watching the sexy Raquel skate around that roller derby rink in black, tight-fitting leather pants was almost like having a spiritual experience. So I instantly fell in love with the movie business.

Our next film which we made the following year put us on the map. It was a true story called *SERPICO* and starred Al Pacino as the biggest whistle-blower in the history of the New York City Police Department. Frank Serpico, an undercover cop, had been outspoken in his complaints about corruption among "the city's finest." That made him a pariah on the force and set a number of dirty cops out to get him. During a drug bust one December day in 1970, as he shouted for back-up, one of the patrolmen shot him in the face. No one called for an ambulance until they thought it was too late.

But Serpico pulled through. His testimony became the centerpiece for the famous Knapp Commission's investigation of dirty cops. It sparked the biggest shakeup in the history of the New York City Police Department. Still fearful of the death threats against him, the whistle-blower fled to Switzerland where he lived for the next twenty years. We tried to entice him back for the premier of the movie promising him armed guards, but he was still too fearful to come. The film turned out to be a smash hit.

We followed that up in 1975 with another big hit called *DOG DAY AFTERNOON* which also starred Al Pacino. This time he played a young homosexual bank robber trying to steal enough money from a Brooklyn bank to get his lover a sex-change operation. It wasn't quite my cup of tea but it was a helluva movie. The film, which also starred John Cazale and Charles Durning, was nominated for several Academy Awards and Golden Globe Awards. It was directed by one of the best in the business, Sidney Lumet. Writer James Pierson won an Academy Award for best screenplay.

As if being a partner in a film company producing big hits wasn't enough to swell my head, two other things happened around the same time that should have insured my becoming a certified ego-maniac.

First, Bernadette and I managed to buy a twenty-two room house on three and a half acres in one of the nicest sections of Rye. Second, because I was a partner in Artists Entertainment Complex that was producing successful movies, I was invited to join some very well known people who were recovered alcoholics to celebrate sobriety at a major public forum called Operation Understanding.

As for the large new house, we simply needed more room. We had our ninth child now, Angela Marie, who was born on August 3, 1970. With eight other children plus ourselves, we had run completely out of space in our tri-level home so Bernadette began looking around Rye. She found what some people would call a "white elephant", a place where a wealthy widow lady lived alone on the first floor and had closed off the top two floors. With ten bedrooms and nine bathrooms it suited us just fine. It required a lot of fixing up and Bernadette thoroughly enjoyed hiring home improvement contractors, painters and interior decorators to get it done.

As for Operation Understanding, I believe it was late November of 1974 when I received a call from my good friend Walter Murphy who was then the President of The National Council on Alcoholism. He was also a neighbor of mine in Rye.

The organization he headed had been started many years before by the first woman to recover in a twelve step program for alcoholics. Her name was Marty Mann. Walter had once been an agent and talent manager for actors like Robert Young and singers like Rosemary Clooney before he blew his own career on booze. But he had been sober now a number of years.

Like Marty Mann, Walter's major goal was to eliminate the stigma associated with addiction. He believed the shame people felt prevented them from seeking help. In addition, the general public had little understanding of the disease and looked down upon active alcoholics the way "the swells" did at Sammy's Bowery Follies. While he knew such a stigma couldn't be erased overnight, he was determined to at least start the ball rolling. He asked for my help and participation which I was delighted to give.

Walter's idea was to have the National Council host a ground-breaking event in Washington, D.C. in May of 1976 where many prominent Americans would stand up at a major press conference and tell the world they had recovered from the disease of alcoholism. He believed the courage and example of such people would help reduce the shame and denial that goes with the malady and open the door for others to come forward and get well. It turned out to be an enormously successful event.

On May 8 of 1976 my wife accompanied me to the nation's capital where we witnessed fifty-three well-known celebrities admit to the world they had recovered from a fatal disease called alcoholism.

Those who participated included people like Astronaut Buzz Aldrin; movie stars Dana Andrews, Dick Van Dyke and Mercedes McCambridge; television celebrities like Gary Moore, Jan Clayton and Tom Ewell; singers Guy Mitchell and Johnny Grant; baseball greats Ryne Duren of the Yankees and Don Newcombe of the Dodgers; politicians including Senator Harold Hughes and Congressman Wilbur Mills as well as a number of clergymen, physicians, attorneys and businessmen. I was included as a film producer but it was mainly because I knew and helped my friend Walter Murphy.

The weekend after we returned from Washington, my mother and father came for a visit. We had just gotten a large new trampoline which we put in the backyard. My folks enjoyed watching the children tumbling high up into the air, especially the older ones.

My mother got nervous watching, especially when my dad decided to give it a try. After a few jumps he started coughing rather heavily and had to stop. He was still smoking those Camel cigarettes and was developing a slight case of emphysema. Fortunately I had quit smoking my Lucky Strikes several years before when the U.S. Surgeon General announced the discovery of a connection between cigarette smoking and heart disease.

It would have been a lovely dinner that night except for my constant palaver about Bernadette and me rubbing shoulders with Buzz Aldrin, swapping jokes with Dick Van Dyke and having dining with Dana Andrews and his wife. Then I had to impress my parents with some talk about the new movies we were thinking of making.

In addition to the boring look on my father's face, I had a hunch Bernadette was also getting fed up with my conceited rantings. I think she was already concerned about my growing lavish lifestyle outside of the house like taking my friends to the fights, handing out cigars and eating in fancy restaurants where there was always plenty of booze. Perhaps all this was bringing back some painful memories from the past when I was "the big shot writer" who thought he should be treated special.

After dessert, the children went off to watch TV and my mother went into the kitchen to help Bernadette with the dishes. I made sure I told my dad that "the maid" was off that weekend. That was the last straw. My father knew all we had was a nice Italian lady in her sixties named Lena who came in a few days a week to help Bernadette with the kids and do some cleaning.

I noticed him staring at me with a deep frown on his face. Then he asked: "When did you hire a maid?"

He caught me off guard. Suddenly I remember being miffed that my father knew I was exaggerating. Actually I was sure he knew I was lying. We had no maid. I felt like I was ten years old again when lying had become part of my survival mechanism. But I wasn't ten and I had no reason to lie anymore.

"I meant Lena," I said, compounding the falsehood. "She was going to help Bernadette tonight, but…"

"You don't have to explain," my father said, interrupting me with an understanding smile. "I was only asking because…well, I wouldn't have been surprised. You already have so much in your life. You've been very successful. You've made so much out of all the opportunities you've been given. I'm really proud of you.

"That's why," he added after an uncomfortable pause, "that's why I don't understand why you have to exaggerate sometimes…especially with me, your father."

I turned my head away. I just sat there tapping my fingers on the table. That same old maniac in my brain suddenly opened up. Who the hell does he think he is my maniac said, preaching to you like that. You were the one who helped him get sober in the first place. Now he's so high and mighty. Here once again was my ego at war with the truth. I still hated being found out. Thank goodness before my growing anger could turn into a harsh resentment, I heard my father continue:

"I was just thinking about what Benny and Charlie always say, that they never saw a really grateful man pick up a drink. I sometimes realize I'm not always as grateful as I should be. I also think it's more difficult for us alcoholics to handle success than it is failure. Maybe that's because we're more used to failure.

"It's probably none of my business but you've got so much to lose. I'd hate to see you lose it by taking it all for granted. I love you, son, and I pray for you every day that you'll never forget where it all comes from, a loving God, not taking the first drink and being very active in the program."

We sat there in silence for another moment or two. I could tell my dad was getting uncomfortable, probably fearing he may have said something that upset me. He did, but then I suddenly became aware that he was simply acting in a way he hadn't in a long, long time. He was being my father. He was sitting there sharing his experiences and insight with me, something he hadn't been able to do when I was a child growing up with a father who was a drunk. But now, sitting here sober in my dining room, he was finally able to express his concern and his love. And for that I will be forever grateful.

That's when I simply looked at him, smiled and said: "Thanks Dad. You're absolutely right. Benny also tells me I have so much humility that I'm proud of it. Thanks for pulling my covers."

I don't think my dad and I were ever closer than we were that night.

Not only did I start becoming more active in the program, but my father and I began going out speaking together at various twelve step meetings in Queens and Westchester County. I looked forward to being with him. There's just no possible way to explain how it made me feel developing such a close and intimate relationship with a man who had been a stranger to me for so many years.

Sure we once drank together and bragged to everyone in Moochie's bar how important we were to the newspaper business. But that was drunk talk and surface stuff. This was far different. This was real. This again was hope and love springing eternal.

My father was retired now and living on his pension from the Pressman's Union supplemented by his Social Security. Bernadette and I were also very generous to my parents on their birthdays and various holidays. Being sober, my dad had been able to save enough money to get a mortgage and buy the two-story building where we had all grown up. The produce store had closed and there was a beauty parlor downstairs now that did quite well. The rent it paid helped my parents carry the mortgage. Finally my mom felt comfortable and secure.

Over the ensuing years, my wife and I were able to spend considerable time with my parents. We were also in a position to send them on trips to places like West Palm Beach, Florida, Paradise Island in the Bahamas and several extravagant casino hotels in Las Vegas. I mention this only because it was all part of healing past wounds and repairing family relationships. Whether necessary or not, it made us all feel better.

For example, every time my parents would return from a trip, they would tell Bernadette and me it was just like they had been on another second honeymoon. It was so satisfying to see how the last fifteen years of their marriage, starting with the day my father got sober, were the most wonderful fifteen years of their lives together. And they always said so, especially to Bernadette who had taken the brunt of many past upheavals.

I think it was in the summer of 1980 when my mother had surgery for intestinal cancer. She had to wear a colostomy bag for awhile and hated it. It was my father who changed it all the time and never complained. He just wanted her to get well and she did. A few months after her initial surgery, she had the colostomy reversed.

Then it was my father's turn. I believe it was Thanksgiving Day of 1981 when my sister, Marilyn, called to my attention that dad wasn't looking very well. He was losing weight and his emphysema was getting worse. My mother was also concerned because he was still sneaking off to have one of his Camel cigarettes when she wasn't watching. So I talked to him. What he said stunned me at first, but then I understood.

"Every day I ask God to take me before He takes your mother," he said. "There's no way I could live without her. So don't worry about me. Just promise that you will take care of mom when I'm gone."

The first week of January my father was diagnosed with inoperable liver cancer. He started taking chemotherapy treatments on an out-patient basis. I think it was the first or second of February when he called me at the office to say his doctor wanted to continue his treatments in the hospital. He asked if I could drive him and my mother since she was so upset he didn't want her taking the car. When I arrived at their place, my dad ushered me quietly into my old back bedroom which was now his office so that my mom couldn't hear us. He whispered quite calmly:

"Please don't tell your mother, but I don't think I'll be coming home from the hospital. This thing's really gotten to me. I guess all that drinking finally caught up with me. Just remember what I asked you, okay? Take care of your mother for me just in case."

My eyes filled with tears. He grabbed me gently by the shoulders.

"No, it's okay, Billy. Really it is. It's my time, and if God wants me, I'm ready to go." Then he hugged me and whispered again: "I love you, Billy. I always have. I've been a lousy father but you've always been a good son."

My sisters, my brother and I spent as much time comforting our mother at the hospital as we did our father. She cried so often she would have to take long rests in a nearby private room which they allowed us to use. By the fourth day, the doctor told us the treatments were no longer working. All they could do was keep him as comfortable as possible. Then he slipped into a coma.

At that point my mom refused to leave his bedside. She was sure he would wake up and she wanted to be there when he did. But the strain on her was too much. One evening she almost collapsed and we had to practically carry her to the private room so that she could sleep for awhile. The rest of us took turns watching over my dad.

It was around nine o'clock one evening when I relieved my sister Patty at my father's bedside. My mother was resting. I sat down next to the bed and took his hand into mine. He was struggling to breathe without life support. I also knew he was in a great deal of pain which was why they were giving him fairly strong doses of medication. The doctor had told us it was just a matter of time.

What I'm about to share was one of the most emotionally painful yet satisfying experiences of my life. It was truly a gift from my Higher Power.

I squeezed my father's hand. I remember saying:

"Dear God. Don't You think my father's already suffered enough? I know he's ready to be with You. He told me so. That's why I'd like to ask You to take him now. We'll all miss him terribly, especially my mother. But he'll always be with us in spirit."

Then I leaned in close and whispered in my father's ear:

"Dad. I know you can hear me. Why don't we say The Lord's Prayer together like we do at meetings. Then you can let go. I have a feeling God's right here waiting for you."

As we began to pray… "Our Father Who art in Heaven…" I was suddenly moved to see my dad turn toward me ever so slightly and his eyes slowly open just a wee bit. Then a small, barely perceptible smile appeared on his lips. Before we were halfway through the prayer, his eyes slowly closed once more, his head slumped down into his pillow and I heard him take his last gurgling breath. I could actually sense his spirit leave his body. I knew exactly where he was going.

I sat there for another moment or two with tears running down my cheeks. Then I wiped my face and walked back into that private room to tell my mother and my siblings that dad had just passed away.

After the funeral when I took my mother back to her house, she allowed me to go through my father's private papers. They were mostly notes he had written down from things he had heard at twelve step meetings and stories and prayers he had saved over the years that meant much to him. They were in two cigar boxes and a small leather case.

"Please take them," she said, trying to hold back the few tears she had left. "I know your father would want you to have them. You meant so much to him. He used to say he could never find the words to express how he really felt about you but hoped his actions would make up for it."

"As you always said, mom," I replied as I put my arm around her. "A good ending always makes up for a bad beginning."

"I never thought my prayers would be heard," she murmured. "I never thought I would have a sober husband. And now he's gone."

"No he's not, mom," I said. "Dad's not gone. He'll always be with us. Look, we're still talking about him and he's still listening."

So I took the two cigar boxes and small leather case home with me. What my dad had written on scraps of paper has enabled me to keep things simple in my life most of the time. His words have often helped me understand what it means to be happy, joyous and free. That's why I'd like to share some of the simple yet insightful thoughts and concepts my father lived by:

"The most exciting thing in the world for me is to see another human life change for the better right before my eyes."

"The most lovable quality anyone can possess is tolerance. It is the generosity that concedes to others the right to their own opinions and their own peculiarities. It is the bigness that enables us to let others be happy in their own way and not our way. Tolerance of others' beliefs and opinions is an important ingredient for everyone to have."

"I try to love my fellow man because we are all children of God. I try to put this kind of love into action by no severe judging of anyone, no resentments, no malicious gossip, and no destructive criticism. To me this love means patience, understanding, compassion and helpfulness."

"All that God asks of me is simply to act justly, to love tenderly and to walk humbly with Him."

"Consider how hard it is to change yourself and you'll understand what little chance you have trying to change others."

"Show me the way not to fortune and fame, not how to win laurels or praise for my name; but show me the way to spread The Great Story that "Thine is the Kingdom and Power and Glory;" this is my prayer that I faithfully say, to help me to meet the new dawning day; for I never could meet life's daily demands unless I was sure He was holding my hand; and priceless indeed would be my reward to know that you shared my prayer to the Lord."

"A tiny smile on your face cheers your heart, keeps you in good humor, preserves peace of mind, promotes good health, beautifies your countenance, produces kindly thoughts and inspires kindly deeds."

"I pray that I never become so wise that I can't listen to what others have to say nor so dumb that I believe everything that I'm told."

"Habits are to the soul what veins and arteries are to the body."

"Youth is not a time of life. It is the attitude of the mind. It is not a matter of ripe cheeks, red lips and supple knees. It is a temper of the will, a quality of the imagination, a vigor of the emotions. Youth means a temperamental predominance of courage over timidity, of the appetite for adventure and the love of ease. This often exists in a man of fifty more than in a boy of twenty. Nobody grows old by living a number of years. People grow old by deserting their ideals."

"Lord, please give me the peace to listen to Your voice within me rather than to the confusion around me."

"Laughter is the song of Angels, the voice of joy, the speech of the happy and the window into my soul."

"Since there is no charge for human kindness, why not spend one day being kind to everyone you meet. Put away all ill feelings you may have for some other day. It is absolutely free of charge to be good so why not try it just for today."

A few days after my father's funeral, my younger brother and I had lunch. Naturally we reminisced about our lives growing up with him, comparing the past with the present. He told me the day he left the Montfort Missionary Order after realizing, as I once had, that he wasn't cut out to be a priest, the only thing my father said to him was: "Many are called but few are chosen." He said mom was disappointed again but this time she got over it rather quickly.

"Dad was a completely different person sober," Bobby said, recalling the large crowds at his wake. "He came to love everyone, especially other alcoholics who needed his help. He turned into a gentle, spiritual man who always gave of himself whenever he could. Certainly he was far from being canonized a saint but I was glad to witness so many of the good things he did."

The rather dramatic change that had taken place in my father's life as a result of his sobriety, his relationship with his Higher Power and his dedication to helping others had a profound effect on his whole family. For example, Marilyn became closer to him than ever. By then my sister had a lovely daughter and three bright and successful sons.

Dad and her husband, Eddie, frequently went fishing together and had family cookouts at their comfortable home on Long Island, New York. Tragically Eddie died of a sudden heart attack while he and my sister were vacationing in Bermuda. Marilyn loved her husband so much that she never remarried. Instead she also moved to South Carolina and surrounded herself with caring and interesting friends.

My younger sister Patty's husband, Herbie, also died of a heart attack while hunting deer in New York's Catskill Mountains with fellows from his hunting club. He left Patty with a young son and daughter. Marilyn, Bobby and I spent a lot of time with my sister consoling her during this terrible time just as my father would have done had he still been with us.

Then tragedy struck again. My sister Patty developed Alzheimer's disease at a relatively young age. As it grew worse, she had to be confined to a nursing home.

Bobby, who I still call my kid brother, left the seminary and, believe it or not, married an attractive girl named Leslie who had been one of my secretaries when I was in the public relations business. They have a charming young daughter and four very athletic sons.

My younger brother has his own consulting business which deals primarily with hospitals and related enterprises helping them find ways to reduce their healthcare costs. His oldest son and his wife work with him.

They say when two people are deeply in love like my mom and dad, when one dies the other follows soon after. That proved to be true with my parents.

My mother's cancer returned a year after my dad passed away. This time it was in her ovaries and the disease spread quite quickly. As I've said, my mom was a strong woman who also had a deep faith in God. Never once did I hear her moan or groan or express any self-pity as I was apt to do when I'd get a tiny splinter in my finger.

Despite the serious differences they once had, Bernadette began spending a great deal of time caring for my mother. She would read her books, have long talks, clean the house and cook what little she was able to eat. I always knew I had married someone very special, but there's no way to explain how much I admired my wife for putting another part of her painful past behind her.

I was planning a business trip to Europe and taking Bernadette with me. My mother's spirits were buoyed when I told her we would be spending a few days in Lourdes, France. We promised to bring home some sacred holy water from the famous grotto where the Blessed Mother was said to have appeared eighteen times to a peasant girl named Bernadette Soubirous. The holy water had been credited with many miraculous cures.

The apparitions were said to have taken place between February 11 and July 16, 1858 at a cave or grotto near a garbage-filled hillside just outside the small French town of Lourdes located in the foothills of the Pyrenees Mountains.

At first the young peasant girl was only able to describe the vision she saw as "the beautiful lady." Sometime later the apparition told Bernadette she was "The Immaculate Conception." There was considerable skepticism in the Catholic Hierarchy at first that such a poorly educated child could be chosen to witness the appearance of Mary, the Mother of Jesus Christ, the Son of God in a filthy grotto.

However, as more and more miracles began to flow from a stream Bernadette had created from a hole "the beautiful lady" had told her to dig in the ground, the Holy See in Rome changed its mind. A Vatican group appointed to investigate the startling events finally declared the young girl's visions "worthy of belief."

Bernadette Soubirous was declared a Saint by Pope Pius XI on December 8, 1933. Lourdes went on to become a major site of Roman Catholic pilgrimage and of miraculous healing with thousands of verified cures over the years. More than five million people visit annually, many hoping for a miracle, some to reclaim their spiritual lives and others simply out of curiosity.

My wife had been eagerly looking forward to our trip, particularly since she was named after St. Bernadette. It was strange that we initially had two entirely different reactions to our visit.

As we stood on a high parapet looking out over more than a thousand sick and disabled people lying on pallets and gurneys in front of the enormous shrine, I could tell that Bernadette was shocked by what she saw. To be honest, I was very surprised by her reaction. She turned to me with tears in her eyes.

"How could God let this happen?" she asked with a look of confusion and what I might call indignation on her face. "If God is so loving and caring, how can He allow so much sickness in the world? Look at all these poor people. I don't understand it."

As I said, I was stunned at first by her reaction. I had only experienced Bernadette's great faith in God before this. What she was expressing now was completely different from what I was feeling as I witnessed the same scene.

"What I see is an incredible display of faith and hope," I replied, trying not to sound too critical of her remarks. "I see hundreds of people here who believe that God can cure them if that is His plan or help them in some other way, like giving them the strength to accept His will."

"But why all this suffering," my wife kept asking. "It doesn't seem fair."

I was about to say more when I realized we were on the verge of arguing over something neither of us really understood...God's plan for all of us. So instead, we accepted our different feelings and spent the rest of the day touring the beautiful shrine.

We spent time at the actual grotto where the Blessed Mother appeared, lighting candles, bathing in a special bath of holy water and filling small bottles with water from the shrine to take home to my mother. Because she still couldn't shake her initial reaction, the day turned into a very emotional one for my wife. By late afternoon she was so tired she took a nap on the sprawling lawn near the large Basillica dedicated to St. Bernadette that had been built on a nearby hill.

That evening my wife felt a little better so she decided to join hundreds of visitors in a candle light procession from the Basillica to the grotto during which people prayed and sang hymns in six different languages. I decided to cross a small brook nearby so I could lie on the grass, watch the procession and admire the grotto. Two marvelous things happened that evening.

First, Bernadette was touched by the great faith of those around her. She recognized some of the hymns being sung were from her childhood. She said she could almost feel the presence of St. Bernadette. All those disturbing, angry feelings she had that morning left her and she felt nothing but joy and peace in her heart.

As for me, my father paid me a visit. That's right. As I lay there on the grass listening to the processional hymns and feeling more grateful than I had ever felt before, there he was. I know it sounds crazy, especially to anyone still struggling with the God thing or any kind of belief in the great beyond. But he was there alright. And he looked great, wearing his favorite blue suit.

There was no conversation, only an exchange of thought and feeling. He wanted to let me know he loved me and that everything was okay, both with him and with me. He gave me a sense that my mother would be with him soon and appreciated that Bernadette and I as well as Marilyn, Patty and Bobby were taking good care of her in the meantime. And then he was gone.

Mom was delighted when we brought her the holy water from Lourdes. She had refused to go back to the hospital for more treatments and was bedridden now at home. She had lost more than fifty pounds and was sickly pale. But she kept up a great front. She had us sprinkle the holy water all over her bedroom and on herself as well. Whether she believed or even hoped it would help, she never let on. I believe it helped her to peacefully accept the inevitable.

As things got worse, we brought in nursing care for my mother around the clock. She was rarely without other company as well. Aunt Helen would come for a few hours every single day. I would visit as often as I could. I will never forget the last time I saw her. Marilyn had been there and told mom I was on my way. My sister had something important to do so she had to leave before I arrived.

As I entered the kitchen, I heard my mother calling to me from her bedroom: "Billy! Billy! Hurry! Your father's here!"

She was so excited when I entered. Her eyes were agape and she had this huge smile on her now shrunken face. Then all of a sudden it turned into an expression of disappointment.

"If only you had come quicker," she said. "I told daddy you were coming. I don't know why he couldn't wait. We had such a wonderful talk."

That wasn't the first time my mother said she had seen my father. But it was her last. My mom passed away a few days later, on April 17, 1984.

The crowd wasn't quite as large at my mother's wake as it was at my father's. But it was very well attended. My brother helped me make all the funeral arrangements. I don't recall if it was a sunny day or a cloudy one when we laid her to rest next to my father in Evergreen Cemetery in Brooklyn. What I do remember quite vividly was what happened a short time later.

After all the mourners left the luncheon we hosted, I drove back to my parents' place. I wanted to look around one last time. Bernadette understood so she drove home with the children. I remember my siblings and I had agreed to meet the following weekend to make a list of mom and dad's possessions and assets and divide them appropriately. But this day I wanted to be there alone. Maybe I still had a few ghosts to exorcize.

As I strolled through the empty apartment which seemed so small to me now, memory after memory after memory came swirling through my head. I could almost hear the arguments and the yelling, the plates being thrown against the wall, my father tumbling down the hall stairs, my mother crying at the kitchen table as my dad headed for Monahan's saloon. Then it got quiet. I walked slowing into the living room.

As I glanced toward the parlor windows, I could still picture my mother hanging out, shouting at my sister Marilyn and her date for missing her curfew. I could still see poor, polite Bill Barry running for his life while mom screamed at my sister for coming home in his car. I started to chuckle as I walked back into the kitchen.

It was easy to recall the white kitchen walls blackened by the smoke I created when I set fire to the house. I think I felt a slight streak of fear shoot up my spine when I recalled that red-faced fire marshal staring at me and asking why I did it. I had to laugh at myself again because, after all these years, I still didn't have the slightest clue as to why I did it.

I saw a framed picture of my sister Patty and her husband Herb on a nearby counter. It brought back memories of those pain-in-the-ass days when I had to drag Patty to school. Thinking about it now gave me another chuckle. So did a picture of my kid brother in the bathtub covering his private parts with a yellow rubber ducky.

As I continued to look around, I began to feel a touch of joy that the images of a drunken father and an out-of-control screaming mother were now simply faded memories of long ago.

Then I walked into my old bedroom. My father had taken out the back window and put in a door leading onto the small porch. It had given my mother easy access since she used to plant flowers out there in orange colored tile pots. I went out onto the porch and just stood there. Suddenly I had the strangest feeling. I felt more alone than I had ever felt in my entire life.

Even though I had my own loving family to return home to, I couldn't shake the feeling of being totally alone. That's when I realized I no longer had a mother and a father. I started to weep uncontrollably. I couldn't stop. Then I began to sob so painfully I had to sit down and put my face in my hands. I don't remember how long I sat there sobbing.

When I finally stopped and started to leave, I noticed one of the last pictures my parents had taken together. It was in a large silver frame sitting on top of my mom's bureau. They had their arms around each other and were smiling as though they were newlyweds.

That picture helped me realize that through the precious gift of sobriety, I had finally been blessed with both a mother and a father who truly loved me. It can't get any better than that.

CHAPTER FOURTEEN

Carrying the Message

I'm fairly certain it was a Thursday afternoon when Bernadette received a phone call from the student counselor at Rye High School. He said one of our sons had been caught drinking a can of beer on the school grounds which was prohibited. Also, he wasn't even close to the legal drinking age.

I took the next day off and went with my wife to meet him in his office. The student counselor whom we knew quite well said he wouldn't come down hard on our son since it was his first serious offense against school regulations. He simply suggested we keep a closer eye on him because he was beginning to pal around with "the wrong crowd."

That was the day I began to realize how little I had been doing to help educate even my own children about the insidious ways alcoholism can creep into your life. And by now, pot and other drugs had invaded our schools as well.

My dad once warned me that, being so busy, I had a tendency to take some things for granted. This apparently was one of them. I would sometimes joke about certain aspects of my past and invite my children to a twelve step meeting once a year when I was celebrating another sober anniversary that this made them aware of the dangers of drinking. We should have been talking about it more at the dinner table.

Even knowing that children of alcoholics have a fifty percent chance of becoming addicted, I don't think I related that seriously enough to my own family. Instead, I thought sharing my own personal experience and offering guidance from time to time while reviewing their report cards was enough to protect them at such a young age from the enticement of "social drinking." And what about all those other families and kids who knew far less than we did? How were they being informed and protected?

I had to ask myself whether or not what some people told me was true, that I was completely powerless to help my children stay away from addictive substances. After giving it some thought, I refused to accept that premise. And I didn't believe it had anything to do with my ego. It had to do with the way I was carrying the message of recovery.

Going to meetings and sponsoring newcomers was essential for my own sobriety, but I knew in my heart it wasn't enough to help those still in denial or completely uninformed. In order to do that, I realized I had to become as active outside of the program as I was in it. But how? What should I do? The answer soon became quite obvious.

As a writer by trade, I had years of experience working in many aspects of the media—newspapers, magazines, radio, television and now my current gig with an independent film production company. I knew that stories in the media were a very effective way to spread any message. Why not use that route to help educate the public about the plague of addiction and the solution to the problem?

I was sure others were already doing it so why don't I try my own hand at it too. It could be the best way to inform those who were suffering and didn't know where to go for help. That's what a quiet voice inside kept telling me.

In a way, I had already started down that path. I had written my first book, *THE SKYLINE IS A PROMISE* which was published by Holt, Rinehart, Winston. It was a motivational narrative about finding a good life by setting one's goals higher than one's reach and trying to accomplish something new and better one day at a time. So I thought that perhaps I should try writing a movie about finding a good life through recovery from addiction.

But again, where would I start? What would the story be? How would I find a tale dramatic enough to attract a large movie audience and reviewers to help spread the word? It was right in front of me all the time—the miraculous stories emanating from the twelve step program of recovery I was already in.

I've always loved doing research because it would usually lead me to some very interesting places and introduce me to some of the most interesting people. My initial shock was discovering that there were more than two hundred programs based on the twelve steps. Let me list just a few of them for you:

Adult Children of Alcoholics

Narcotics Anonymous

Alcoholics Anonymous

Cocaine Anonymous

Al-Anon/Alateen

Overeaters Anonymous

Clutterers Anonymous

Gamblers Anonymous

Nicotine Anonymous

Crystal Meth Anonymous

Debters Anonymous

Emotions Anonymous

Heroin Anonymous

Neurotics Anonymous

Marijuana Anonymous

Sexaholics Anonymous

Workaholics Anonymous

Breast Cancer Survivors Anonymous

Smokers Anonymous

Co-Sex and Love Addicts Anonymous

Pills Anonymous

Food Addicts in Recovery Anonymous

Computer Gaming Addicts Anonymous

Tough Love Anonymous

Lost Children Anonymous

Survivors of Incest Anonymous

Co-Dependents Anonymous

And the list goes on.

What I also discovered was that the twelve steps were originally written by a man named William G. Wilson, a once highly successful Wall Street stock broker who lost everything through years of alcoholic drinking. His destructive downfall followed by his dramatic rise was a story that grabbed me. So I extended my research into his life and personal experience with booze.

Born in the small town of East Dorsett, Vermont, Bill Wilson was a go-getter from an early age. His patriotic grandfather who raised him once challenged the boy to outdo their nearby Australian neighbors. Young Bill built a boomerang that soared high into the air and returned almost to the very spot where he stood.

Following boarding school, he married Lois Burnham, the daughter of a wealthy New York physician. She fell in love with him at first sight. Bill went off to World War I as a young Army Lieutenant and returned home to a hero's welcome. But he had met good old John Barleycorn while in Europe and also returned addicted to alcohol.

He set out to make his fortune in the industrial boom of the Roaring Twenties. As a Wall Street stockbroker, he was soon living it up and drinking far too much. By the time he and his wife were picked clean by the stock market crash of 1929, Bill was already a chronic alcoholic. Forced to move in with her parents, Lois found a job at Macy's Department Store while Bill spent his time guzzling booze in Speak Easies and on park benches.

Lois continued to believe that her love for her husband could help him conquer his disease. Only when strapped to a hospital bed in a dry-out hospital did the former stock broker begin to confront his malady. However, it took more drunken rampages, three more trips to the hospital and the threat of confinement in a mental institution before he finally hit his bottom.

As he laid sweating and shaking in his hospital room one night convinced he was dying, Bill reached out in desperation, pleading:

"If there is a God, please help me."

He later described the room as suddenly being saturated with a brilliant white light as he experienced the presence of a great Spirit filling his mind and body with peace and joy—"the kind of peace and joy I had never felt before," he said later. When he asked his doctor if he might have been hallucinating, he was told:

"I don't really know, but from the looks of things you seem fine. Whatever happened, hang on to it because it's so much better than what you had before."

Bill quit drinking. He came to believe that faith in a Higher Power would keep him sober along with helping other drunks find what he had found, a "Spiritual Experience." However, during an unsuccessful business trip to Akron, Ohio, he was tempted to drink again. Instead, he phoned a local preacher who introduced him to another alcoholic in need of help.

That man was an inebriated Akron physician by the name of Dr. Robert Holbrook Smith. They soon discovered that by sharing their experiences and supporting each other through regular close contact they could stay sober.

So they began spreading that message to other drunks around Akron. Based upon his and Dr. Bob's experience and that of their early converts, Bill penned twelve suggested steps to guide them and a growing number of others along the road to recovery. It was the beginning of Alcoholics Anonymous and the birth of twelve step recovery programs that, over the ensuing years, multiplied into hundreds of others all around the world.

Bill Wilson passed away in January of 1971. It was no coincidence in my opinion that his widow who was approaching eighty lived only twenty minutes away from Bernadette and me in a town called Bedford Hills, New York.

I knew from more than twenty years working in the media business that the best way to get the real story was directly from the horse's mouth so to speak. So I called Mrs. Wilson to see if she would meet with me. When I explained what my goal was and that I was in a twelve step program myself, she generously invited me up to her home the following Saturday afternoon. She called her place "Stepping Stones."

Bernadette came with me. I needed someone who could make an objective judgment of the lady and the dramatic story I hoped to hear. Neither of us was disappointed. We not only met a gracious and charming woman who welcomed us with genuine warmth, but someone with great humility even though she had played a major role in the life-saving program her husband had given the world.

Lois Wilson lived in a quaint, cedar-shingled home surrounded by eight acres of tall pine trees, full-grown maples and very large oaks. The outside of her house was adorned by carefully manicured beds of lovely flowers which we learned she planted and cared for herself.

I'll never forget seeing the warm smile on the charming face of this gracious, gray-haired lady when she opened the front door of her home to greet us. Like my late mother-in-law, Lois wasn't quite five feet tall but she appeared larger than life.

"Please come in," she said. "I hope you enjoyed the drive up. Come. Let us sit in the living room."

There was another lady there named Harriet who had been the Wilson's housekeeper, cook, traveling companion and good friend for many years. She also greeted Bernadette and me warmly and offered us some tea and fresh baked cookies which we accepted.

"Tell me about yourself, Bill," Lois said as she nestled into a comfortable white couch near a large stone fireplace while pointing us to large, high back chairs across from her. "And is it Bernadette?" she asked, smiling at my wife.

"Yes," Bernadette nodded politely.

"I hate formalities," our hostess smiled again. "I believe we're simply friends who hadn't met yet."

"Thank you for taking the time to see us, Mrs. Wilson," I began. "From what I hear, you must be a pretty busy lady."

"I said I hate formalities," she shot back. "Please call me Lois. And yes, I used to be quite busy, especially when my husband was alive. We traveled all over the world together. People couldn't wait to meet him. What he did meant so much to everyone in recovery wherever we went.

"I was what you might call his trusted companion. I made sure he always had enough sleep and enough to eat. And a change of socks." We all laughed.

"I'm sure you did much more than that," Bernadette said in a very supportive manner.

"Maybe so," Lois replied, "but not really until Anne Bingham and I started Al-Anon. Then I was real busy."

"Al-Anon?" I asked.

"Yes, the Al-Anon Family Groups to be official," she explained. "Many wives get almost as sick as their husbands from living with the disease. I know I did. That's why my dear friend Anne and I started a twelve step program for spouses of alcoholics and their families. To help them recover. It's based on the same twelve steps my husband wrote. It's also an anonymous program.

"Should I seriously consider your proposal for doing a movie about how all this began, you would have to promise that you wouldn't break my anonymity as a member of the program."

For a moment I thought that could cause a problem, but then I realized we were still so far from the starting gate at this point it really didn't matter.

During my research for doing a possible movie on this subject, I remembered coming across something the famous, internationally-renowned writer, Aldous Huxley, once said about Bill Wilson's great achievement in creating the first twelve step program:

"When the history of the twentieth century is finally written, the greatest thing America will be known for giving the world will be Alcoholics Anonymous."

When I mentioned this to Lois, Bernadette and I were both struck by the simple way she described her and her husband's enormous dream.

"I know it may sound immodest," she said very quietly, "but I believe Mr. Huxley is right. At least I hope so, for Bill and I always dreamed that one day everyone would come to live by the twelve steps and there would be true peace and harmony throughout the whole world."

Before the afternoon was over, the story I heard from this extraordinary woman was far more dramatic, exciting and meaningful than I could have possibly imagined. She said if I promised to tell the truth of that story in a movie, she would gladly cooperate and give me her permission to do so. She also agreed to meet with me on a regular basis so that I could tape record all the memories of her life with Bill and how he created one of the greatest spiritual movements of the twentieth century.

I couldn't wait to tell my partners at Artists Entertainment Complex. While this film project wouldn't have blood running in the streets like *SERPICO* or the FBI putting a bullet in the brain of a bank robber as in *DOG DAY AFTERNOON*, I felt sure the importance of the story and how it could help millions of people would certainly draw just as big an audience. At least that was my pitch. My partners didn't agree.

Marty Bregman synthesized their combined negative opinion by quoting those immortal words of Louis B. Mayer, one of the founders of Metro Goldwyn Mayer Pictures:

"Movies are made to entertain. If you want to send a message, call Western Union."

I refused to be discouraged. So I decided to leave the partnership, set up my own firm and make the film myself. It was a decision dangerously based one more time on a big ego and self-will. In other words, the "big I am" was going to pick up the gauntlet from Bill Wilson and make sure everybody in the world got sober. And they would know that I did it with just a little assistance from Mr. Wilson. Thank goodness I had a Higher Power Who loved me enough to protect me from myself and a great sponsor who eventually pulled me back down to earth. But it was a struggle.

After meeting with Lois and taping her recollections for more than six months, I sat down and wrote a movie script which I called, *A LOVE THAT*

NEVER DIED. I used that working title because Bill Wilson's wife always thought her love could get him sober and keep him sober. Unfortunately it could not.

The first person I approached about the film project was one of the corporate directors at Columbia Pictures in Manhattan whom I knew very well from my days in public relations. He really liked the idea and arranged for me to pitch it to his nephew, Peter Guber, a brash young executive who ran Columbia's California studios at that time.

"I love drunk stories," Peter shouted at me as I was ushered into his huge Los Angeles office. He was seated behind a large glass desk that sat atop a platform so he could look down upon his visitors. "I love your script but it needs a few touches. We need more action and more sex.

"We should have this big shot guy...what's his name...oh yeah, Bill Wilson, cockeyed and bare-assed drunk, chasing gorgeous half-naked broads in and out of hotel rooms. Then the police show up and haul him off to the drunk tank where he tries to cure all the bozos in there. And that's the start of AA. What do you think?"

"Are you sure you read my script, Peter?" I stuttered out of shock.

"Sure," he said rising from behind his desk so he could look even further down at me. "Why the hell you think you're here?"

"I don't know," I replied, "because my script tells basically a spiritual story of how Bill Wilson created a program that's helped to sober up millions of people around the world."

Peter frowned at me. "You're kidding," he said, half sneering. "That's hot shit. But I don't make spiritual stories. They suck."

I tried a few other studios but struck out there too even though I had a much more polite reception. Not only didn't they really understand the spiritual aspect of the story, but I just couldn't go along with the severe changes they were suggesting. Since I had promised Lois Wilson I would tell the truth of the story, I put the script under my arm and headed back to New York to find some other way to make this movie. Lois was as disappointed as I was. So was Bernadette.

After spending much more money than I could afford trying to get it done, my sponsor Benny finally convinced me to get off the pink cloud, come back down to earth and turn it all over to my Higher Power. Then he reminded me that the best way to find a little humility and a lot of self-honesty was to start working again with other alcoholics.

So I put the script on the shelf, found some other ways to bring in a few bucks and began spending a lot of time at Casa Serena, an alcoholic rehab run by my good friend Joe Piccolo in Golden Bridge, New York. I not only loved sharing my experience, strength and hope with his patients but I really enjoyed his spaghetti and meatball dinners every Friday night. Before I knew it, I was sponsoring Joe's cook, a tall, rugged-looking guy in his late forties by the name of Ed McCormack.

One night after a meeting, Ed asked if we could speak for a few minutes.

"I decided to take you up on your suggestion," he began.

"What suggestion was that?" I asked.

"You said I probably wouldn't be spending the rest of my life as a cook in a rehab, that I should start thinking about what I really want to do with my life. I've made a decision."

I was almost afraid to ask, but did anyway.

"What's that?"

"I think I'd like to go to Hollywood and become an actor."

I was immediately concerned that my past activities in the film business might have had an influence on his decision. I was concerned because Ed wasn't exactly what you would call the leading man type. Of course, with his facial scars, touch of acne and deep set eyes he had possibilities as a character actor. Since I couldn't budge him off his risky decision, I simply said:

"If you decide to go, make sure you get to a twelve step meeting as soon as you arrive and join a group. And be prepared for a lot of rejection because that goes with the territory."

Ed and I had shared many of our experiences and accomplishments during our relationship at the Casa Serena. He knew about the script I had written about Bill Wilson and the important role he played in the recovery movement. Still, I was a bit surprised when he asked:

"Would you mind if I took a copy of your script with me just in case I bump into somebody who would like to make it?"

While it was an innocent enough request, it sounded damn stupid to me.

"Sure Ed," I replied with a touch of sarcasm. "That's the way movies get made. A cook from a rehab in Golden Bridge, New York takes a movie script with him to Hollywood, California. One day he bumps into a half-baked producer in a cheesy diner. He says to the producer, 'I have this great movie script here. Would you like to make it?' The producer says. 'I've been looking for a script like that all my life.' So he goes ahead and makes it because, like I say, that's the way movies get made in Hollywood."

I should have apologized immediately to this really nice sober fellow for my sarcasm. But it didn't seem to sway him. He wanted to take my script with him anyway.

Like I said, Ed's request sounded totally idiotic at first. It certainly wasn't the way movies get made, at least not by smart, energetic, experienced film producers. Right? But how can we mere mortals conceive the ways of Providence, for whether you'd like to believe it or not, this was very close to how this movie actually came to be made. It's what I call "my God story."

Ed McCormack, the cook from Casa Serena, went off to Hollywood. One night my wife and I were watching *ALL IN THE FAMILY* featuring a character called Archie Bunker on television. Archie's house had been burglarized and he called the police. Guess what? One of the detectives who showed up to investigate was my friend Ed.

On another night we were watching *SANFORD AND SON*. The junkyard caught fire. Fred Sanford called the Fire Department. Guess who came charging in as the lead fireman? That's right, Ed. He was going around tinsel town knocking on producers' doors and winding up with bit parts in their shows. He was such a hustler that he was getting to know practically every production company in Hollywood and what projects they were developing.

Then one day Ed called me. He was very angry.

"There's a production company out here that's trying to steal your movie," he snarled

"Ed," I replied trying to calm him down. "Anybody can make a film about Bill Wilson and what he did. It's what you call public domain."

"But you have Lois Wilson's special permission to do it," he continued to protest. "That must mean something."

"I wish it did," I said rather sadly.

"Well I'm getting to the bottom of this," my friend snarled one more time. "You worked too hard on that script to have someone steal your idea. I'm getting to the bottom of this."

Ed discovered that a production company named Garner-Duchow had been trying to bring the story of Bill Wilson and his accomplishments to the screen without any success. The company headed by actor James Garner had retained five different screenwriters and had not come up with a satisfactory script.

My pal Ed immediately befriended Garner's secretary, Mary Ann, handed her my script and asked her to read it. She did and liked it so much she sent it right over to her boss. The actor thought the script was written by a new writer his partner, Peter Duchow, had hired. Garner read it himself and called to congratulate Peter for finally getting an excellent script. They could now make their movie. Peter said he had never heard of and certainly never hired anyone named Bill Borchert. Still, they both liked the script.

After finally unraveling the puzzle created by the former cook from an alcoholic rehab , Peter Duchow called me early one Saturday afternoon. Bernadette and I were just finishing lunch. The film producer began by apologizing for reading my script without my permission. He said the script I wrote was exactly what they were looking for with one big exception. I had written it as a feature film. They had a deal to produce a two-hour TV movie for The Hallmark Hall of Fame. Peter wanted to know if I would be willing to rewrite it as a television film.

I kiddingly told him I was kind of busy at the moment but if he would give me about five minutes, I would get right to it. We both laughed. I later learned that Peter wanted to do this movie for essentially the same reason I wanted to do it, to carry the message of recovery. He convinced me that by doing it for television, it would reach millions more people. After thinking it over, I fully agreed.

He flew into New York City the following Wednesday with Norman Stephens, a senior creative executive with Warner Brothers who was overseeing the project. We met at the Waldorf Astoria Hotel, reached an understanding, agreed upon certain changes that enhanced the story and I set off to write the final draft. We decided to call the movie, *MY NAME IS BILL W.*

We started shooting in Richmond, Virginia the first week of February, 1989, turning that southern community into Manhattan in the Roaring Twenties and Akron, Ohio into the Depression days of the 1930's. James Woods starred as Bill Wilson, James Garner as Dr. Bob Smith and JoBeth Williams as Lois Wilson.

MY NAME IS BILL W. debuted on ABC-TV on Sunday night, April 30, 1989 as a Hallmark Hall of Fame Production. It drew a very large audience. Bernadette and I had hoped our dear friend, Lois Wilson, would have lived long enough to see the movie. But she died from a prolonged illness on October 5, 1988 at the young age of ninety-seven.

The movie garnered seven Emmy nominations. James Woods won the Emmy for Best Actor and April Ferry won for Best Costume Designer. James Garner was nominated for Best Supporting Actor and I was nominated as Best Writer.

The critical reviews were many and great. Alcohol and drug recovery centers across the country were permitted to record the film free of charge and they continue to use it for patient education programs. Hallmark Hall of Fame had the movie translated into several languages and it continues to play on television all over the world as well as in millions of homes.

In fact, Warner Brothers Studio, "The Hallmark Hall of Fame" and ABC-TV all claim that since its production in 1989, *MY NAME IS BILL W.* has become the most watched television movie ever made. When all those fine tributes are mentioned, I no longer worry about getting a big head. I've long since come to accept the simple fact that I was simply a useful tool for my Higher Power in all of this as was my dear departed friend, Ed McCormack, the former cook in a rehab.

As the old adage goes, once you accept the truth, the truth will set you free. Not only did it unleash me to some degree from the bondage of self, but it opened up a whole new opportunity to write even more movies and books to carry the message of recovery.

At the same time, I've learned a great deal more about life being a series of ups and downs, highs and low, successes and failures, happiness and sadness. The day my sponsor, Benny Michaelson, passed away was one of the saddest times for me. I've often said he saved my life or at least led me out of the darkness that was suffocating me. My good friend and my dad's sponsor Charlie Alexunis once reminded me that people like Benny, who had given me so much of himself, never really die. Their guidance and their spirit stay with us forever. He was right. I've had three other sponsors in my program since, but Benny is still with me and still trying to keep me on the straight and narrow.

As for my family, since our children were now either married or out on their own, we no longer needed a twenty-two room house to kick around in. Also, Bernadette had undergone quadruple by-pass heart surgery and her cardiologist suggested she would be better off living in a warmer climate. Freezing cold New York weather and huge snowstorms had been getting to me too.

After looking around for almost a year, we decided to build a home in Little River, South Carolina, eight minutes from the Atlantic Ocean and twenty miles north of the resort area of Myrtle Beach. We moved into our southern abode early in 2001.

One day I was unpacking boxes in my office at our new house and came across a stack of old tapes. They were my interviews with Lois Wilson from years before. When my wife asked what I planned to do with the tapes, the answer became quickly apparent to both of us.

First of all, there hadn't been enough time in the Bill W. film to tell Lois's moving story. We weren't able to show how she became the co-founder of two other worldwide twelve step programs, Al-Anon Family Groups and Alateen for the children of alcoholics. That disappointed Bernadette and me.

I knew Lois's tale had to be told because it would hopefully help millions of suffering families impacted by addiction find a solution. So with all these old tapes in hand, I sat down and wrote another book, *WHEN LOVE IS NOT ENOUGH: THE LOIS WILSON STORY.*

The title illustrated the fact that Lois's belief that her love could keep her husband sober was a heart-breaking misconception. She had nurtured and supported her beloved Bill sometimes beyond rationality as his addiction took over their lives. She covered up for him, lied to her family out of shame and hid from her friends, just like my wife Bernadette did. Lois finally had to accept that her love was not enough as Bill's drinking spiraled out of control.

One day as her husband dragged the Bowery into their home once again, Lois lost complete control of her emotions. Seeing the devastation of alcoholism all around her, she began beating on her husband and screaming:

"You don't even have the decency to die!"

When Bill finally got sober and began working with Dr. Bob to organize a fellowship to help others, Lois only felt worse because she couldn't understand why he wasn't spending more time with her. They began to argue. She was also worried about losing her parents' home because he wasn't making any money.

One night she got so angry she threw a shoe at her husband, an action totally foreign to her grace and dignity. Overwrought, Lois went outside to calm down. There she met some women who had driven their husbands to the recovery meeting Bill was holding at their house.

She invited the ladies in for a cup of tea. As they sat around her kitchen table, she heard and witnessed from those wives of alcoholics the same kind of pain and frustration she felt herself. That's when Lois came to recognize she had been seriously affected by her husband's disease and that she and these other women around her needed to find a way to recover. Lois suggested they try practicing the twelve steps Bill had written and they worked.

Sometime after the book was published by Hazelden Publishing Company in May of 2006, I received a phone call from Brad Moore, the president of Hallmark Hall of Fame. We had become good friends during the shooting of *MY NAME IS BILL W.* He told me he had read my new book and blithely asked if I believed lightning could strike twice in the same place.

"If you say it can, Brad, I'll believe it," I blithely replied.

He then asked if I'd be willing to sell Hallmark the film rights to my new book about Lois Wilson and write the screenplay for another Hallmark Hall of Fame movie based on her story. I told him it would be an honor and a privilege.

Academy Award nominee, actress Winona Ryder, told me on the set she was eager to play Lois Wilson since she so admired what she had accomplished after all she had been through. Winona had read the book twice and was totally prepared from day one. So was Golden Globe winner, actor Barry Pepper, who played Bill Wilson. The director, John Kent Harrison, had a special interest in making the movie. His mother had died from alcoholism.

The movie *WHEN LOVE IS NOT ENOUGH* debuted on CBS-TV as a Hallmark Hall of Fame Production on Sunday evening, April 25, 2010. It was nominated for three Emmy awards, two Golden Globes, two Satellite awards and a Prism Award. It came away with an Emmy, a Golden Globe, a Satellite and a Prism Award.

Four days after the film's debut, I was given the great honor of receiving The Marty Mann Founder's Award from The National Council on Alcoholism at a luncheon in New York City. I was told it was for my efforts to help eliminate the stigma of alcoholism and carry the message that there is recovery for those who seek it.

I accepted the award with a great deal of gratitude and humility— well, as much humility as I was capable of at the time. It helped me to remember what my old sponsor Benny used to tell me—I had so much humility I was proud of it. That's the way he would always try to keep my feet on the ground

As I've said, Marty Mann was the first woman to recover from her disease in the twelve step program created by Bill Wilson. I met her through Lois when I was doing my research for the "Bill W." movie. Since she had known the AA co-founder very well, she had given me some very interesting insights into his character, a number of which I used in the film.

Marty Mann came from an upper middle class family in Chicago. She attended private schools, traveled extensively and was a debutante. She moved in a fast-living social circle and gained notoriety for her capacity to drink without serious consequences. That was, until she married into a wealthy New Orleans family that was wiped out in the stock market crash of 1929.

Through her social connections, the hard-drinking debutante found a job in public relations which became her only source of income. She fell into a deep depression from all her misfortunes and started drinking around the clock. She even tried to commit suicide. Her psychiatrist, Dr. Harry Tiebout, knew Bill Wilson and got Marty into his program. She found sobriety there and a renewed desire to do something with her life.

Once sober, she became disturbed by the stigma and the lack of knowledge that the disease of alcoholism was killing people. So she gathered support from some wealthy friends and started The Yale School of Alcoholic Studies in 1945. Several years later she organized The National Council on Alcoholism. Marty Mann passed away on July 22, 1980. Three main ideas formed the basis of her message:

1. Alcoholism is a disease and the alcoholic is a sick person.
2. The alcoholic can be helped and is worth helping.
3. Alcoholism is a public health problem and therefore a public responsibility.

I was sitting in my office one day trying to decide what my next project might be when I received a call from one of the executives at Hazelden Publishing Company. He asked if I would be interested in writing a meditation book for them based on the Eleventh Step of the addiction recovery program. It reads:

"Sought through prayer and meditation to improve our conscious contact with God as we understood Him, praying only for knowledge of His will for us and the power to carry that out."

Since I was and still am far from being any kind of spiritual or intellectual giant, I had to give it some serious thought. Soon I realized there was a great deal of source material available that I could delve into. It also occurred to me that writing such a book might help improve my own spiritual well-being. So I accepted the challenge. It proved to be one of the most satisfying experiences of my writing career and something I really needed at that time.

After digesting more than forty spiritual books ranging from The New Testament to *THE JUNKIE PRIEST*, I put together a treatise called *SOUGHT THROUGH PRAYER AND MEDITATION*. It consisted of fifty-two different reflections, one for each week. My concept was that if one meditates on the same subject matter for a whole week, some of it might stick. The book was well accepted. Some twelve step groups even use it in their discussion meetings.

Sometimes people ask which book among those that I've written is my favorite. I have no problem telling them it was my "Miracle" book.

Like my mother-in-law, I had always wanted to see a real miracle. But a miracle for me had to be accompanied by claps of thunder as someone rose from the dead or a crippled child getting up and walking or someone riddled with cancer suddenly being pronounced cured by a bunch of doctors standing around totally baffled. I had no idea that God was constantly performing "quiet little miracles" each and every day until I began attending and listening intently at twelve step group meetings.

I had been hearing recovered men and women talk about so-called coincidences in their lives which they referred to as God Shots. Just listening to them share their experiences helped strengthen my belief that God was actually "here and real" in my life. So I started jotting down their stories. Then one day I had a God Shot myself. I quickly came to recognize it as one of my own quiet little miracles.

We were living in Nashville at the time. It was a Sunday morning and we were all getting ready to go to church where our new son, Daniel, was to be baptized. Mama was in the kitchen warming the baby's bottle. As I entered, she was sniffing the air. She said she smelled smoke.

I looked around and suddenly spotted a plume of gray smoke sifting in from under the door that led to the garage. When I opened it I saw one side of the garage ablaze. I shouted to my mother-in-law to get everyone out of the house. Then I opened the roll-up garage doors, jumped into the station wagon and backed it out so it wouldn't catch fire and explode.

Next I grabbed the garden hose to put out the fire. It didn't have a long enough reach to make a difference. I was in a panic. I had forgotten to call the fire department. Suddenly two men came running up the steep driveway at the side of my house. Both were very stocky, wore beards and coveralls and each carried a large fire extinguisher. They rushed into the garage and in very short order had the fire completely out.

In the few moments it took for me to toss the garden hose aside, take a deep breath and then turn to thank them, they were gone. I walked quickly to the top of my driveway figuring I could catch up to them, but they were nowhere in sight. Neither could I see a car or truck in the street below. I stood there for a long time scratching my head before ushering everyone back into the house. That puzzlement stayed with me for days.

By the way, it was obvious which of my young sons had set that fire. There was the same look on his face that the Fire Marshall had seen on mine years before when I did the same dastardly deed. And also like me, he burst into tears when I asked why he did it. My son didn't know either. He was playing with matches near a pile of old newspapers in the garage when the papers caught fire. We had a long talk and, like my father, I didn't punish him either. His fear and regret were punishment enough.

I waited until I had gathered enough of these God Shots and then wrote a book titled, *50 QUIET MIRACLES THAT SAVED LIVES*. I included my own miracle story in it which I called, "Two Bearded Angels." That book was also published by Hazelden Publishing Company. In my Preface I wrote:

"I have learned that miracles come in all sizes, shapes and forms, from unexpected phone calls to chance meetings. They are small enough to simply produce a warm glow and dramatic enough to create awe and wonder. If we allow ourselves to look beyond the glow and focus on the wonder, we will recognize that, in moments such as these, we are in the presence of God."

Next on my agenda was a book called, *1,000 YEARS OF SOBRIETY*, another Hazelden-published book. It contained inspiring interviews with twenty men and women who had stayed sober more than fifty years. It focused on how they did it and the advice they had for the newly sober.

I was originally going to write a book called *500 YEARS OF SOBRIETY*. Then a friend of mine, Mike Fitzpatrick, asked if he could work with me on it. We decided to extend the number of interviews with long timers in recovery which made the book more interesting and attractive.

Then came the book *WHEN TWO LOVES COLLIDE* which I felt told a story far more dramatic and uplifting than the well-known tale called *WHO'S AFRAID OF VIRGINIA WOOLF*. The story I wrote recounted the chilling saga of a heroic surgeon in World War II named Dr. John Mooney who was severely wounded several times in battle and took alcohol and drugs to kill his pain so he could operate on thousands of casualties and save their lives. He came home not realizing he was addicted to alcohol and drugs.

He married a beautiful Georgia country girl who loved to party. As a renowned surgeon, success, fame and fortune initially filled their lives. But then their passionate love for each other began to collide with their passionate love for their addictions. Even though he went to prison for using illegal drugs and she got hooked on electric shock therapy, they never lost their commitment to each other. In the end, they both found recovery in the twelve steps and dedicated their lives to helping others recover. I came to believe so strongly in their commitment that I wrote in the book:

"The word commitment was once almost synonymous with a sacred oath. It was the grip of a handshake that closed a deal, the anvil of confidence that brought things to fruition. Most of all, it was the mortar that solidified relationships, the one thing that made them strong, whole and lasting. It was the virtue that engendered hope and faith in the idea that tomorrow would be a better day.

"A true commitment transforms a promise into reality. It is what boldly clarifies your intentions and makes your actions speak louder than your words. It is making the time when there is none…coming through time after time…meaning when I say 'I love you' that I am committed to working to love you even when it's hard to do.

"But that was then and this is now. It's sad to see that something has happened to the meaning of that word. It has lost some of its luster, some of its pride, some of its reverence. For many in this day and age, true commitment is no longer one of the most essential ingredients in our character even though it is an ingredient that affects every aspect of our lives."

The more I learned, the more I came to understand that a true commitment to recovery was essential for those fighting addiction. Without it and a strong faith in a Higher Power, there will always be the threat of relapse hanging over them like the Sword of Damocles.

I use the word addiction here because more and more people today not only drink alcohol but take drugs ranging from heroin and cocaine to pot and prescription medications. When we look around, we can see that the crisis of addiction has not ebbed one single bit. It has only grown worse.

According to the American Medical Association and the Federal government, there are more than forty-four million active alcoholics and drug addicts currently in America. And using the fabled rule of thumb, every addict affects at least five or more people in their lives—spouses, children, relatives, neighbors, co-workers and others. That means there are over two hundred and fifty million people in this country alone impacted by the disease and most of them don't know where to go or what to do about it.

Teenagers are dying. College students are flunking out. Senior citizens are caught in the plague and the consequences of their drinking and over-medicating is falling on their children who already have their own families to care for. It is a fight that has to be won and it is a fight that requires a constant wake-up call in order to win it.

My wake-up call comes every time I attend another twelve step recovery meeting or read about another fatal drunken automobile accident or hear about a neighbor's son or daughter over-dosing on drugs. It pains me because I understand from painful, first-hand experience how this terrible disease of addiction can be arrested. I also know that no matter how much damage it has caused, one can find a whole new life in recovery—a life beyond our wildest dreams.

I was reminded of that again one evening when I went to one of my favorite speaker meetings in Surfside, South Carolina, which is just below Myrtle Beach. A handsome young man in his early forties named Howie was there celebrating his third year of sobriety. His lovely wife Maria was pushing him in his wheelchair with their two kids tagging along.

Three years ago, Howie, who had been a great college football player until booze took over his life, was nearly killed when his car collided head-on with a large delivery truck. He was intoxicated. His best friend who was in the passenger seat was thrown through the front windshield by the impact and died instantly. The truck driver was unharmed. Howie wound up a paraplegic, paralyzed from the waist down. He became a man who believed he had nothing left to live for. One day a sober nurse introduced him to the twelve steps of recovery and his whole life took on new meaning.

Over coffee and cake that evening, the young man excitedly told me he had started a sign business about a year before and it was doing very well. He said he and Maria were even looking forward to buying a small house.

I could tell how their lives had changed by the big smile on his wife's face and the way he kept squeezing her hand. Howie expressed his gratitude to everyone at the meeting for helping him through his many bouts of self-pity so that he could stay sober, face his challenges and overcome them.

When I left and headed for my car, I couldn't get that young couple out of my mind. As I started the engine and began driving home, I suddenly realized why. I had once again experienced something that had taken me a long while to believe and accept myself. I had just witnessed one more time that hope and love really do spring eternal.

Because of that, my life is pretty good these days. Bernadette and I are still very much in love. We have a wonderful family that now includes twenty-three grandchildren and two great-grandchildren. And while we have financial security, a lovely home and I'm still able to write, there's one thing that still worries me a great deal.

As I've mentioned, we have nine children and now all these grandchildren. Knowing a great deal about the high incidence of addiction in families, I can't shake the nagging fear that some in our family may wind up a drunk like my father or me or worse. More than three million people die annually from alcohol and drug addiction.

I decided to write this book not only to share my experience, strength and hope as well as my father's awesome recovery, but also to let families everywhere know there is a solution to the terrible curse of addiction. There is the opportunity to heal relationships, restore families and, as I've said before, find a life beyond our wildest dreams.

This experience of recalling the past has been at times a rather painful yet healing journey. I hope it has been worthwhile for all of you who have taken it with me.

The disease of addiction can attack any of us at any time. It is cunning, baffling and powerful. For parents with alcoholism or drug addiction in the family, it is a special burden we must bear. While treatment and twelve step programs work well to arrest addiction, perhaps one day soon medical research will find a cure and perhaps even prevent the onset of this often fatal malady. With scientists at The National Institute of Health and elsewhere focused on genetic markers and manipulation, it may happen sooner than we think.

And as the Irish who suffer mightily from this disease might say, "Wouldn't that be just grand!"

The brothers of William Borchert, Sr. made up half a sandlot baseball team. (Left to right) Hennie, Freddie, Herbie, George and young Bill, Sr. Three brothers died of alcoholism. Bill found sobriety.

Frieda and Henry Borchert, parents of William Borchert, Sr.

The wedding of Ruth and William Borchert, Sr., parents of William Borchert, Jr.

Hennie Borchert with his only child and his pride and joy, Henry, Jr., who died of a football injury received in a championship game. Deeply depressed and very drunk, Hennie died when he crashed his car into a tree under the influence of alcohol.

The wedding of Catherine and Freddie Borchert. Some years later, Freddie committed suicide under the influence of alcohol.

Bill Borchert, Sr. (right) helping his drinking buddy Tommy Murphy
repair tires for his jalopy.

A typical beer party in the basement of Monahan's Bar and Grill. Ruth is second from left on bottom tow and Bill is fourth from right on top row. Grandmother "Lizzie" McLintock can be found in the center of the bottom row sitting on the lap of Charley the Vegetable Man.

Bill, Sr. loved to sing and once tried to make a career out of it.
But his drinking created too many sour notes.

Marilyn Dean with her pet, Candy and children (left to right)
Billy, Eileen, Craig and Eddie.

Patricia Borchert marries Herb Gass.

Bill Jr.'s mother-in-law, Mrs. Angelina Forcina, seated at her dining room table.

Following the elopement, Bernadette and Bill get married in church
as Mama Forcina had requested.

Their first daughter Judy was born eleven months later—on Valentine's Day.

Robert Borchert (top) with his family. In the middle are Tim, Don and Brian, and at the bottom his wife Leslie, daughter Sally and son Stephen.

Bill relaxing on their honeymoon in Maine—with a bottle of beer.

Bernadette and Bill always loved dancing together.
Here they are celebrating their 25th wedding anniversary…sober.

This family photo was taken outside their Rye, N.Y. home the day before Larry got married. (left to right in front) Walter, Robert, Father Bill, Angela, Judy and Larry. (left to right behind) John, Charlotte, Bernadette, Bill and Daniel.

Nominated for an Emmy as Best Writer for scripting the film *My Name is Bill W.*, Bill poses at Emmy party with (left to right) Executive Producer Peter Duchow, film star James Woods and Director Dan Petrie.

Bernadette with movie star James Woods at Emmy celebration for *My Name is Bill W.*

When Bill, Jr. became successful in the motion picture business, the family moved into this twenty-two room home in Rye, N.Y. His sobriety continues to pay dividends.

Ruth and Bill at their grandson Robert's graduation. This was two years before Bill Sr.'s passing. Ruth died Less than two years later.

Here are Bernadette and Bill dancing together again only this time at
their 50th wedding anniversary—and still sober.

Bernadette and Bill remain very active today, traveling abroad as well as throughout the United States, carrying the message of sobriety at meetings, conventions and special events. Here they are sailing down the Mississippi—and still very much in love.

Dear Reader,

Without your interest in reading my book and taking this intimate journey with me, it would not be possible to reach out to so many people in need of help. I would be additionally grateful if you would take a minute or two to review my book on Amazon. No matter what authors might tell you, we do want to know what our readers think.

Sincerely
Bill Borchert

William G. Borchert began his career as a journalist in New York City, working as a reporter and writer for one of the country's largest daily newspapers. He covered and wrote some of the most important stories of his time—from Martin Luther King's struggle for racial equality to the nation's space race to the last execution in Sing Sing Penitentiary's electric chair.

After working as a feature writer for national magazines and creating syndicated shows for radio, Bill became a partner at Artists Entertainment Complex, a new independent film production company that went on to produce a number of box office hits. These included *Kansas City Bomber* starring Raquel Welch, *Serpico* starring Al Pacino and *Dog Day Afternoon* also starring Al Pacino.

As a screenwriter, he was nominated for an Emmy for writing the highly acclaimed Warner Brothers/Hallmark Hall of Fame movie *My Name Is Bill W.* based upon the founding of Alcoholics Anonymous. It stars James Garner, James Woods and JoBeth Williams and won three Emmy Awards. Bill also won The Christopher Award, The Paul Newman Award, the Vince Lombardi Community Service Award, and the Marty Mann Founders Award.

He wrote the screenplay for the Entertainment One/Hallmark Hall of Fame movie *When Love Is Not Enough*, which was based upon his book about Lois Wilson, the co-founder of the worldwide fellowship of Al-Anon. The movie stars Academy Award winner Winona Ryder as Lois Wilson and Golden Globe winner Barry Pepper as Bill Wilson, the co-founder of Alcoholics Anonymous.

Bill has written a number of other books including *The Skyline Is a Promise, 50 Quiet Miracles That Changed Lives, Sought Through Prayer and Meditation, When Two Loves Collide*, and *1,000 Years of Sobriety*.

He is often invited to speak around the country at major business conventions, college campuses and civic and social organizations about the nation's struggle to combat the plague of alcohol and drug addiction and its social stigma that kills thousands, young and old, every year.

Bill and his wife, Bernadette, live in Little River, South Carolina and Stratford, Connecticut. They have nine children and twenty three grandchildren.

32232994R00202